Critical Acclaim for
From My Sisters' Lips

'To some, [Islam] represents suicide bombers and honour killings and the oppression of women. How to change this perception? Na'ima is a pretty good start ... *From My Sisters' Lips* is an extremely thought-provoking book that challenges Western preconceptions of Islamic women' *Daily Telegraph*

'More and more women are making the remarkable decision to convert to Islam. A stereotypical view paints this as the religion which represses women and forces them to hide behind floor-length robes. But this is not the full picture, as one British woman, Na'ima B. Robert argues in her new book' *Daily Mail*

'Spiritual awakening is at the core of *From My Sisters' Lips* ... Robert shows how Islam has made a positive difference to the lives of women from wildly different backgrounds, with fascinating results' *Image*

'One of the main strengths of this book is the clear and lucid presentation on the main tenets of Islam ... You can't help but be throughly engaged when you read it. There is a sense of vibrancy, of headiness about it' *Emel Magazine*

'*From My Sister's Lips* sheds light on why women choose Islam ... An interesting and informative book ... it is only by questioning preconceptions and stigmas that we – both individually and from a societal point of view – wil grow' *The Program*

Na'ima B. Robert is the daughter of a white South African father of Scottish descent and a black South African mother of Zulu descent. Born in Leeds, she grew up in Zimbabwe and went on to gain a first-class degree from the University of London. She has worked in the travel and tourism industry, was a teacher and has written and illustrated children's books. Following her conversion to Islam and her marriage to a Ghanaian revert, she settled in South London, where she now lives with her husband and two small sons.

For further information visit www.nrobert.com

FROM MY SISTERS' LIPS

A unique celebration of
Muslim womanhood

NA'IMA B. ROBERT

BANTAM BOOKS

LONDON • TORONTO • SYDNEY • AUCKLAND • JOHANNESBURG

FROM MY SISTERS' LIPS
A BANTAM BOOK : 0553817175
9780553817171

Originally published in Great Britain by Bantam Press
a division of Transworld Publishers

PRINTING HISTORY
Bantam Press edition published 2005
Bantam edition published 2006

3 5 7 9 10 8 6 4

Set in 11/14pt Sabon by
Falcon Oast Graphic Art Ltd.

Bantam Books are published by Transworld Publishers,
61–63 Uxbridge Road, London W5 5SA,
a division of The Random House Group Ltd,
in Australia by Random House Australia (Pty) Ltd,
20 Alfred Street, Milsons Point, Sydney, NSW 2061, Australia,
in New Zealand by Random House New Zealand Ltd,
18 Poland Road, Glenfield, Auckland 10, New Zealand
and in South Africa by Random House (Pty) Ltd,
Isle of Houghton, Corner of Boundary Road & Carse O'Gowrie,
Houghton 2198, South Africa.

Printed and bound in Great Britain by
Cox & Wyman Ltd, Reading, Berkshire

Papers used by Transworld Publishers are natural, recyclable
products made from wood grown in sustainable forests. The
manufacturing processes conform to the environmental
regulations of the country of origin.

For my husband,
the wind beneath my wings

CONTENTS

ACKNOWLEDGEMENTS

Firstly, I thank Allah, Lord of all the worlds, for making this book possible. I ask that He accepts it as an act of worship from me and places it in the scale of my good deeds. To my sisters: a big '*Jazakunna Allahu khairan*' to all of you who shared your time, your innermost thoughts and feelings with me. In spite of all the children and missing Dictaphones, we did it, *masha Allah*. Take this book: it is yours. To the memory of my mother: dear Mama, you would have loved this book. You live on in all of us. A 'big girl' thank-you to my wonderful Daddy: your hopes were not in vain. I am so glad we were able to share this most 'harrowing' of journeys. Hugs to my brother and sister: thanks for believing in me and being there – with the Hoover and the babysitting! To my loving family, aunts, uncles, cousins and grandparents: thank you for your support and for loving me and accepting me in spite of the many challenges. A good cup of coffee for Miriam, my sounding board and debate partner – so much of this book is you! A 'shout out' to all my companions on this journey from Africa, Europe and the States: I salute you. *Tatenda*, Sisi Priscilla and Mai Ethel: you deserve medals for your patience! Thank you, Mishti (Chatterji), for taking a chance on an unknown author.

Kisses for Sheri Pie (Sheri Safran), my agent, the woman who made it all happen. Thank you, Brenda (Kimber), my editor, for letting me flow – and for all those thought-provoking questions!

AUTHOR'S NOTE

This is a personal book and, as such, it focuses on a small slice of the Muslim experience. As Muslim women, we are comfortable sharing our experiences and speaking candidly about our private lives and thoughts because we have a great example in Aisha, the wife of the Prophet Muhammad (s), who shared the intimate details of her life with him (s) so that we could learn from her experiences. Perhaps some will learn from ours.

The opinions expressed in this book are the result of personal experiences and understanding and are therefore not representative of every Muslim woman. Nor is our experience as reverts (converts to Islam) a reflection of all Muslim women's experiences. Muslims consider accepting Islam to be merely 'reverting' to the human being's natural disposition of acknowledging and worshipping the One God, thus the use of 'revert' instead of 'convert'.

Also, although I have tried to explain Islamic concepts as clearly as possible, there are some things that will be difficult for non-Muslims to understand. The Muslim accepts these things because of his faith and grounding in Islamic knowledge – the same cannot be expected of those who have not entered the faith.

Muslims are required to send greetings of peace and blessings to the Prophet Muhammad (*sallallahu alaihi wasallam*) whenever his name is mentioned. For that reason, there is an (s) after his name, although the greeting should be said in full. Muslims also express respect for the Companions (r) of the Prophet (s) by saying 'RadhiAllahu anhu/anha' (May Allah be pleased with him/her) when mentioning their names.

According to Islamic terminology, the head-scarf is called a *khimar* in Arabic. However, as the word *hijab* is more commonly used, the two have been used interchangeably throughout the book.

Although my sisters' stories are true, all their names have been changed.

INTRODUCTION

Catching sight of a Muslim woman on Western city streets, covered from head to toe, rarely fails to provoke a strong reaction. Feelings of shock, horror, repulsion or pity are not uncommon, especially upon seeing this strangest of sights for the first time. Comments range from the patronizing ('Poor woman, doesn't she know she's in England now, she doesn't have to dress like that?') and the insulting ('It makes me sick to see them dressed like that!') to the ridiculous ('I bet she looks like a dog under there!').

Without doubt, the assumption is that this poor woman was forced by her husband or family to dress as she does, that she is an uneducated immigrant who probably speaks little or no English or that, steeped in ignorance, she has yet to experience the delights of Western freedoms. She is, in essence, desperate to be liberated.

Such is the common perception of this woman, who remains faceless, nameless and voiceless – a non-person.

But what if this woman had a name, what if she had a voice? What if she could tell you about herself, her history, her family, her thoughts and feelings? What if, by sharing herself with you, you grew to see beyond the exterior, beyond the veil, and see for yourself in what ways you are alike and in what ways you are different?

By 1977, my parents had left apartheid South Africa and settled in Leeds, where I was born. We then travelled to Ethiopia and then Zimbabwe, where I spent the next twelve years, attending primary and high school, living the life of your average middle-class Southern Africa teenager. My peers and I played, partied and preened in accordance with our cultural influences, namely, American music videos and films. At seventeen, I left what I considered the 'small-town mentality' of Harare and came to London to study. While at university, I was exposed to new ways of thinking and living – I became more aware of world issues and, like many Social Sciences students, became more radical and politicized, becoming quite a militant Afrocentric Black Nationalist. However, it was on a trip to Egypt that I first encountered Islam and was struck by the *hijab*, the covering of the Muslim woman. This trip proved to be a turning point in my life, causing me to question my lifestyle, my beliefs and my purpose in life. After much reflection and many air miles, I took my first tentative steps on the path of Islam.

Since accepting Islam, I have been blessed to meet many wonderful women who, like me, converted to Islam: honest women, caring women – strong women. Through our blossoming friendships, I have got to know the many sides of their personalities. They have taught me about faith, about patience, about themselves and about myself. But, for so long, we have been defined by others, in words that are not our own.

For a long time, the idea of writing about my experiences and those of my sisters had appealed to me. I thought that it was important to tell our story, both for those who know us and for those who don't, the strangers who see us and so misunderstand us.

I invite you now to accompany me into my heart and the hearts of my 'sisters in Islam', to find out who we really are – not what the stereotypes say, nor what the media says – what *we* say. We have spoken candidly about many aspects of our lives, trusting that you will listen without prejudice.

I also hope that, while you read, you will

address your own ideas and challenge your pre-conceptions about Islam. By showing the Islamic faith at work in the lives of the women in this book, I hope to show a personal and private side of Islam, one that is only seen by those privileged enough to be admitted to its inner circle.

This book is a celebration. It is a celebration of womanhood. It is a celebration of sisterhood. It is a celebration of courage, warmth and friendship. It is a celebration of laughter, patience and love. It is a celebration of Islam.

Na'ima B. Robert
December 2004

Part One
Finding Islam

This is the story of how we came to accept Islam.

These stories are only slices of personal history.

Part of us wants to keep them that way, to keep them private, to protect them.

But another part of us, the stronger part, wants to share this history with you, to take you on this journey too.

To show that Islam speaks to the hearts of people from a thousand diverse backgrounds, in a thousand different ways.

To show how Islam enriches the lives of millions of people, every day, in every way.

To share the heartache and joy of leaving what you know for what you can only imagine.

To show that we have chosen to be and are proud to be Muslim women.

To show that we are striving to hold on to our Islam with all our strength and that we will hold on, even when it burns like hot coals.

To show that we are of you, that our roots spring from where yours do.

It is only our fruit and flowers that differ, for we are nourished by a different source.

I

MY PATH

I was born in the north of England, in Leeds, where my mother and father went on to buy a little terrace house, on a narrow road of other terrace houses just like it. Three years later, our family moved to Ethiopia and then to Zimbabwe when I was six. By this time, I had a brother and an extremely chubby baby sister, whom I adored. We lived in a lovely house in one of the 'low-density' suburbs of Harare, with a swimming pool and two acres of flowers, a vegetable garden and banana trees. For the first eighteen years of my life, I lived like every other middle-class Zimbabwean youth that I knew.

I went to a girls' school in Harare, complete with blazers, boaters and Head Girls, as I became in the Sixth Form. My mother and father tried their best to teach us about our Scottish and Zulu roots, our Southern African culture, to appreciate who we were and where we came from. We were never sent to exclusive colonial-style private schools, we learnt traditional Zimbabwean dances and would often sing anti-apartheid songs while we walked to school. Indeed, we were politically aware from a very young age although, as we grew older, the desire to fit in with our peers and emulate what we saw on television often overrode our parents' best intentions!

I enjoyed school a great deal and routinely won academic, art, public speaking and drama prizes at the end of each year. I was an outgoing and confident girl, full of energy and ideas, always on the go, always developing new projects. However, alongside my squeaky-clean school persona, I was also a party girl, as were all my friends. We all lived a double life in a way, many of us excelling at school while remaining a permanent feature of the Harare party scene. Our role models were not classical writers or feminist thinkers, although we did subscribe to the flirty, in-your-face, *Cosmopolitan* magazine brand of feminism! Nor did we model ourselves on the heroines of the Zimbabwean liberation struggle, the *Chimurenga*. Our role models were American actresses, singers and entertainers, among them the girl groups TLC and Salt-N-Pepa. Our 'moral guidance' came from R'n'B, ragga music and 'gangsta' rap – not much guidance, as anyone who has ever listened to 2 Live Crew, Snoop Doggy Dogg or Shabba Ranks will tell you! In fact, the sexual mores and social aspirations of the majority of 'cool' Harare youth were wholly imported from Western shores – we were like young people in so many places, carefree and careless. I often shudder to think of how many times we came close to danger because of the way we lived and our lack of caution. Carelessness due to drink, drunk-driving, getting lifts with strangers, being out alone at night with no money, at the mercy of guys as foolish as we were, drugs, STDs, HIV, early pregnancy, abortions, you name it, we came close to it. However, I came out of my teenage years unscathed, with good O and A Levels to boot! Not all my friends were that lucky.

Unlike the majority of Zimbabweans, I was raised in a non-religious household. My mother, a strikingly beautiful Zulu woman, had been born and raised a Christian but lived a glamorous city life in Johannesburg, working as a nurse while winning beauty titles and ballroom dancing championships. Going against tradition (and the apartheid laws), she fell in love with my father, a White South African. Having been groomed for privilege and supremacy in exclusive White boarding-schools, he had

21

rejected the racist premise of apartheid and embraced the anti-apartheid struggle through grassroots theatre. If ever there was a 'White African', he was one! My father was a committed Marxist and an agnostic at that. So, as children, we were told that the Bible was full of fairy tales, and that was what we believed. However, I sang the hymns and said The Lord's Prayer like all the other children, even though it didn't mean anything to me.

In my final year of high school, I decided to apply for a university place in London. I was determined to get out of Zimbabwe. I didn't want to fall into the trap of thinking that the city life of Harare was all there was and that the Circus nightclub was the most sophisticated place on the planet. So I applied and was accepted at one of the colleges in the University of London. All I had to do was find the money to get me there! After about eight months working in the travel industry and singing in a successful local band, I saved enough money for my ticket and my first few months in London. So I left Harare to study French, Politics and Business Studies in London. It was there that I met my first close-knit group of girlfriends and began to discover the true meaning of friendship between women. We read together, worked together, ate together and partied together. We explored

Frantz Fanon, Alice Walker and Descartes. We nodded our heads to Puff Daddy's crew, Maxwell and Erykah Badu. We let our hair 'go natural', no chemicals, twisted it, braided it and wrapped it in Afro print. We talked about Black issues (on which our views were to become increasingly militant), about the state of the world, about our families and our pasts. My social circle was a group of beautiful, confident young Black women, getting an education, having fun – on top of the world, or so I thought!

In the summer of my first year at university, I took a trip that was to change my life for ever. And it all began with an innocent invitation to participate in a music festival in Egypt as a Zimbabwean representative, alongside one of my musician friends who was a professional singer and mbira player (a traditional Zimbabwean instrument). Although I was not a trained musician, I could sing and play the African drum, *ngoma*, as well as perform many traditional Zimbabwean dances.

Egypt was hot and noisy and it bustled in shades of sand and sunlight. Of course, we explored the pyramids, museums and markets as all tourists do. But I also remember being very aware of women in headscarves, in *hijab*, wherever we went and, quite frankly, I was appalled. All my budding feminist instincts raged

23

against the whole idea of a woman covering herself – I thought it a symbol of female oppression, of male dominance. But most of all, I thought it made them look terribly ugly. Usually, when we see things that are foreign to us, we base our opinions on our own experiences and knowledge. It is rare for us actually to step outside our own perceptions and try to understand what we see through the eyes of those living it. For some reason, on that trip, I dared to ask about what seemed so incomprehensible to me.

One evening, we were performing at a concert in a village out of town. After our set, I remember seeing a young woman, the organizer's wife, who was wearing a creamy coloured headscarf – a *hijab*. It framed her face and then fell in folds over her neck and chest. I looked into her face – she was beautiful. It seemed to me that her face was glowing and, somehow, in some way, the *hijab* only accentuated that. I was so taken with that sight that I stopped to speak to her. After exchanging pleasantries, I asked her the question that had been burning in my brain since I had arrived in Cairo: 'Why do you cover yourself? You are so beautiful.' To this day, her answer hits me with its clarity and simplicity.

'Because,' she said, 'I want to be judged for what I say and what I do, not for what I look like.'

BAM!

Ever since I can remember, I have been aware of my looks – not so much because I am particularly beautiful (although my friends and family would attest to my vanity!), but because of how people reacted to me. Throughout my teenage years, my friends and I were totally comfortable with the notion of using our looks as leverage, of wielding power over men in this way. In that world, every woman knows the drill: when you go for that job interview, you make sure you look your best, and if it's a man you're meeting, perhaps even show a bit of leg, laugh at his jokes, pout a bit to be taken out to lunch – that sort of thing. Most women grow up knowing these tricks and use them both consciously and unconsciously.

So on that night in an Egyptian village, when that lovely woman told me that she was not interested in being judged on her appearance, but on what she said and thought, I had to sit up and take notice! What did she mean? Remove physical looks from the equation? I felt nothing but admiration for this woman. What is it about Islam, I thought, that can make a woman so strong that she no longer strives to be noticed by men, no longer needs the admiring gaze to feel attractive, no longer puts herself on display when the rest of the world is doing just that? These questions affected me deeply. I began to think about my life, about my own self-image and how I wanted to grow and develop. I asked myself whether I had the courage, the confidence, and the self-esteem to get by on my character and intellect alone.

And so it was, on that fateful trip to Egypt in the summer of 1998, that I began to think about Islam and set in motion the wheels of change. It was as if speaking with that beautiful woman who had so impressed me with her quiet strength of character had opened my eyes. Suddenly, I saw worship all around me – in mosques, on the streets, everywhere. All at once, I became aware of words of devotion, uttered in Arabic – 'bismillah' – in the name of Allah, 'alhamdulillah' – all praise is due to Allah, 'insha Allah' – if Allah wills, 'masha Allah' – it is as Allah wills. I was both surprised and intrigued, for I suddenly realized that I had a spiritual side that I had never bothered to explore. And it worried me that I knew so little about one of the world's great religions. I had had my fill of Christianity. All those religious education lessons at school had left me cold, the memory of the Bible-bashing, gun-toting colonizers indelibly etched on my brain. It was near impossible for me to divorce the Christian message from all its cultural baggage and from the imperialism that had brought it to Africa. Growing up in Zimbabwe, one of the frontline states bordering apartheid South Africa and conflict-ridden Mozambique, Angola and Namibia, we were very much aware of the way in which Christianity had been used as a smokescreen to cover the wholesale theft of our land. Although this did not (and still does not) deter the majority of Southern Africans from following the faith, it bothered me. This unease was only increased by my involvement with Black and Africanist thought at university – becoming a Christian was akin to selling out. But Islam? Islam was completely new to me then and came with no history as far as I was concerned. I started to ask questions about the faith, what Muslims believed in, what they did, what they didn't do. I resolved to read the Qur'an on my return to London. And the Bible too – I felt I wanted to give Christianity one more shot.

I left Egypt shaken: my encounter with the Islamic faith had affected me to the core. I couldn't put my finger on what had touched me so, but whatever it was had thrown into question all those long-held assumptions and expectations about my future ambitions. What was my life about? Would I finish university and get a high-powered job, working nine to nine? Would I spend my money on clothes and home furnishings, visiting Zimbabwe every year? Would I eventually return there, get married to a local 'mover and shaker' and live in a leafy suburb with a maid, a cook and a gardener, far away from the common folk, the *povo*? Would I wait until I was thirty and then have children, making sure to send them to the best colonial-style private schools and take them on overseas holidays every year? In essence, would I live the life that I had decided on during my teenage years, the life that all young Zimbabweans in my social group aspired to? Somehow, all that I had seen and heard in Egypt had awakened something in me, a yearning for direction, for depth and substance – a yearning for something more than the vapid existence I had been planning for. For the first time, I began to wonder about the world and my place in it: I began to wonder about the meaning of life.

On my return to London, I was already convinced that I wanted to give 'dressing modestly' a try. So I wrapped my head, much as the singer Erykah Badu was doing that year, and wore loose-fitting clothes – tunic tops and wide pants in muted colours. Alternatively, I would always make sure that I kept my coat on if I had tightish trousers on. My transformation from disco diva to 'African sistah' did not go unnoticed on campus. One of the rumours that reached me was that I had joined a cult and had to wear the head-wrap all the time. However, the rumours didn't faze me because my instincts told me that I was doing the right thing, no matter what wild conclusions other people jumped to.

I bought a translation of the Qur'an by Marmaduke Pickthall, the English writer who became a Muslim in the early twentieth century. To my dismay, however, I could not grasp its magnitude. Apart from uninspiring religious education lessons in school, I'd grown up outside the biblical tradition and could not relate to the stories of the prophets and the peoples of the past. And, as I could not read Arabic at that time, I had to make do with the English version, which, as anyone will tell you, is a poor substitute. No one had ever explained its origins to me – I did not know how it had come to exist in its present form, whether it was the original revelation itself or whether someone, the Prophet Muhammad (s) or his followers, had actually composed it themselves. I thought it very much like the Bible, in that it contained some of the same stories and that it had been written by different men over a number of years. In fact, my initial reaction was quite irreverent and my first copy is full of underlining, question marks and exclamation marks. There were some concepts I just could not grasp at that time and it was only when I learnt more about the Qur'an that I began to understand them.

But there were aspects of Qur'anic law that I readily understood. I could see the beauty and wisdom of establishing the prayer five times a day. It meant that the first action of the day was worship, *Salat al-Fajr*, as was the last, *Salat al-'Isha*. In between those two prayers were the other three, *Salat adh-Dhuhr*, at about lunchtime, *Salat al-'Asr*, mid-afternoon, and *Salat al-Maghrib*, prayed when the setting sun turned the clouds crimson. Those five prayers were a constant reminder of God and a chance to renew one's relationship with Him.

There were other laws that made sense to me as well. Although my friends and I had been known to indulge in a tipple occasionally, I had no problem accepting the prohibition of alcohol and other intoxicants. It is a well-known fact that Zimbabwean men love their beer; throughout my childhood and adolescence, I had seen for myself the drunkenness, the squandering of wages, the violence, the promiscuity and the devastating consequences that accompanied excessive drinking in the African context. But anyone anywhere in the world who has smelt the reek of stale beer on their breath, felt the throb of a hangover, tasted the sickening slime of drunken vomit, seen the pathetic pain of an alcoholic's need or suffered the consequences of a drunken 'bit of fun' will understand, at least a little, the way in which alcohol can debase the human being. Although these scenarios do not accompany all alcoholic (mis)adventures, the prospect of them was enough to convince me of the wisdom of staying away from it altogether.

However, it took a nasty surprise to stop me eating pork. My flatmate and I had bought some and had put it in the fridge. To our horror, when we took it out to cook the next day, the pale lump of meat was crawling with maggots. That was enough to make me swear off pork for life. To this day, even the sound of the word makes me feel sick.

To me, the injunctions for men and women to be modest and treat each other with respect meant an end to unwanted male attention, to catcalls, to wolf whistles, to innuendo and sexual harassment. It also meant an end to seeking male approval for my looks or clothes. That meant that I changed how I dressed and how I interacted with men, keeping a certain distance between them and me. It was a new way of being, a new way of looking at the world. It meant that I called the shots: I shared as much of myself as I saw fit and no more – no man had any *right* to me. What can I say? It was empowering.

So, slowly but surely, my lifestyle was changing. However, I was not convinced that I needed to actually convert to Islam in order to benefit from the Islamic way of life. I thought that I would merely continue to change a few things here and there while maintaining my own individual lifestyle and goals. I still felt much more loyalty to my Black 'brothas' and 'sistahs' than to the Muslims I had met. Indeed, although I was being drawn towards Islam, Muslims themselves were still a mystery to me. My university was in Mile End, just up the road from Whitechapel and the now (in)famous Brick Lane, densely populated by Asians, most of them Muslims. They were all around us there – in the estates and terrace houses, chicken-and-chips shops and storefront mosques. I would often see the men, stern-faced, many with grey and white beards, walking purposefully to the little house near campus that served as a mosque – a mosque where, I was later to learn, there was no space for women to pray. Although women have the choice between praying at home or at the mosque, it is a sad feature of some more traditional mosques that they do not allow women to make this choice for themselves. The Muslims there were mainly Bengalis and I would see the women too, their saris peeking out from under their black cloaks, their scarves perched precariously on their heads, their lips and teeth stained deep orange by the betel nut they liked to chew. And then there were the young girls, fresh-faced with neat lace-trimmed scarves and feminine Pakistani trouser suits, *shalwar kameez*, and the young boys, thin and wiry, with gelled hair and the ubiquitous mobile phone. I saw all these people, these Muslims, and I knew that they believed in Allah and that they no doubt read the same Qur'an that I battled with every night. And yet, I felt no kinship with them at all – I did not see myself reflected in their eyes. And so I kept away.

My religious solitude was to end when I saw a girl from university who was in the year above me. Her name was Sandra and I had been trying to get her to come to the African Caribbean Society (ACS) for a long time. However, her best friend, Hanah, was an Arab, a Muslim, with an Egyptian father and Zanzibari mother. I remember she had always been dead against what she saw as the exclusionist and racist premise of the ACS, so I had pretty much given up on the two of them. But, one day, I was walking through the canteen and I caught sight of Sandra, sitting with a group of friends. They all looked the same, except for the strange look on Sandra's face and the scarf that was tied around her head. It was one of those lace-trimmed *hijabs* favoured by the Bengalis, but she had wrapped it around her head instead of letting it fall over her neck and chest. She looked so different. What has she done? I asked myself. I was so curious that I could not resist going up to her and asking about her new look. That was when she told me that she had taken her *shahadah* that weekend – she had affirmed the Muslim testimony of faith:

'*Ash-hadu an-laa ilaaha illallah wa ash-hadu ana Muhammad ar-rasoolullah.*'

'I bear witness that there is nothing worthy of worship, in truth, except Allah and that Muhammad is the Messenger of Allah.'

She was a Muslim now. I was shocked and envious at the same time – she looked so happy, as though she knew that she had done something important and meaningful, that she had done the right thing. She had taken a brave step, a step I was too frightened to take.

'Well,' I managed to say, 'you were braver than I was.' Then I told her about my tentative steps towards Islam and my reservations. That was when she asked me if I would come to her room in the halls of residence and show her how to tie a headwrap. I was happy to oblige. The very next day, I went over with some material, a beautiful gold and red striped weave from Egypt, a thick black fabric perfect for solid 'wraps' and a length of navy chiffon. And that night, amidst the trying, the tying and several failed attempts, a friendship began to blossom, a friendship that was to change my life for ever.

All of a sudden, I had someone to share my interest in Islam with, to discuss and debate the ins and outs of the faith with and I relished it. And just as my interest in all things Islamic began to grow, so my passion for 'Black issues' began to wane. The more serious issues were hardly ever addressed at the African Caribbean Society meetings and I was particularly frustrated by the repetitive way in which we discussed the same topics, year in, year out. As the same old debates about African vs. Caribbean identity, the dangers of Black–White relationships, and misogynist and violent song lyrics continued to raise temperatures during our meetings, my heart began to feel strangely restless. It all seemed so shallow, so meaningless – were these really the most important issues facing us as human beings? My growing interest in Islam had exposed me to a radically different world view and a new understanding of the purpose for human existence, and I found it increasingly difficult to ignore all that I now knew. The last straw for me was when the Society organized a viewing of the Jamaican film *Dancehall Queen* as a cultural event. Sitting in the darkened auditorium, with the ragga music blaring, gazing at the writhing bodies on the dance floor, legs splayed, clad in 'batty riders' and thigh-high boots, I felt so distant, so apart. This is not who

I am any more, I thought to myself. I no longer belong here.

So I got up; I left and went to the student prayer room on the other side of the campus. I needed to be around other people who were on the same wavelength as me. I needed beneficial company. I needed depth and meaning. I needed *soul food*! And it was then that I realized that I no longer felt completely at home with my old persona and that, little by little, my heart was inclining towards Islam.

But, for all my heart's yearnings, there were practicalities to consider. And ideologies. And politics. How could I, a Black African woman (as I saw myself then, never mind my mixed parentage!) be part of a religion like Islam? As far as I could see, it was a religion for Asians and Arabs! After all, they were the only Muslims I had ever really seen. I failed to picture how I could fit in to that way of life without losing my sense of identity. And to espouse a faith that would risk estranging me from my family, friends and the traditions of my ancestors filled me with apprehension.

My new friend, Sandra, was always very patient with me when I brought up these objections. I think that part of her could see where I was coming from but a larger part of her wondered why I was so hung up on the whole

'African identity' thing. To her it was simple: if Islam is the truth, all these other things are of secondary importance, so why let them get in the way of following what you know to be right?

But I had more questions for her. I remember very clearly crying out one day, 'What if I give my life to Allah and He does something I don't want with it?' After all, I had plans: the fancy job, the money, the big wedding back home, the children in striped blazers and braids – I had it all figured out! But if I accepted Islam, I knew all that had to change. Was I ready to let go of my ambitions and plans for the future? No, I was not ready for that change – not ready to give up a carefully planned future that had been dictated by my past. I was being held back by the fear of the unknown, the fear of uncertainty, the fear of submission.

It was around this time that I started working as a temp for a major shoe company in London. There I met a woman of West Indian descent and, pleased to see another Black face in the office, I became friendly with her. I found her to be very down to earth and welcoming, and I was extremely impressed when she told me that she had taken an 'X' after her name as a substitute for the family name that she would never know. In the West, almost every Black person whose ancestors were slaves has a European surname,

37

the name of their ancestors' owner, the slave master. Their original African names were changed and are now, for the most part, lost for ever. I was soon to discover that the practice of replacing the slave name with an 'X' was what the followers of the so-called Nation of Islam did, just as their charismatic one-time spokesman Malcolm X had done. So when Monica told me that she regularly went to the Nation of Islam's Temple One in Shepherd's Bush and invited me to go with her, I was eager to go and experience it for myself. Maybe this was where I belonged – in a 'Black version' of Islam? So, on the evening of the next meeting, we went together and I had my first encounter with the controversial Nation of Islam.

We got to the meeting hall. The Nation of Islam bodyguards, tall and broad in their smart suits and neat bow ties were there to greet us. Amid a chorus of 'Asalaamu alaikum, my Black sisters', 'Asalaamu alaikum, my Black queens', they directed us to the booth at the top of the stairs where we were to be searched, as was the somewhat paranoid practice at Nation of Islam meetings. The woman in the booth wore what appeared to be a uniform: a navy blue dress and a cape on her head, much like a nun's habit, which covered her hair and lay behind her ears down to her back. We were searched and I remember being impressed by her efficiency and seriousness, something that I had rarely found in the Black organizations I knew. When we entered the meeting room, the women were seated on the rows of chairs closest to the entrance and the men on rows of chairs on the other side of the room. A narrow aisle separated them. Everyone was looking up at the stage, where recruits from the Fruit of Islam, the Nation of Islam cadres, stood with their legs apart, gazing impassively into the middle distance, much as they had in the 1960s, in Elijah Muhammad's day. The other men were all dressed in suits, many with bow ties, and the women wore the same capes as the first woman we had met. The visitors sat in the rows further back, some donning headscarves for the occasion.

The meeting began with the greeting of 'Asalaamu alaikum' and a reading from the Qur'an, the first verse, Surah al-Fatihah. What followed then was a mixture of evangelist-style preaching (for which the Nation of Islam speakers are well known), personal anecdotes and a presentation by the children who attended the Nation of Islam school. The meeting and its content evoked powerful emotions in all of us, especially the more 'Black conscious' ones in the gathering. I went again, a few weeks later, taking with me my flatmate, Efua, and my colleague, Nichelle. Nichelle was far from impressed with the racist ideas espoused by the speakers but they didn't put Efua and me off too much. But it was only when I went to a third meeting with a Muslim friend that I began to have doubts as to whether the 'Nation of Islam' was the right thing for me. For a start, I was not convinced by their premise that all civilizations in the world had been established by the 'Asiatic Black man'. I found it ridiculous that a movement that claimed to espouse Black advancement chose to wear suits and natty bow ties as their uniform. Even more incredible was the routine use of the name 'Muhammad' – an Arabic name if ever there was one – while still claiming to be neither African nor Caribbean, but 'Asiatic' in origin. On the train home, our Muslim friend said, 'That's not real Islam, you know.' And, though I knew very little at that time, I knew that he was right. Compared with the doctrine of the Nation of Islam, 'real' Islam seemed measured, balanced, welcoming and open. Instead of concentrating on the relationship between the Black man and the 'White devils', Black empowerment and other social problems that Black communities faced, Islam stressed the relationship between all human beings and their Creator – in belief, in manners and in worship. The two ways of life and belief systems seemed miles apart. My search was not yet over.

The sense that I was reaching a turning point in my life just wouldn't leave me. While on the one hand I sensed that I could not continue picking and choosing the aspects of Islam that fitted in with my world view, on the other, I knew I could not go back to my old lifestyle. The time had come for me to make a decision. Sandra, who had become a good friend by now, told me that I would have to make a choice or risk dying in disbelief, as a non-Muslim. I was agonized. But the Christmas holidays were around the corner and I had received my pay from the department store where I worked part time. What would I do? Would I go to spend Christmas with my family who were in the States? Or would I go somewhere that would help me understand what I was meant to do with the rest of my life? I chose the latter. I decided to go to Muslim Africa, to Guinea, the land and life so vividly etched in my mind by Camara Laye's book, *L'Enfant Noir*. I also chose Guinea because I knew that it had a largely Muslim population and also because, on my way to Egypt, I had met the director of the Guinean postal service and he and his people had impressed me with their firm faith and strong sense of identity. He was to be my contact as I made preparations for my trip.

All my friends were appalled. To them, the whole idea was crazy: I hardly knew my host, had never visited the country, would be travelling on my own and would have no one to look out for me. So strong were their objections that I almost called the whole thing off, until, by a twist of fate, a few things happened that made me believe that I was destined to make that journey. The first was a chance meeting with a group of Nigerian Muslim women while at work in the department store. I recognized them immediately as Nigerian because they were wearing tie-dyed *boubous*, those voluminous African outfits usually known as kaftans. But on their heads, instead of the common starched headwrap, they wore the same lace-trimmed *hijabs* favoured by the young Asian girls in my area. I was intrigued and, as was my practice in those days, immediately went up to them and said, '*Asalaamu alaikum*' – peace be upon you. They all answered with bright smiles and, '*Wa alaikum salaam*' – upon you be peace. I went on to ask them where they were from and what they were doing. One of them, the one with the brightest smile, told me that they were from Lagos and that they had come to London on holiday. It turned out that she was the owner of a travel agency back home in Nigeria. During the course of our conversation, it emerged that she had a colleague who ran a travel agency in Conakry, the capital of Guinea! When I told her that I had been planning a trip there but had no other contacts, she insisted that I take her card and the name of the lady in Conakry and look her up as soon as I got there. That made my heart smile – was this a sign that I was meant to go after all?

Then, on my way home on the tube, I met a woman who, for some reason, gave me the feeling that she believed in what I was looking for. I felt compelled to talk to her.

'Are you a Muslim?' I asked her after introducing myself, to which she replied, 'Yes.' It turned out that she was from Sierra Leone, but I think it was her father who was from Guinea. It was just like a game show, as if two bells had gone off in my head, indicating that I had the right answer. Although it may sound foolhardy, I made up my mind there and then that I was going to Guinea. I remember saying to one of my friends at the time, 'I am going and if I die out there, I know that it is only by the will of Allah.'

So, taking my month's wages, which included some overtime and an overdraft, I bought my ticket, packed my bags and said goodbye to my brother and sister who were in transit in London. I then boarded the plane for Paris. There I was to catch a flight to Dakar, Senegal, and from there, make my way to Conakry. All the while, I was consumed by a strange sensation. I felt like I was floating on the waves of destiny, of the *qadr*, swimming with the tide, drifting far out to sea. I was serene and unafraid, although I was well aware of the potential danger. The director of the Post Office could have been lying all along, there could be no wife or children, it could all be a ploy to get me out there and take advantage of me. But my mind was untroubled by these thoughts. I had no misgivings, and by the time I got to the transit lounge in Paris, I knew I wanted to be a Muslim. I wanted to be like those people around me who exuded so much confidence and who seemed to be sustained by their faith in Islam. This is an excerpt from the journal I kept while I was out there:

13/12: Overcome by emotion at the first sight of Senegalese Muslims – they look like my people! My chest trembles and my eyes fill with tears – *alhamdulillah!* . . . The men are bickering about something now – is it Arabic they are speaking? Silver rings everywhere, an Adidas trainer peeks out from one old man's outfit. The old man with the brown *boubou* and matching Burberry scarf kills it!

I was completely seduced by the look and feel of these Muslims who were so different to the ones I'd encountered in England. As someone still steeped in the ideals of Black nationalism, these Muslims appealed to my own African identity and my sense of Black pride. They were proud to be African, in their looks, manners and dress, a quality all too rare in many parts of Southern Africa. There, the legacy of British colonialism manifested itself in the way many people sought dignity and prestige by trying to be British. In stark contrast, I was impressed by what I saw as the confidence of the Muslim people of 'French' West Africa.

After a brief stopover in Dakar, I flew to Conakry and found myself, safe and sound, in the home of the director of the Post Office with his wife, Madame, and two little sons. And that was the start of four unforgettable weeks. In that time, in the sticky heat of Conakry, I took to wearing my headwrap with a kaftan, *un boubou*. I found them loose and comfortable and, although they were still very beautiful, they hid the shape of my body and I revelled in that. I was cool, at ease, and passed almost unnoticed amongst the locals. I was loath to wear the few Western clothes I had brought with me, always eager to go back to the comfort and security of my folds of starched fabric. However, not everyone felt this way. My hostess did not cover Islamically at all and there were many times when she and other women would try to convince me to shed my 'old women's' *boubou* in favour of jeans from the market. Needless to say, I was appalled by the idea and refused every time. Firstly, I was not interested in going back to wearing jeans and, secondly, I was not about to go 'wearing jeans from no Guinea market'. After all, I still had to keep up some sort of image! The desire to 'protect myself' with the *boubou* was strengthened by an incident that took place concerning one of the wealthiest men in Guinea at the time. Ever since I had announced my desire to become a Muslim, there had been one issue on everyone's mind: who was I going to marry? Now, to be honest, marriage had not been at the forefront of my mind but here, all of a sudden, it consumed my waking hours. Everyone had a brother, an uncle, a cousin who would make me a wonderful husband – it drove me absolutely crazy! One such prospect was this particular specimen, '*un des serieux de Conakry*' (one of the big shots of Conakry), a mover and shaker of immense proportions and nearly twice my age. My host family genuinely thought that he would make a good match for me and encouraged him to come to the house and talk his foolishness with me. One evening, he invited us to visit his football team, which was staying at one of the city's five-star hotels. Madame, upon seeing that I intended to wear one of my *boubous* as usual, made a tremendous fuss and insisted that I change into something younger, smarter and less voluminous. Stupidly, I gave in to her. I then spent one of the most uncomfortable evenings of my life: ignored by the men as they talked football, I was obviously the arm candy and not there for conversation. It is so strange to me that women are often expected to accept this role. They must be with a man to be looked at, admired and flattered but not to speak or to express any kind of intelligent thought. Strange too how the man gets his kicks from his friends admiring 'his woman', envying him and secretly coveting her. It makes him feel like a man, macho, as if her good looks validate him and his good taste. I was never comfortable with that, although like many impressionable young women who are seeking approval, it was often par for the course when I was growing up. On that warm evening in Conakry, I felt humiliated and was furious with myself for capitulating, for not standing by what I believed in. I abruptly left the men and went to the shoreline, at the edge of the hotel garden, where I could taste the salty mist from the waves breaking on the rocks. At least I still had my headwrap. It is strange, but although the headwrap is by no means an Islamic form of covering, it became my lifeline in those days. As long as I had that, I felt that I could hold on to my dignity and my principles. And I knew that if I lost that, I would have lost more than just the covering on my head – I would have lost the fight for my new identity. That evening, I resolved never to be put in such a compromising situation again. My days of being a man's trophy were over.

My reputation for intransigence spread throughout our community of family and friends and I was affectionately dubbed, 'Al Hajja', the one who has made Hajj, the pilgrimage to Mecca. The reason for this was that it is common for people in the Muslim world to live the most un-Islamic of lives until middle age when they then perform the Hajj. As the reward for Hajj is the forgiveness for all one's sins, many come back from Mecca with their consciences clear, ready to start living an Islamic life, now that the fiery desires of youth had been spent. So, because I eschewed clingy, revealing clothes, boyfriends and showing my hair, I earned myself that title.

In Guinea I was once again surrounded by the ebb and flow of worship – prayers uttered aloud at dawn while mist still blanketed the ground, the call of le muezzin, Friday rituals and the

Jumu'ah prayer (the Friday congregational prayer) at the mosque. Five times a day, I would make *wudhu'*, put on a scarf that covered my head, neck and chest, roll out my prayer mat, face the *Qiblah*, the Ka'bah in Mecca, and pray – the five daily prayers became the natural rhythm of my day.

It meant a lot to me that this ritual was the same one practised by the Prophet of Islam (s) and his followers, and by Muslims all over the world since then. Later, it was at such times that I would think of the *ummah*, the Islamic nation, and I would feel proud to be part of such a wonderful community.

Every Friday, I would go to one of the many mosques with my host's mother, Hajja, a formidable woman with a great sense of humour and a wonderful personality. We would drape a wide piece of fabric across the top of our headwraps and across our necks and over our shoulders. In that way, we would make ourselves suitably dressed for the prayer. The first time I ever prayed in the way that the Prophet Muhammad (s) himself had prayed over 1400 years ago, I simply followed what my neighbours were doing. When they raised their hands, I raised mine: '*Allahu akbar!*' ('God is the greatest!'). When they bent forward from the waist in *ruku*, I did the same: '*Subhana Rabbi al-Adheem*' ('glorified be my Lord, the Most Great'). When they knelt down, faces and palms pressed to the floor, I prostrated with them: '*Subhana Rabbi al-A'laa*' ('glorified be my Lord, the Most High').

Can there be a posture more symbolic of man's relationship with God than the prostration? The human being, who normally walks so tall and proud, bends his body willingly – his waist, his knees, his ankles – until his face is pressed to the ground in humility before his Lord. I found this posture extremely moving. It was at that moment, in *sujood*, that I felt closest to Allah, whose name now rolled off my tongue with ease. It was then that I was able to speak to Him, to call out to Him, to confide in Him, to cry tears before Him. It was while in *sujood* that I learnt to love Him.

On that first Friday, when we returned to Hajja's house, one of the men taught me how to recite the first verse of the Qur'an:

> *In the Name of Allah, the Most Beneficent, the
>   Most Merciful*
> *'All the praises and thanks be to Allah, the Lord
>   of all the worlds.*
> *The Most Beneficent, the Most Merciful.*
> *The Only Owner of the Day of Recompense*
> *You (Alone) we worship, and You (Alone) we
>   ask for help.*

Guide us to the Straight Way.
The Way of those on whom You have bestowed
  Your Grace, not of those who earned Your
  Anger, nor of those who went astray.'
Surah al-Fatihah 1:1

Although the unfamiliar words tested my tongue, I persevered, learning that verse and two others phonetically. My hosts bought me a booklet from a roadside vendor that explained the postures and recitations that were involved in the prayer, the *salah*, and they gave me a velvet green prayer mat to use in my room. They also taught me how to make *wudhu'*, a form of ritual cleansing that Muslims make before approaching the prayer.

In the blue-tiled bathroom, I made my intention to make the *wudhu'* and then I washed my hands three times, the cool water slipping through my fingers and over my wrists. And, with a cupped right hand, I brought water to my face and took a mouthful and inhaled at the same time, emptying my mouth and nose with the left. I did that three times. Then on to wash my face three times. The water ran into my hand and, as I raised my arm, it flowed down it as I washed, first the right then the left, three times. I passed water over my hair, backwards, then forwards, then I wiped my ears with my fingers and thumb.

Lastly, I poured water from the jug onto my feet as I washed them three times. There are few things as refreshing as the *wudhu'*, particularly, I found, during the humid days in Guinea. It left me feeling clean and alert, ready to pray in the cool of my room, the shadows from the tree outside my window playing pretty patterns on my green prayer mat and the terracotta floor.

The days passed quickly in Conakry, peppered by trips to the market, prayers, buying new *boubous* and conversations – in French – with the neighbours and other people we met. I also learnt a few phrases of one of the local languages, Sousou, and used them often, much to my hosts' delight. And then, all at once, the month of Ramadhan was upon us and I could feel the excitement in the air.

> The month of Ramadhan, in which was revealed the Qur'an, a guidance for mankind and clear proofs for the guidance and the criterion [between right and wrong] . . .
> Surah Al-Baqarah 2:185

To my mind, there is nothing like being in a Muslim country during Ramadhan. There is nothing in the Western Muslim experience to rival it, no ritual, no sense of solidarity, nothing like it. To this day, I remember the camaraderie that came from knowing that everyone (well, almost everyone!) was abstaining from food, drink and sexual relations from dawn until dusk. And, like most parts of the Muslim world, we ate very well after the sun had gone down: aromatic rice and spicy fish, fresh sweet bread from the best baker in town, sweet-sour *bissap*, made from sorrel leaves and rose water, steamy couscous and roasted chicken and Madame's speciality, sweetcorn salad. After eating our fill, we would make *wudhu'* and walk through the now-damp dust to the mosque on the corner where the *'Isha* prayers were held. Women, dressed in *boubous* of many colours with translucent scarves thrown over one shoulder, always filled the upper section of the mosque at prayer time, particularly when it was time for *Tarawih*. These are the long prayers that are per-formed in almost every mosque during Ramadhan, during which the whole Qur'an is habitually recited over the course of the twenty-nine or thirty days of the month.

So, day by day, I came to feel comfortable as a Muslim amongst these people who, a month before, had been strangers to me. My hosts treated me as if I were their own daughter and I felt a strong sense of belonging. I was one of the family, present on family visits, shopping trips and weddings; they never left me out. That is not to say that there was no tension – obviously there were personality clashes of sorts and I witnessed many things that I knew were un-Islamic and *haram* (prohibited), even with my own limited knowledge of the *deen*. But I also saw that Islam was something that people *lived*, that it was not just an ideal. And I now knew that I could live it too. (The only question now was who to marry!) But I should mention here that although I prayed, fasted and covered my head, I had not yet taken my *shahadah* – I was not even a Muslim yet.

I came back from West Africa a changed woman. I had no doubts that Islam was for me. I had begun the process of surrender, of submission. It was on a bleak day in London, a few weeks after my return, that my friend Sandra and I made our way to Central Mosque in London's Regent's Park. It was there, after months of searching and questioning, that I finally accepted what had been in my heart for the longest time: 'I bear witness that there is nothing worthy of worship, in truth, except Allah and that Muhammad is the Messenger of Allah.'

In essence, I was the last person anyone would have expected to become a Muslim. I came from a completely non-religious background; I was young, and living a fun-filled, busy life. I was getting an education, planning for the future, politically aware and active. I was passionate about what I believed in. And then Islam came along and turned my world upside down. It made me ask questions, demand answers and learn to accept the undeniable. There was no way I could have turned away from Islam and been at peace with myself. For me it was quite simply the truth. And so I accepted it.

2

MY SISTERS' PATHS

But surely I am an aberration. After all, aren't most women who 'turn to Islam' easily influenced, brainwashed, no-hopers who need something to believe in to make up for their own deprived existence? Or else they do it for a man, to keep him and, hopefully, bear his children. Surely the world is not full of beautiful, intelligent women, successful in their chosen careers, with active social lives, who willingly leave all that and embrace Islam? It will come as a surprise to many to discover that the new breed of Muslim women do not fit neatly into any pigeon holes – their stories are far more varied and interesting than the stereotypes.

Why Tell Them?

Muslims never tire of hearing stories about how people from distant places and with different faces came to embrace Islam. It is often an inspiration to be reminded that individuals from such different backgrounds came to unite upon a common understanding of the meaning of life. As sisters within Islam, as part of the inner circle, we are familiar with these fascinating stories – they are part of our history. For the non-Muslim, however, they remain a mystery, even though these are women who cross our paths every day, who live down the road, whose children attend our children's schools. I feel the time has come to open that inner circle. I want to share what I have been privileged to be a part of for the last six years, so that others may share in the wonders of a spiritual journey that unites so many people from so many ages, colours, places and backgrounds.

Girls Next Door

The one thing that binds the women quoted in this book is that they are all products of this society. They were born into it, they were schooled in its ways, they imbibed its beliefs, they lived up to its expectations. There was a time, not long ago, when the only 'veiled' Muslim women one would see were the Arab women in Oxford Street and Edgware Road. However, one glance at the sisters in this book will show that the face 'behind the veil' in contemporary London is no longer necessarily Middle Eastern. Since becoming Muslim, I have met English, Welsh and Scottish reverts, as well as Black sisters from Africa, the Caribbean and the Americas, sisters from the Far East – China, Malaysia and Taiwan. I have even met Muslim reverts from as far afield as New Zealand – yes, a real Kiwi – and Australia. The Muslim woman is no longer necessarily from a different culture, although the idea that she is makes it easy to generalize and stigmatize: 'Well, she's not like us, is she?'

The truth is that this woman could be your next-door neighbour, the girl your daughter went to school with, the woman your son had hoped to marry. She could have been brought up in a terrace house or a penthouse apartment with a view. She could speak with a cut-glass accent or in the best Cockney rhyming slang. She could put the 'ruffest ragamuffin' to shame with her Patois or speak French, Spanish and Italian – with no trace of an accent. She could cook the best steak and kidney pie you've ever tasted – and you'd never know it was *halal*! These are fish 'n' chips, rice an' peas, spag bol and coleslaw women. They are Jalof rice, paella, fried plantain, spring rolls and wonton soup women – not 'those people who eat curry all day'. With so many women living in the West embracing Islam, from every sector of society, the old prejudices just won't wash.

Uprooted Muslims

However, it is not only Western non-Muslims that 'find' Islam. Although most born Muslims grow up with some form of Islam in their lives, it is very common in this day and age to find girls and boys with Muslim names who are as 'Western' as Peter and Jane. The name 'Allah' is new to them, the Islamic beliefs and practices completely alien. There are parents who make a conscious decision to bring up their children without Islam for a variety of reasons. Some want their children to fit into the society they live in and to get ahead, others want them to focus on education or a career instead of being 'side-tracked' by religion, others still don't want to 'burden' them with cultural baggage that will only hold them back, perhaps secretly doubting the value of Islam in their and their children's lives. So there are women of Muslim parentage in this book who went to the same schools as their non-Muslim counterparts, who had the same manners, held the same values and were exposed to the same cultural influences. They too are products of this society and their entry into Islam is no less strange or unexpected than that of any other Western woman.

Sara grew up in a home devoid of any Islamic influences whatsoever.

'My father was not a practising Muslim at all,' she told me. 'The only restriction of his that came from Islam was that he didn't eat pork but, other than that, I never heard him talk about Allah or praying or fasting in the month of Ramadhan or anything. It was something completely alien to me. My father was really enamoured with European culture: compared with the chaos of Pakistan, the organization of European society appealed to him and fitted in with his mentality. He liked the art, he liked the music, the languages, and he enjoyed travelling to centres of "high culture".'

Indeed, Sara's only encounters with Islam were through friends at school and, although she acknowledged their shared identity, she had absolutely no idea of what that identity entailed.

'I remember that I had a Pakistani friend who was looking for a gift for her brother and she found this ring with "Allah" on it.

'"What does that mean?" I asked her.

'"Well, that's the name of God," she told

me. "That's what we believe as Muslims."

'I was like, "Ah, right . . ."

'I was completely disconnected from my Muslim identity. I had never seen a Muslim praying in my life – for me, praying was putting two palms together in front of me!'

Far from attending *madrasa* (classes to teach children how to recite the Qur'an and read and write Arabic) in the evenings, like most Pakistani children, Sara went to church and Sunday school with the Brownies and Girl Guides.

Brought up in France, Hajar was also divorced from her roots. She did not grow up on the largely Arab estates as so many French North African immigrants do, nor in the Muslim enclaves that other Algerians gravitated towards. The *harqis* were Algerian Berbers who fought for the French during the Algerian liberation war and Hajar's father was one.

'The children of *harqis* were brought up French,' she told me, 'because they couldn't really be anything else, as if they had no more right to an Algerian identity. My father always moved us away from any Arab influence – we lived in areas where people were very French. In our home, there was no tension whatsoever between an Algerian identity and a French one: we really grew up French. I never had a good Arab or Muslim friend, ever. My friends were always Karine, Eveline, Isabelle: French, French, French.'

Not only were there hardly any Arab influences around, but there was precious little Islam too. 'There was no Islam in our home at all, no religion, although there were Berber traditions that my parents followed, like weddings and circumcisions.'

Although her parents were from Bangladesh, Jameela was raised in a completely non-Islamic environment too.

'I grew up in an Asian household that was meant to be a Muslim household but wasn't. Hence, my name was Jane and my brother's name was Gavin. Yup, Jane and Gavin!'

These women encountered Islam as something new, something strange, just as their non-Muslim counterparts did. There was nothing in their background that made them predisposed to being a practising Muslim. They had to discover Islam for themselves and embrace it anew.

Church and Temple

Unlike me, most sisters grew up with some form of religious belief. These beliefs ranged from staunch to lapsed Christianity, from Taoism to Judaism, from Sikhism to Hinduism – I have met sisters from every religious background. A few sisters shared their religious backgrounds with me.

Like most Caribbean women of her generation, Umm Tariq was brought up a staunch Christian. As she puts it, 'Our parents were always God-fearing and they always taught us to give thanks to God and to acknowledge our Lord. So we always had the fear of God in our hearts when we were growing up.'

Umm Muhammad also grew up with strong religious influences: 'My mum brought us up as Christians: we went to church and Sunday school. We were always taught to fear God and to remember that God can see you. It was a very West Indian upbringing.'

However, Aliyah grew up in a non-religious West Indian family, a fact that could be attributed to her grandfather's harsh, dogmatic take on religion.

'We weren't religious, probably because my mum's dad was Seventh Day Adventist and he was such a staunch follower that he ended up driving all his children away from any kind of religion whatsoever.'

Mei Ling had believed in God from a very young age: 'The belief that there was a God had been instilled in me when I was little, for as long as I can remember.' She spent the first years of her life with her paternal grandmother, who was a strong believer in the principles of Taoism, visiting the temple regularly and praying to be reunited with her parents who had settled in the United Kingdom.

'My parents were Taoists but not really practising ones – my grandmother was really into it and we just followed her – she was very powerful. We would take part in all the rituals just to keep her happy. However, I never liked the statues in the temple – to me, they were decoration, they were not God. I felt that God was in me, He certainly wasn't those gold statues.'

However, once in Britain, Mei found herself drawn to the teachings of Christianity, partly due to her exposure to it at the Church of England school she attended. But, while studying Theology at A Level, she found her faith sorely tried by what they learnt about the Bible and its origins.

'I was shocked and horrified to discover that the Bible, the New Testament, was fabricated, that Christianity was like a farce. The New Testament was made up of bits and pieces and the material that they used to write the texts on had deteriorated . . . it was like dropping a book on the floor and all the pages falling out and then putting it back together without knowing the page numbers. It just didn't make sense. Many of the girls in the school were daughters of vicars and, during a class discussion, they stood up and said, "Even though the Bible is fabricated, I still have my faith, I am still firm on this religion." That was the day that I took my crucifix off and thought, Forget this.'

But, while Mei made a conscious decision to shed the beliefs she had grown up with prior to embracing Islam, the majority of sisters did not: they continued to be known as Christians, Hindus or Sikhs – the religions they had been brought up in.

Deprived Children?

As many people view 'turning to Islam' as a last resort, there is possibly a feeling that there must have been certain factors, an unhappy childhood perhaps, that triggered it. I know that, in my case, this could not have been further from the truth, having enjoyed a happy and fulfilling childhood and adolescence in Zimbabwe. But maybe other sisters had different stories to tell? For this reason, I asked the sisters to tell me about their backgrounds and their childhoods.

It came as no surprise to discover that some came from fairly sheltered, middle-class, two-parent families, with strong traditions and high expectations. Claire, for example, told me about her idyllic childhood on her parents' farm in

Ireland: 'I was brought up as a practising Catholic in Ireland. I had a very sheltered upbringing, a very white, Irish, Catholic upbringing, very family-oriented as well, lots of cousins, lots of aunties, lots of extended family. I grew up carefree . . . running round, gathering up the sheep, running up and down the fields . . .'

Mei Ling too spent her early life in a rural environment, albeit one quite different from the Irish meadows.

'I grew up with my maternal grandmother on a farm in Taiwan, in a country village. Occasionally, I would go up into the mountains to be with my maternal grandparents where life was really basic: bath time was out in the open, in the courtyard . . .'

When she was about four and a half, her parents sent for her to come and live with them in England. But life there as the eldest daughter of two hard-working, traditional Chinese parents had its own challenges.

'At the beginning, it was a bit difficult for me to settle into life in England – a new language, a new culture, and my parents didn't speak some of the dialects that I knew. There was a strict routine and I had grown up without one – I had to eat and go to bed when they told me to, whereas in Taiwan I had been very spoilt. Also, in England, I was always with Mum and Dad, whereas in Taiwan I had been with Granny and Grandpa, this uncle, this auntie, these cousins – "Mum and Dad" was a routine I wasn't used to.'

Some, like Sara, grew up in homes where both parents occupied traditional gender roles.

'When my parents first got married, it was not a problem for my mother to work. They entertained a lot and did all the things that young European couples do. But when my mum had the children, my father said to her, "Right, that's it, you stay at home with the children and do the cooking, the cleaning. Your place is in the home." And my mum just didn't know what to do with herself. All of a sudden, he had reverted to this traditional Pakistani man and that wasn't how she had expected him to be. But there was never any doubt that he loved my brother and me. He was very caring and he loved us to bits. He had a lot of time for us children, even when they separated.'

Others, like Aliyah, were raised solely by their mothers: 'Both my parents are St Lucian but I grew up in a one-parent family, just my mum, my brother and me. I don't have any bad memories of my childhood. My mum was not someone who beat us or raised her voice a lot. I don't remember any of that during my childhood.'

Listening to sisters describing their childhood experiences, I realized that their backgrounds did not fit any particular mould. It could not be said that all these reverts came from broken homes, or were the result of absent fathers, or abusive mothers, or a lack of routine or stimulation. Like the women themselves, their childhoods were varied and encompassed all manner of experiences. Certainly, these young women's experiences dispelled the myth that Islam was a last-ditch attempt to escape from unhappy backgrounds! Nor would it be fair to say that all Muslim converts are essentially no-hopers with few prospects and little ambition. In fact, for many sisters' parents, education was of the utmost importance. As Jameela told me, 'Education was the focus of my parents' lives, it was the be-all and end-all. Us being educated was their primary goal and everything was secondary to that. I think that the reason for my parents' attitude was that they had come here from overseas and realized that to get anywhere in this country, you needed to be a professional. So education was everything.'

Mei was also sent to a private school and expected to perform well, albeit without much parental support. She told me about her parents' attitude to her schooling and their own responsibilities.

'My parents wanted me to be perfect, with the spotless frock, clean socks, polished shoes . . .

but they were always really busy with work, with running the restaurant. They were very motivated and they wanted to succeed. That is a part of Chinese culture: when you die, you have to leave something for your children, for your family, and if you haven't, then you've failed. Even though you love your children very much, if you have to work twenty-four hours a day and don't see them, that is the price you will pay.'

Aliyah, on the other hand, did not thrive at school, where she found herself living up to the negative expectations that others held of her and 'her kind'.

'I was one of the "bad girls" at school,' she told me. 'I went to a grammar school where there weren't very many Black girls; the majority were White, and there was always this expectation that if you were Black, you were bad. I started out being good, which was what my mum sent me there for in the first place – to make something of myself. And then after always being accused of doing things you didn't do, you started to do them. And that was the way I became – I got a bit of a reputation. And we were really bad – we bunked off school, smoked, bullied the other children and older people, did graffiti everywhere. I left school on the last day of the term, never to return!'

However, it was only when exam time came

that the enormity of her actions hit her. But she was determined to salvage what she could of her education – determined to make something of herself.

'I wanted to go to college because I felt like I had messed up big time. Towards the end, I realized that it was too late to pass any exams or anything like that. But I had developed a love of cooking while at school and although I got bad reports in every other subject, I always got good grades in Home Economics. I had had the ambition to be a chef from a very young age so I went to college to study that.'

Although Umm Muhammad started off loving school and the whole learning experience, problems at home started to affect her attitude to her work.

'I had always been top of my class, doing really well in all my subjects and, all of a sudden, I couldn't get any homework done. I didn't want teachers telling me what to do and what not to do and I started playing up in class, bunking off school. A girlfriend of mine and I would usually go and register and then leave, not attending any lessons at all. I just wasn't interested because there were too many things on my mind – I just couldn't see the point. In the end, I turned up to one O-Level exam, didn't turn up for the others and never ever went back for my results.'

Mei went on to university to prepare herself to take over the family business.

'After school, I went on to study at the university in Nottingham. I was advised by my parents to do something that would help when it came time for me to take over the business so I took Business Studies.'

Claire left Ireland to study Law in Bristol; Sara, having attained a degree in Geography, decided to take time off to travel. On her return, she completed a Masters degree in Development Studies.

Far from the common stereotype of the un-educated, inadequate convert to Islam, there are sisters who thrived in a public-school environ-ment and others who dropped out, some who went on to pursue Masters degrees and others who left university to establish successful careers. There is no way of fitting them into one stereo-typical category – these were not ignorant, unsophisticated women incapable of making informed decisions.

Career Girls

Not only did many sisters go on to higher education, but a good number of them also worked hard at building careers for themselves.

After dropping out of university in France,

Hajar came to London and spent six years building a successful career in the music industry, working for a record company in marketing.

'I had worked my way up from independent record and PR companies . . . I lived in, with and for music. I guess it was my religion. My partner, a DJ, and I both shared this passion and I found myself spinning records at clubs and on a community radio station where I presented a weekend breakfast show.'

Picking up Aliyah's story again, it is clear that, although she had had a poor start, she soon distinguished herself as a competent and enthusiastic chef, landing a job at a top hotel while still on her college course. At the time, her ambition was to be head chef and, eventually, to run her own restaurant. After taking time out to have a baby and recover from a heartbreak, she returned to her chosen field and continued to excel.

'I went back to work at the hotel, got my baby into a nursery, lost a lot of weight and enjoyed dressing up – got my life back on track. At that time, I was doing well in my job and I felt like I had everything: I had the child, my child had everything that he wanted, clothes were not a problem, wine bars on the weekend, if I wanted to travel, I could do that.' She was living the life she had dreamt of, or so she thought.

Mei was also a hard worker, dividing her time between her regular job and her parents' restaurant, squeezing her social life in between. She described her schedule for me: 'I would come home from my nine-to-five job about six, six-thirty, get dressed up, have something quick to eat and work in the restaurant until eleven-thirty at night, go to sleep, wake up again, go to work – that was how I got my money and pleased my parents as well. If I wanted a social life, I would go out after I finished work. I was living in Central London and I had a great time, made loads of friends, had money . . .'

Good Times and Party Girls

In addition to work and study, these women had active social lives – some of them extremely so!

Umm Muhammad told me about some of her exploits: 'By the time my sisters and I were of age, there was no stopping us. We loved the music, the fashion, the glamour, the excitement, the drama and the whole carry-on. Those were the Eighties and it was all about the leggings, the ra-ra skirts, the baggy trousers and the junk jewellery. We were all big on the rave scene and we raved a lot!'

When she left Ireland to go to university in Bristol, Claire found herself struggling to find others who could keep up with her wild ways.

'I was up for drinking every night, up for taking drugs every weekend but I couldn't really find anyone to keep up with me. I used to think, For goodness sake, who am I going to get to come to the pub with me at two in the afternoon? No one would do it. I wanted this whole mad experience and I wasn't satisfied that I was getting it one hundred per cent. When I used to go back to Belfast for my holidays and be with my old friends, then that would be quite hardcore.'

Hajar and her friends were also regulars on the London club scene, DJ-ing, hobnobbing with hip-hop stars and other celebrity clients, organizing events and parties. She was also able to indulge her tastes in classy restaurants and designer clothes.

Others, like Sara, had tamer pursuits, such as seeing art-house films and visiting galleries. Sara also had a passion for travel and, as soon as she had the time and money to do it, she visited several European countries and the Americas.

'I was travelling, seeing new things, learning new languages – trying to make the most of my experiences,' she told me.

Although Jameela was of Muslim parentage, she too had a social life that was unchecked by traditional restrictions.

'I lived a very, very Western lifestyle in every

way. It was not a problem for me to wear Western clothes, I could wear what I liked. There were no restrictions placed upon my brother and me. Having said that, we had our own boundaries, we weren't excessive – I mean we weren't on any hard drugs or anything. We basically had a very free, liberal upbringing.'

Feminists and Rebels

Many converts to Islam are seekers – seekers of meaning, seekers of the truth. As a result, it is not uncommon to find them being drawn to several different ideologies en route to Islam, as I was to Black Nationalism.

Sara's journey to Islam was full of detours and lay-bys, as she told me: 'I was always journeying, trying to find some kind of truth. I never gave up on that. I was convinced that there had to be the right way to live but I just didn't know what it was. So that was when I started exploring and I became very political. I was particularly interested in development issues in the so-called "Third World" and that led me to take an interest in Socialism. Also, from the age of about seventeen, I became an ardent feminist. One of the reasons for that was, when I lost my father, I realized that that unconditional love from a man had gone because he had been completely devoted to me. That triggered a lot of things in my mind and I started reading about different theories of feminism. I devoured all the books, discovering Shere Hite, Naomi Wolf, Germaine Greer and the classics like Simone de Beauvoir.'

Claire found her own form of self-expression in the young underground feminist movement, the Riot Grrrls, as she had always been 'a rage-against-the-machine type person'!

She explained the attraction to me: 'The Riot Grrrls appealed to me because I was really into music, and I used to play the bass guitar with my friend who played lead guitar. I found some Riot Grrrl records at a friend's record store and I got into it that way. Also at that time, I was into poetry as well and so I identified with their lyrics too. And there was a tongue-in-cheek side to it as well, as in "We're not really good at singing, we're not really good at playing any of these instruments, we're just going for it because who cares?" It's that rebellion thing I was talking about.'

What Now?

But for all their education, money, friends and fun, there was still something missing in these women's lives. Some were aware of it, others tried to ignore it but, without a doubt, there was a hole somewhere that all the good times in the world just couldn't fill.

Aliyah was acutely aware of the aimlessness of her lifestyle: 'In the last year before I became a Muslim, I was really low. It seemed to me that I had everything but there was still something missing. I was thinking, There has to be more to life than this. Men who drove Porsches were offering to take me here and there but all that just didn't appeal to me. I felt like a robot at that stage: you go to work, you get this money, you spend it, you come home – that kind of life didn't seem like it was going anywhere. So for a long time, I was searching for something – searching for answers to questions like, why do we exist?'

Umm Muhammad told me about coming home from raving and sitting at the window, looking out into the night sky, wondering whether there wasn't more to life than this, whether her life didn't have a higher purpose.

Even Claire's hardcore lifestyle began to lose its charm after a while. 'We went out clubbing one night and everyone was taking drugs. But then everything wore off. I just felt, I can't do this any more. It just doesn't feel right. I was coming home at night and feeling totally empty: it just wasn't "doing it" for me any more. Everything had lost the glitz and the glamour. In the cold light of day, it all looked really awful to me.'

Umm Tariq had a different story to tell. Having reached her fifties, after all the distractions of raising a family and working, she began to think again of the religious faith she had been brought up with.

'What if I die? I thought. You grow up hearing about Hell Fire and you know that it is not a nice place to end up. And you know for certain that you are going to die and what will happen to you after death. I started to think more seriously about worshipping God.' This led her on a journey of discovery, trying to find the true church, the one that truly worshipped God.

In every case, there was one moment of clarity, a moment of lucid thought that led to questions and those questions, in a myriad different ways – from spiritual yearning, to life-changing experiences, to a search for the truth – led to answers, the answers of Islam.

Encountering Islam

Hajar's encounter with Islam was as unplanned as it was unexpected. While DJ-ing in a jazz club, she met a new Muslim revert and became friendly with him. On numerous occasions, she expressed her apprehensions about schooling her three-year-old little boy. She wanted him to be schooled amongst well-brought-up children but, at the same time, did not want to send him to a private school and 'end up with a snotty little brat in my home who would have little or nothing in common with his parents'. Her friend suggested she try sending him to a Muslim school.

'No way! I thought at first. I won't have him brainwashed by those religious people!

'But, many a conversation later, I decided to pay a visit to our local Muslim school. I was received by a sister, completely covered in black. I stood there, unsure as to whether I wanted to go through with it but curious about this welcoming voice behind the veil. I was invited inside and the headmistress, whose face I could now see, satisfied my curiosity and I left, relieved at the fact that there weren't any places available in the nursery.'

However, a week later, Hajar received a call from the school, informing her that a place had become available, inviting her and her son for an interview. After assuring herself that it was only on a temporary basis, she enrolled him and little Faris began attending the Muslim nursery.

'I don't really understand what made me put him in that Muslim school in the end. I suppose I thought that at least he wouldn't be around those rude children that swear and throw tantrums; he would be around these people who were religious and they seemed cool. But I didn't want him coming home a religious person – I just wanted him to have nice etiquette, to be a nice boy, that was it.'

Indeed, Faris grew to love his new school and came home with all sorts of interesting tales. But he also came home with Islamic rules and etiquette, something Hajar wasn't quite prepared to accept.

'Whenever he would tell me that something wasn't allowed Islamically, I would say to him, "Faris, these people aren't going to dictate our lives to us. This is how we live and you go to school there, that's it, full stop." But then one day, I heard him reciting the Qur'an and it sounded really beautiful. And he came home one day and told me the story of Abraham (Ibrahim), when he was thrown into the fire and Allah made it cool for him. He brought home this piece of artwork that he had done to illustrate the story and it was really beautiful. By the way he told me the story, I could tell that it had really touched him – and it touched me.' This led Hajar to make efforts to find out more about what her son was learning at school.

She also began to spend time with Faris' head-mistress and her children, who were her son's playmates. Soon, she was attending the Friday sermon at the mosque, making sure no work appointments were ever booked at that time.

'The sermon there was always a revelation to me and I made it a weekly event. I used to go wearing this linen designer coat and a matching chiffon scarf and, when I returned to work, spiritually fulfilled, I would park somewhere isolated and remove them without being seen. This was such a difficult experience every time as I was beginning to enjoy the comfort of those garments. I felt as though I was developing two personalities, two identities, and living two lives. I decided to observe the two lifestyles and decide which was more rewarding and satisfying. Eventually, after reviewing the pros and cons of each, I decided that, without a doubt, my new-found lifestyle had so much more to offer than the life I had known up to then. My cocoon was ready to burst.'

Umm Tariq encountered Islam during her search for the church that truly worshipped God. Having decided to become more religious, she had made enquiries about different churches.

'The Pentecostal Church was recommended to me. I went there for a while and the songs that they sing are very catchy and I thought, Yes, this is it. But I soon realized that, no, these people are not worshipping God. How did Jesus pray? Who did Jesus pray to? These people were praying to Jesus, not to God. But Jesus always prayed to God, as the Bible says, to "the Father". So I thought, This can't be right. I never actually questioned Christianity, I was thinking more in terms of different churches. I thought to myself, There must be the truth out there – how can I find it?'

Her son and daughter-in-law had already embraced Islam and, as she said, 'I was upset when my son became Muslim because I had never heard of Islam. I thought, That is strange; I've never heard of it. It must be something new.

'So I would say to them, "I don't think it is you who have the truth, I think it is Christianity. It is only a matter of finding the right church." My son would say to me, "Mum, one of us is in the wrong road."

'I said, "Well, it's certainly not me."

'And although I was often angry with him, I had a burning desire to know who had the truth. But what really changed things for me was when my son came home with the Book of Barnabas. Well, I read it with an open mind and it said that Jesus did not die on the cross and that, to be honest, was how God guided me. That made me stop and think. I thought, God can do anything: why would He let Jesus, a noble Prophet, die such an agonizing death? And I kept reading that book and that was it for me. Allah just lifted the veil from my heart – and I believed.'

Mei was introduced to Islam by her university friends, many of whom had embraced Islam while she was at home during her year out. When she went back up to campus to see them, they asked her whether she was interested.

'I said, "I'm not interested in this kind of religion. It's not for me." I had learnt a little about Islam at school – the five pillars, that sort of thing. But, other than that, I had completely forgotten about it. Then they asked me whether I had a religion, what my religion was. I told them that I did have a religion but that it didn't have a name. So they asked me what it was.

'I said, "I believe in a God, but we don't know what He looks like – he doesn't have a white beard or white hair or anything like that. He can hear everyone when you need Him. He has the power to do whatever you want."

'At that time, I was doing yoga because I had a really bad back and they say that the moon position is the best thing for your back. And my friends said, "You know what? When Muslims pray five times a day, they go into that position too."

'I was like, "No! Really?"

'So my friend said that maybe my religion was similar to Islam – I told her not to be silly. But we started talking about Islam and it all started making sense. So we talked about Islam, all night and all day, about nothing but Islam. But I still thought that Islam wasn't for me because I didn't feel Muslim. Then someone gave me this sheet of questions – do you believe in one God? (Yes.) Do you believe in angels? (Yes.) Do you believe in the Prophets? (Oh, yes.) Then at the end of the questions, it said, "If all the answers are ticked, you are a Muslim."

'I gasped: "Ahh, I'm a Muslim. Oh my God, I can't be Muslim! My parents will kill me!" But I had made my decision and, suddenly, I realized it wasn't about my parents any more – it was about my Lord.'

Not everyone welcomes Islam into their lives or accepts it as soon as it is presented to them. Islam's entry into Jameela's life as a teenager was more like an intrusion. Having been away at university, her brother, whom she adored, came back talking about Islam.

'My brother basically stumbled upon Islam and that was what he came home to the family with. Of course, they thought he was stark raving mad!

'At that time, I went with the flow because of what my brother meant to me. He was like my mentor – he was the be-all and end-all at that time in my life and I simply followed in his footsteps. However, it was not something I found

84

myself comfortable with because of all that it asked of me.'

Being young, Jameela felt torn between living up to her brother's high expectations of her on the one hand and living the life she was used to on the other.

'While he was home on holiday, I would be playing this double role. It was like there were two people: Jameela and Jane.'

But this situation proved to be unsustainable and, following a major confrontation with her mother over wearing the *hijab*, she decided to leave home.

She Must Have Done It For Him!

Almost without exception, if a woman embraces Islam while involved with a Muslim man, it is assumed that she only became Muslim to please him, to keep him, for his sake. However, I have discovered that this is far from the truth. In most cases, although the partner may have been a catalyst, the women themselves researched and studied the *deen* independently before deciding to embrace the faith.

When Claire met Gareth at university, for example, he told her that he was a Muslim, albeit a non-practising one. But, one year, when he came back from the summer vacation, 'The rough time he had had with drugs over the summer had pushed him to clean up his act – to find out a lot more about Islam – so by the time I saw him again, he was doing a lot of serious thinking. We spoke a lot about spiritual things when we got together and then, slowly, he started to actually practise Islam. He would talk to me a little about the *deen* but I wasn't really interested – I had gone through my phase of thinking deeply about religion and that was more or less behind me. My attitude was, So what? Just believe whatever you want, you don't have to go on about it. He used to encourage me to read these books but I would never read them because I felt, I am Catholic, that is what I am and that's fine for me – it's not like I get a great deal of solace from it but, hey, that's what I am. I don't want to be anything different.'

But Gareth kept talking to her about Islam, encouraging her to talk about her beliefs, explaining Islamic beliefs to her.

'To be honest, I could see Islam was the truth but I couldn't get away from seeing all the restrictions that it entailed as well.'

On their first visit to Gareth's home town, he sent Claire to see another revert with his sister, who had also become Muslim. It was a disastrous visit and, on the train back to Bristol, Claire said to him, 'Look, I'm not a Muslim, I'm

not going to be a Muslim and you have to understand that. And I don't want to talk about it
again.'

'And he said, "OK." So that was it for quite a
while. About six weeks.'

But before they spoke about it again, Claire
had actually been thinking about Islam and
becoming a Muslim.

'A few things happened that made me start
thinking about the lifestyle that meant so much
to me. I guess I fell out of love with the clubbing
and the drugs but I wasn't talking to anyone
about it – I was just keeping it all inside. Maybe
I felt that accepting all Gareth was offering
would be like giving up the battle – there was still
that stubbornness there. My Celtic roots, no
doubt! However, I was working in the university
bookshop at the time and I was reading some of
the books on Islam he had left in my room ages
before. Then, one night, all my friends had left
my flat and Gareth and I were sitting in the front
room. And he asked me, so tentatively, "Do
you think you are ready to become Muslim
now?"

'And the funny thing was, I *was* ready. And so
I took my *shahadah* – the testimony of faith. I
can't explain why, but Allah had just changed my
heart. I was now a Muslim.'

Umm Muhammad was also introduced to

Islam by her partner, Abdur-Raheem, the father of her child.

'I knew that Islam was something Abdur-Raheem was interested in – he used to speak about it occasionally – but I never realized how serious he was. Then, one day, I was coming down the High Road, fresh from one of my Saturday-morning shopping sprees, and he was coming the opposite way. He told me that he had just been to the mosque and that he had taken his *shahadah*. So I was like, "Oh, OK, this is what you believe." After he became Muslim, he bought me a Qur'an.'

The more Umm Muhammad read about Islam, the more convinced she became that it was the truth – but she was loath to give up her party lifestyle and so resolved to do nothing about it. However, when her son Muhammad was born, his father decided that he wanted to practise Islam properly and he began to tell Umm Muhammad more about Islam, showing her how to pray.

'I was still interested but I was afraid of making the move. I had begun to understand that Islam came with a lot of obligations and I was afraid I wouldn't be able to fulfil them. Also, I was afraid of no one being like me – that everyone would be older, speaking Bengali or Urdu or Arabic. I was definitely afraid to make that move. But then I started to pray. I also watched the video of *The Message*, that told the story of the early days of Islam, and that put more things into perspective for me with regards to all that I had read in the Qur'an and the *hadith*. Then two months after I had the baby, Abdur-Raheem decided to leave and go and live in the mosque. He didn't want to keep living as we were so we separated. I was devastated because I loved him but I understood what he had done because I wasn't ready to change yet. He would still come up, on a Saturday, to see Muhammad but he wouldn't stay and spend time with me because we weren't married. As far as he was concerned, he was going to be a Muslim now and nothing was going to stand in the way of that.'

Umm Muhammad then met a group of young Muslim women, from different races and backgrounds, who answered a lot of questions for her and invited her to their Arabic class. And then, on her birthday that year, she was out hunting for clothes as usual when she met a Muslim man at the incense stall where Muhammad's father normally worked. He was surprised to learn that she was the mother of Abdur-Raheem's child and unimpressed to hear that he had left the two of them. He began to ask her what she knew about Islam and was surprised at the fluency of her answers. He then suggested she go down to the mosque to speak to the brothers there. 'They asked me what I knew about Islam and about Allah. Then they asked me, "Do you believe this to be the truth?"

'And I said I did. And they said, "Well, what are you waiting for then?"

'So then I thought, What *am* I waiting for? There was nothing stopping me, except getting dressed up to walk down the street. So they asked me whether I thought I was ready to become Muslim.

'And I thought, Why don't I just take my *shahadah* now? So I did.'

Aliyah met Ahmad while she was enjoying a successful career and hectic social life. But his conversion to Islam in the early days of their relationship was to prove its biggest test and a bittersweet introduction to Islam. Ahmad had taken Aliyah's son, Jameel, to the dentist but was over four hours late coming home. Aliyah was worried sick.

'Then he came in with a great big smile on his face – I remember it well; he was glowing,' she told me.

'I said, "Where have you been?" I was so worried!

'And he said, "I've become a Muslim." Just like that. He had met a brother in the park and he had talked to him about Islam. He had been so convinced that they had gone to the *masjid* [the mosque] together and he had taken his *shahadah*. I was just shocked. I was full of all sorts of emotions.

'"What do you mean you've become a Muslim?" I asked. "You went to the dentist's, for crying out loud, and now you're telling me you're a Muslim!"

'He said, "Listen to this tape, listen to this tape!" and he put on a tape of Qur'an recitation. To me it just sounded like some weird Asian music. He was so high, he could talk of nothing but Islam. It was as if, within a few hours, the past six months had disappeared. I felt like I had nothing in common with him any more.

'And I said to him: "This isn't going to work."

'Early the next morning, he went out to the mosque to pray. After that, all the Islamic things he was doing just seemed weirder and weirder and weirder to me. It was as if someone had abducted him, taken him up in a spaceship and brought him back down again as this stranger. I just felt like I was faced with a totally different person. He was so close to the mosque, he was there practically all the time and he was learning a lot from the brothers. He would come home and try to relay it to me but I just wanted to scream. Then he started saying that he couldn't do certain things because they were . . . he was using these words like "*haram*" (unlawful) – I didn't even understand him any more! He started telling me that I couldn't wear these skirts, that I couldn't dress like that and I wasn't having it! I remember packing my bags and standing by the door and saying, "I can't do this. I'm not ready for this. You can't become a Muslim and then just expect me to follow you."

'Also, I had known a Black girl who used to cover her face and she just looked like a freak to us. We used to stand there in amazement, looking at her, because she was the only person I knew in the world who dressed like that. And I just thought, You want me to be like that? No way!

'But he persuaded me not to leave and we talked and talked. He invited me to come down to the mosque. He bought me a scarf and said I should wear it to show respect to the place. I remember holding it underneath my chin and, when I got there, a sister said, "Why don't you pin it? It's easier . . ." And she pinned my *hijab* for me. Then they asked me whether I was Muslim and I said no. And then we started talking. And I started to attend a lot of the Muslim events because there was something on every day – a talk, a bazaar, or something.

'Then one day we went to an Islamic talk in one of the local schools and it was really interesting. I spoke to so many sisters that day and felt so welcome and comfortable. While we were waiting to leave, I got talking to a sister and I ended up saying to her, "I think I may want to become a Muslim, you know."

'A few days later, I was in the *masjid* and I said, "I want to take my *shahadah* now." So they took me upstairs and I took the *shahadah* and all the sisters were so happy – it was like one big party.'

As we've seen, sometimes a man can be the catalyst for a woman's entry into Islam. But it is rare to find a woman who did not study the *deen* for herself, wrestle with it and, finally, accept it for herself.

Brainwashed and Bullied

There is one thing that many of my sisters' stories have in common and that is the role of questioning, reading and study in their decision to embrace Islam. This is an important point to note as many people, especially our parents, tend to think that us young reverts go through a brainwashing process and are eventually bullied into taking our *shahadah*. Most sisters studied the ins and outs of the faith before committing themselves and, for many, it was the intellectual and religious evidence that finally convinced them of the correctness of the *deen*.

When Abdur-Raheem became a Muslim, Umm Muhammad was still very much enjoying her life – 'raving, partying, looking good, coming and going as I pleased.' Her reading of the Qur'an the first time didn't draw her any closer to the faith. Indeed, it was not until her partner bought her a book of *hadith*, the sayings of the Prophet Muhammad (s), that she began to pay attention.

'Reading that book of *hadith* touched me. Reading about different aspects of the *deen* made me think, Hmm, this looks like something that is true . . . I could get into this.

'And then I read the whole of the Qur'an again and I was drawn to the concept of the Oneness of God, the story of how Jesus was raised up and not crucified . . . And then I was given the Book of Barnabas and that touched me in the same way. And after reading lots of other books, I began feeling in my heart that Islam was the true religion.'

Indeed, it was reading that first attracted Hajar to learn more about Islam, after her son told her the story of Prophet Ibrahim and the fire.

She was inspired to buy a book about him and she began reading about the prophets and also the life of the last prophet, Muhammad (s). She found it all so fascinating and took to visiting a local bookshop regularly, keen to discover more.

Umm Tariq, too, found that all her doubts melted away after reading the Gospel of Barnabas. Claire was another sister who took to reading about Islam secretly, while working in her university bookshop, not wanting to let on to Gareth that she was finally taking an interest in the *deen*.

In Jameela's case, it was only when she began to take the initiative and actually think about the *deen* for herself that she was able to commit to it fully. After running away from home and being taken by her brother to live with Assiyah and Siraj, two well-respected members of the South London Muslim community, she recalls her attitude thus: 'I think I was a very difficult character to deal with for anyone who met me at that time. I couldn't be told anything, especially about the *deen* – I was very arrogant in that way. No one could actually sit me down and say, "What are your thoughts on this?" or "Islam says this, what do you think?" It wouldn't even reach that point. I would literally just walk out of the room.

'However, it was the subtle things that I saw that were touching me, moulding me, softening me towards Islam. Assiyah's nature, her manners, the way she dealt with me, the way she dealt with her children, with other people.'

Jameela began to visit Siraj in hospital without

anyone else knowing. It was on one of these visits that she finally took an honest look at herself and her life.

'He said something to me once – it may seem really strange and insignificant, but it was definitely the turning point for me.

'"What is it that you want?" he asked.

'I said to him, "It's not that I don't believe, I do believe in there being only One God and that Muhammad is the Last Messenger. But I just can't do all the rest . . . I can't put that thing on my head, I can't do the rest, I don't want to do the rest – I want my freedom. I want to be able to do this, do that . . ."

'As he was listening, he started sitting up in bed and lowered the oxygen mask that he had to reach for constantly. He was so frail, in a really pitiful state.

'"Look at me," he began, "death is approaching me. My time is limited. I might speak to you now, I might not be able to speak to you again tomorrow . . ."'

Seeing her friend and mentor so close to death had a profound effect on Jameela. The more she thought about it, the more everything she was holding on to seemed to fade into insignificance. It is often said that death gives one a new perspective on life – and that was what happened to Jameela.

'From that point, I decided, I can't really mess around like this, I don't have time to do this. And it all hit me. And this time, it hit me for myself because all along it had been about my brother, but now it was something that I had realized myself and that was the difference. It was very important to make that realization for myself because as long as someone is trying to drum it into you, you will feel oppressed, forced into things. That is until the point that Allah gives you that guidance – and when He does, that's it: that is it. The next day was *Eid* [a Muslim day of celebration] and I started praying, I put on the full covering, the *jilbab*, the *niqab*, everything – I just dived in, headfirst. As far as I was concerned there was no time to waste. My faith and conviction were so strong, just sky high. And I'm glad, I'm glad I did it that way because if I'm not at that point any more, at least I know that I had once been there in my life. It was destiny and I'm glad.'

Stories of Western women accepting Islam are compelling because they go against many people's preconceptions: that the Western way of life and belief systems are far superior to anything that Islam, or any other belief system, has to offer. Secretly, they wonder what on earth would make a woman swap her Western 'freedoms' for, as they see it, a life of submission and restrictions. I believe these stories speak to all of us. These stories are a part of our history, as reverts, as Muslims, as women, as people living in the West – different parts of them will speak to each one of us.

As I read through the few stories I have collected, I am reminded of their value: they show the universal appeal of Islam. The sheer diversity of the backgrounds and life experiences that characterize the sisters in this book show that Islam can speak to anyone. The sisters do not fit comfortably into any stereotype, any mould. They each have their own unique personality, their own voice. They were arch feminists, African nationalists, underground anarchists, music moguls, rock rebels, disco queens, devoted church-goers, designers, athletes, models, singers, career girls, Masters students, cultural Muslims, Christians, Sikhs, atheists, from every racial background and of all ages.

And, most unexpectedly, Islam was able to reach out to each of them, to settle in their hearts and speak to every one of them in a personal way, giving them the answers they were looking for and changing their lives for ever.

3

BEING A NEW MUSLIM – THE JOYS AND THE TRIUMPHS

My journey to Islam was a sensual one – a journey of sights, sounds, tastes and textures. I fell in love with the very idea of being a Muslim, of praying with the first light, of tasting my first morsel of food with the sun's dying rays, of hearing the melodious call to prayer and of prostrating on warm soil. Unlike most of the other women you will meet in this book, I did not study Islam in depth before deciding to become a Muslim so, for me, much of what I now know about Islam was learnt after I actually became a Muslim – and it became a real journey of discovery.

The powerful beliefs that unite all Muslims – male, female, Black, White, rich and poor – were what brought these sisters, from all their divergent paths, together. Some were searching, others were not, but, in the end, there was an inescapable fact, an undeniable truth, which made submission to Allah too powerful to resist.

It is this belief in the Islamic creed that must be understood and I hope that these few paragraphs will serve as an introduction.

Islam – The Fundamentals

Muslims believe in and worship Allah, the One God, the God of Moses, Abraham, Jesus and all the other prophets. 'Allah' is the name of God in the Qur'an, the book revealed to the Prophet Muhammad over 1400 years ago, in which mankind is commanded to worship God alone. This is the cornerstone of the Islamic faith: *tawheed* – pure and unadulterated monotheism.

The Islamic lifestyle revolves around the worship of the Creator alone, without any partners. There are no intermediaries: no all-powerful clergy, no confessional priests, no saints to be called upon, no prophets to be sacrificed to, no deities to be appeased, no ancestors to be consulted. In Islam, worship is holistic, and all forms of worship are to be directed to the Lord of all the worlds: Allah, the One God. Worship is not confined to the ritual acts of praying, fasting, giving charity and reciting the Qur'an. It extends across the spectrum of life to include all manner of daily acts, such as eating, drinking and sleeping, to personal acts, such as grooming oneself, relieving oneself and enjoying sexual relations, to actions of the heart, such as unconditional love, sincere devotion, fear and reliance.

The depth and comprehensiveness of Islamic monotheism blew my mind. I could not think of another belief system that kept worship uniquely and solely for God alone. To me, it only seemed proper that, if I wanted to pass my exams, find a new job, get a good husband, I ask the ultimate authority – God – instead of wasting time consulting the minions of the cosmos.

In a world that revolves around the material and the finite, Islam calls to a life dedicated to the divine and the eternal. In the Qur'an, Allah states the reason behind our creation:

> And I created not the jinns and humans except (that) they should worship Me (Alone).
> Surah Adh-Dhariyat 51:56

That gave me the answer to that most vexing of questions: what is the purpose of life? It meant that, as I had suspected, there *was* more to life than chasing a higher level of material comfort and getting ahead in the rat race. That meant that I wasn't forever looking for approval from my parents, my peers and my society. That meant that every day had meaning, every day was an opportunity to put something forward for my account with my Lord. Every smile, every act of charity, every job well done now counted for something truly worthwhile – the worship of my Creator – and this was the reason for my creation.

Muhammad ibn Abdallah (s) was born in the Arabian peninsula around 570 CE and lived in the city of Mecca, a thriving town on the ancient trade routes and home of the Ka'aba, the structure that Abraham (Ibrahim) built for the worship of the One God. The Ka'aba had since been converted to a home for the many idols that were worshipped by the Arabs at that time. Muhammad (s), who was known as 'Al-Amin' for his trustworthiness and truthfulness, was chosen as a prophet to call his people and the whole of mankind back to the worship of the One God and he began his call in Mecca. Although most members of Muhammad's family and quite a few others embraced this new faith, the majority of Meccans, particularly the ruling elite, did not take kindly to the Prophet's (s) condemnation of the polytheistic ways of their ancestors. In the end, the Muslims were driven out of Mecca, first to Abyssinia where they sought refuge with the Christian king, Negus, and then to the town known as Yathrib. It was there that Islam was to be established as a complete way of life, with worship, justice and social relations reflecting what Allah had revealed in the Qur'an.

The film *The Message* also had a profound effect on me. Although it wasn't a perfect depiction, it did manage to convey, without ever showing him, a sense of the personality and presence of the Prophet Muhammad (s) himself. It brought me closer to the characters that inhabit the narrations and stories about the time of the Prophet (s), the *hadith* – they all became real people to me and, when they suffered, I wept for them. My friends and I were strengthened by the fortitude of those early Muslims, persecuted for their rejection of the idols of their forefathers – it made us strong in the face of the problems we were dealing with because of our new faith.

The five pillars of Islam were one of the first things I learnt about and they are what most school students are taught when studying the religion. They are the *shahadah* (the testimony of faith), the *salah* (prayer), the *zakah* (compulsory charity from one's wealth), the *sawm* (fasting in the month of Ramadhan) and the *Hajj* (the pilgrimage to Mecca).

The Muslim belief, *Iman*, is also based upon pillars – six, to be exact. The six pillars of *Iman* are to believe in Allah, His Angels, His Messengers (all the prophets mentioned in the Torah, the Bible, the

Psalms and the Qur'an), His Books (the afore-mentioned texts in their original forms), the Last Day (the Day of Resurrection) and the *Qadr*, both the good and bad aspects of one's fate.

As my friends and I went to Islamic lectures and study circles, listened to tapes, read our books and discussed issues amongst ourselves, we came to understand the sheer enormity of the *deen* that we had embraced. Although the beliefs themselves were simple, we found that the ins and outs of Islam truly were like a vast ocean of knowledge. And we dived straight in.

> 'One of the best things about those early days was acting upon the things that you read, knowing it all made sense. For so many years, I had been taught by my Christian family about this and that but it had never made sense. But Islam finally made sense to me. It wasn't just a religion; it was a way of life.' Aliyah

A New Muslim

There are many aspects of the new Muslim experience that we remember with fondness – discovering the *shahadah*, the testimony of faith, studying and appreciating *tawheed* (Islamic monotheism), savouring the prayer, experiencing the fast, the comfort of our new dress code – the *hijab* – the new sense of community, and the exciting direction our lives had taken. The daily discovery of our Islam was thrilling. In our manners and attitude, it was as if we were saying: 'Hey, we're Muslims and we have this great *deen* – this faith – and we're on top of the world!' Without doubt, those were happy times, joyful times, triumphant times.

The *Shahadah*

One of the most important elements of our new Islamic faith was, and still is, the *shahadah*, those words that have been uttered by Muslims for over 1400 years and that confirmed our commitment to Islam.

The *shahadah*, which is also known as the *kalimah*, is the first pillar of Islam, and it is:

> *Ash-hadu an-laa ilaaha illallah,*
> *wa ash-hadu ana-Muhammad ar-rasoolullah,*

This statement consists of two parts, negation and affirmation. With the statement, '*laa ilaaha*' ('there is nothing worthy of worship'), the Muslim negates the worship of any other god or anything else, be it a stone, a tree, a statue or a saint. The words '*illallah*' ('except Allah') affirm the worship of Allah alone and that He is the only One worthy of that worship.

'Because I was born a Muslim, I didn't think that I needed to take my *shahadah*. In some ways, I wish I had achieved that milestone, just to mark the difference between the time of ignorance and the time of knowing. But because I didn't formally take it, I spent a lot of time contemplating it, as it is very difficult to grow without that foundation.' Sara

The *shahadah* has conditions attached to it, conditions that make it valid. The first of these conditions is knowledge, *al 'ilm*. The second is sincerity (*al ikhlas*), the third, truthfulness (*as-sidq*), the fourth, certainty (*al yaqeen*), the fifth, love (*al mahabbah*), the sixth, submission (*al inqiyaad*), and the seventh, acceptance (*al qubool*).

Words cannot really express the feelings and emotions that accompany the *shahadah*. By pronouncing it, you become part of the *ummah*, the nation of the Prophet Muhammad (s), you have entered the fold of Islam. You are now part of a community, not because you happened to be born within artificial national boundaries, but because you all share the same beliefs.

For many, a rush of emotions accompanied the *shahadah*: excitement, relief, anticipation and joy.

'When you take your *shahadah* you're told that you are like a newborn baby, that you have no sins. You feel like a different person. You even think that you look like a different person.' Umm Safwan

While taking the *shahadah* was an emotional step for some sisters, there were also many who did not fully comprehend the significance of that statement until they had grown in the *deen* and increased in their understanding. I do not think I became aware of its significance until well into my first year as a Muslim, so much so that I am sure I did not fulfil the seven conditions when I actually pronounced it. But, through reading and asking questions, I began to realize the enormity of those words and how they were to impact on every aspect of my life. This was always made clearer to me when a conflict arose between what my peers expected of me and what I knew Allah expected of me. I would think, How can I justify doing what they are asking me to do when I know, I *know*, that I am here to worship Allah alone? Is their approval more important to me than the pleasure of Allah? And, because I was beginning to appreciate the *shahadah*, I knew what the answer to that question was.

The second part of the *shahadah* or *kalimah* is '*Muhammad ar-rasoolullah*' and it means that the Muslim accepts Muhammad ibn Abdallah (s) as Allah's Prophet and Messenger, following his example and obeying his commands. A Muslim is supposed to love the Messenger Muhammad (s) more than any other human being. This was something I found hard to fathom until I actually started to learn about him, his character, how he treated others. I think the times when I really felt my heart soften towards him were when I would hear about his private life: Muhammad, the family man. Before I got married in 1999, I listened to a tape about how he treated his family members and I wept: the compassion, the humour, the humility, the mercy, the surprising intimacy and gentleness, made me wish that I could marry someone with just a bit of his character. I must confess that part of what appealed to me was how different he was to the general stereotype of the traditional Muslim man – they were poles apart in so many ways and that was a comfort. I knew that I would be proud to one day teach my son the way of our Prophet (s) at home so that my son could be a true Muslim man in his.

Discovering the Qur'an

It is reported in *Sahih al-Bukhari*, the most authentic Islamic text after the Qur'an, that, in his fortieth year, the Prophet Muhammad (s) began to receive divine inspiration in the form of dreams that would come true. At that time too, he grew to love being in seclusion and would often go to the cave of Hira to worship Allah for many days at a time.

One day, while he was in the cave alone, the Angel Gabriel (Jibra'eel), the same angel that God had sent to Moses (Musa) and Mary (Maryam), came to him.

'Read,' he commanded.

Muhammad (s) had been raised for much of his life among the Bedouin in the desert and could neither read nor write.

'I do not know how to read,' he told the angel. At that, the angel caught him up and pressed him so hard that he could not bear it. When he was released, the angel again commanded him to read.

Again he replied, 'I do not know how to read.' At that, the angel seized him and pressed him again, until he could bear it no more.

After releasing him, the angel commanded him to read for the third time, to which Muhammad (s) replied, 'What shall I read?'

For the last time, the Angel Gabriel pressed him tightly and then recited the following words:

'Read! In the name of your Lord who has
   created [all that exists]
Has created man from a clot.
Read! And your Lord is the Most Generous.'

And, with that, the angel was gone, leaving
Muhammad with the first verses of the Qur'an.
The call to Islam had begun.

When I first read the Qur'an, before I was
actually a Muslim, I didn't really get it. Having
not been a Christian before, I couldn't see how it
was different from the Bible, and so I had a
rather cavalier attitude to the rules and injunctions that it contained. I just didn't take
some of them seriously thinking that, like the
Bible, it had been authored by a man and had
probably been changed to suit men, or people in
power.

It was only when I learnt about the divine
origin of the Qur'an that my Islam began to
strengthen. Until then, I would take some bits
and leave others, comfortable in the belief that it
was my opinion that mattered most. And as anyone with any knowledge of Islam will tell you,
that's not quite the way it works!

But as I began learning about the Qur'an, I
became more impressed and felt compelled to
delve further into and draw closer to it. The
words that were revealed to Muhammad (s) by

Allah, via the Angel Gabriel, took the pagan Arabs by surprise. Muhammad (s)'s people were famous for their love of language and poetry and the Qur'an was to them a wonderful example of that – but the Prophet (s) had been born and weaned among the desert tribes and could neither read nor write. How could this illiterate compose such measured prose? He had never studied under the rabbis and monks that were around at that time, so how did he know the stories of the Jews and the Christians? He was not a man of science, so how could he know the secrets of embryology, the details of geography and the mysteries of space? He had no crystal ball – how did he have the knowledge of events of the past and the ability to predict events of the future? Was he really mad, as his tribesmen called him at the time? But Allah Himself offered a clear proof that the Qur'an was from Him and Him alone when He issued a challenge to the whole of mankind to produce something like it. The first challenge was to produce a text similar to the Qur'an, the next, to produce ten verses like it, and finally, to match just one verse from the Qur'an. No one has ever been able to meet that challenge.

The Qur'anic text itself has been passed down through the generations in what is known as the *mutawaatir* form of transmission. This means that it was relayed by such a large group of people to such a large group of people that it is not possible for them to have conspired to corrupt or change the text. This is coupled with the fact that Allah Himself promised to protect His Word from distortion and forgery:

> And if he [Muhammad] had forged a false saying, attributing it to Us, We surely would have seized him by his right hand, and then certainly cut off his life artery!
> Surah al-Haqqah 69:44–6

The Angel Gabriel brought the revelation to the Prophet (s) throughout his life, over a period of twenty-three years. The Prophet Muhammad (s) would then recite the verses that were revealed to him and teach them to his companions, who would memorize, teach and write down what they learnt. Those early fragments were written in Arabic on pieces of cloth, leaves and anything else that was easy to come by. Near the end of his life, the Prophet (s) would spend the month of Ramadhan reciting the entire Qur'an with the Angel Gabriel. One of his faithful companions, Zayd bin Thabit, was with him on those occasions and would recite with him. When the Khalif 'Uthman ordered the Qur'an to be compiled in one text, in the year 24–25 after the

Hijrah, the emigration to Madinah, it was Zayd bin Thabit that confirmed and checked both the text and the order of the verses.

It is for these reasons that the Qur'an as it was revealed is extant – the ancient copy that lies in a museum in Turkey is the same as the one you can buy in any bookshop today.

This was a source of great pride for us new Muslims: the Qur'an had remained unchanged and unadulterated, unlike the Scriptures we had grown up with, and that injected a certainty and confidence into our belief.

Many of us were taken with the Qur'an itself. When I asked Claire about the joys of being a new Muslim and about the things that she had loved when she first came to the *deen*, she answered without hesitation: 'The Qur'an. It was just the most fantastic thing I had ever read. I was always into Shakespeare, literature and poetry, but when I read the Qur'an, it was something else.'

The Qur'an has moved millions through its message, its words and their meanings and its melodious flow when it is being recited. The recitation of the Qur'an is something that Muslims have always prioritized, since the dawn of Islam and in every corner of the world. Even where there is no ink or paper, the verses of Allah's Book are preserved in the hearts of the faithful. It is possibly the only book in the world that thousands of people have memorized from beginning to end ... but for me back then, even memorizing the short opening verse was a source of pleasure and joy.

I had learnt three verses phonetically while in Guinea and, on my return, was keen to learn a few more. Like all new Muslims, I started from the back of the Qur'an, from the short verses in Juz' Amma, the thirtieth part of the Qur'an. I remember taking the train to work, reading the Arabic words phonetically from my little green book, saying the words over and over again so that I would be able to recite them in my prayers. So while others listened to their Walkmans or read the latest bestselling novel, I was reciting to myself, my singing voice finding solace in the ebb and flow of the Speech of Allah.

One day, I was in one of the biggest Islamic bookshops in East London, browsing for books, tapes and other Islamic goods. Slowly, as I picked my way through the prayer mats, tooth sticks (miswak) and perfumed oils, I became aware of the tape that was being played in the background. It was a tape entitled The Life of the Prophet. I stopped to listen as he narrated the Prophet (s)'s last sermon – in which he spoke of the brotherhood of the Muslims, of safeguarding the rights of women, of the equality of the different races, of remaining steadfast upon the obedience of Allah – and the impact of his words remains with me to this day. Those words shook me to my very core. Tears sprang to my eyes and fell down my cheeks as I rushed out of the shop to get money to buy that tape. It was as if I had realized, in a moment, the beauty of the faith I was now a part of. If only, I thought, if only we could actually put those words into practice, how beautiful it would be! The bittersweetness of that day, when I felt the great potential of Islam, was to stay with me for a long while.

The *Sunnah* of the Prophet (s)

The speech, actions and consent of the Prophet (s) make up what is known as the Prophet's *Sunnah*. Muslims are bound by its rulings, and the *hadith* are the reports of these sayings and actions.

Learning about the science of *hadith* was something else that increased my love for and appreciation of the *deen*. One summer, the mosque organized a seven-day seminar, taught by some of the world's best students of Islamic knowledge. There, undisturbed by children and other concerns, we did an intensive course on various Islamic disciplines. One of these was the *science* of *hadith*. And they could not have picked a better word!

I learnt that the *hadiths* were recorded by the companions of the Prophet (s) and passed down to each generation through narrations. These narrations are linked by chains of transmission, where each person in the chain is named and known. For example, a *hadith* narrator will say, 'I heard from so-and-so, who heard from so-and-so, who heard from so-and-so, who heard from Abu Bakr who heard the Prophet (s) say such and such.' A *hadith* is graded according to its level of authenticity – authentic (*sahih*), good (*hasan*), weak (*da'eef*), or fabricated (*mawdhoo'*). This system of verification amazed me at first. I can't explain how reassured and thrilled I was when I had understood the different classifications! I was even inspired to write a poem about it! I learnt that if the chain of narration, the *isnad*, was missing even one person, the *hadith* would not be deemed authentic. This was also the case if there were untrustworthy characters in the chain, if there was no established contact between the narrators in terms of time and place, if the wording was uncharacteristic of what was known from the *deen* or the Prophet (s)'s way of speaking. Indeed, anything else that cast doubt on the soundness of the *hadith* would prevent the *hadith* from being graded as authentic and could even cause it to be classified as weak or fabricated, particularly if there were known liars in the chain.

THE JOYS AND THE TRIUMPHS

I was most taken with the scientific rigour with which the scholars of the past and present studied and graded the *hadith*. It might sound strange to anyone who hasn't been through it themselves, but this was a glimpse into the depths of Islamic scholarship and we were very impressed by what we saw. This sophisticated and wholly Islamic method of study increased our confidence and boosted our faith.

For me, it was only further proof of the beauty of Islam – as far as I am aware, the *isnad*, the carefully recorded chain of narration, is an institution unique to the Muslim nation. It also meant that the *sahih hadiths*, such as those found in Sahih al-Bukhari and Sahih al-Muslim, were to be taken seriously and they often formed the basis of many of our discussions at the time.

'I just loved reading the *hadith* and finding out about all the things I never knew about Islam and the companions. And also the Prophet (s), how he was with his friends and his family and it was so nice, so touching. There's so much history there.' Claire

Days Full of Worship

Another high note of those early days was establishing the various acts of worship. One of these was the prayer, *as-salah*, the second pillar

117

of Islam. Muslims are commanded in the Qur'an to establish the prayer five times a day:

> Verily, the prayer is enjoined on the believers at fixed hours.
> Surah an-Nisa 4:103

I had started praying while in Guinea, where the day itself was measured by the calls of *le muezzin*, floating out over the rooftops and busy streets. In Conakry, there was a mosque on practically every corner so it was easy to drop what you were doing or stop your car, put on your scarf and pray.

'Once, when I was in Times Square, amidst the hustle and bustle, I saw a Muslim man praying, surrounded by the chaos of New York. It was a most spectacular sight, one that really touched me.' Sara

Back in London, at university, we would either go to the student prayer room in the Students' Union or find an empty classroom and pray right there, prostrating on our coats. The midday prayer was particularly tricky, especially during the winter when it was only about two hours away from '*Asr* (mid-afternoon) – we often had lectures or tutorials just when the prayer was due. It took me a while to manage the five prayers every day but I persevered, coming to a stage where I prayed regularly, eagerly reciting the new *surahs* I was learning all the time. Sharifah is a new Muslim and is still new to the *deen*. She told me, 'I just really wanted to learn how to pray in Arabic – and to pray properly, how to make *wudhu'* [ritual cleansing] – it's still exciting for me. Even now when I pray, I get a feeling that I've never had before, I feel at peace after I pray, like I've off-loaded a whole lot of stuff.'

For some sisters, the prayer (the *salah*), was one of the first things that took root in their hearts, paving the way for the rest of their Islam.

Claire, for example, told me the harrowing story of how she began praying and why: 'At my sister's graduation, my friends and I went out and I took this dodgy "E", an Ecstasy pill. I started to tremble and feel really hot. I was sick, like my head was going to explode, like my brain was going to squeeze out through the sides of my head. I was trying to stay calm, saying, "Please let this end, let this end . . . Allah, if You get me through this, I'm not going to do it again." So I took a cab home and I was sick all night. Then, when the sun was coming up, I looked around the room for something to cover my head with and I prayed. And I prayed from that day onwards.

'Even though everything else might have come slowly,' she continued, 'once I started praying, I never stopped.'

For Sara, the *salah* was something that took time to grow on her: 'I didn't immediately feel an affinity with the *salah*. I did it as a matter of course because I knew that I had to do it. But, without even realizing it, I developed a love for it and a need for it. I remember that on my travels, I was completely removed from the Muslims and the Islamic way of life but I would try my best to hold on to the *salah*, just to hold on to something of my *deen*. It was like a lifeline, the only link I had with Allah.'

I had developed a love for Islam while fasting in the humid climes of West Africa, surrounded by others who were fasting too. My first Ramadhan in London was wonderful, albeit very different from Guinea. To be honest, it made me very 'homesick' for the traditions and rituals of the fast in Conakry. However, fasting in London had its own charms: Sandra, Hanah and I, as well as all our friends, were all fasting together. That didn't really mean much during the day, when we had lectures and tutorials to attend, but, after the *'Asr* prayer, when our time was freed up, we began to count the hours and minutes to the time for *iftar*, the meal that is eaten when the fast is opened at sunset. At that time, *iftar* was at about four o'clock and we would eagerly make our way to the student prayer room where dates and water would be served. Ahh, that first taste of sweetness after the day-long hunger: exquisite. The crisp coolness of water after the thirst: heavenly.

It was at times like those that I would be inspired by the wisdom of the fast: the physical and spiritual exercise of keeping away from food and drink, particularly when everyone else on campus was eating the usual baked potatoes and tuna sandwiches all around you, was empowering. It also reminded me that not everyone has food every day, it taught me to be grateful for the food I did have, having felt for myself the gnawing of hunger pangs. This is an extremely humbling experience, which is meant to encourage the one fasting to consider those less fortunate and appreciate the blessing of food. I know that I did at the time and the peace that descended on all of us when we got ready for the sunset prayer told me that the others had felt it too.

'I could really relate to the whole idea of "going without". I thought that we *needed* to feel what it is not to have food and drink for a certain amount of time so that we could relate to those who don't have and appreciate what we have a bit more.' Sara

After this, we would pray *Maghrib*, which is one of my favourite prayers because the recitation is made out loud. We had some sisters who could recite really beautifully and I would immerse myself in the prayer, my eyes moist with gratitude at having completed another day of fasting. And after the prayer, it was time to eat. Many of the students would bring food to share with others and sometimes, we would end up with a real feast! On other days, we would take a walk down to the chicken-shop 'strip', a stretch of main road that was overpopulated by chicken-and-chips shops (amazingly, all the same franchise!), and get a box of greasy, but oh-so-tasty, Southern-fried chicken to eat back on campus.

Sometimes, we would all meet at Sandra's place and she would prepare a delicious meal, served up Caribbean style! But some of our best *iftars* were spent at mosques around the capital where they would lay on a spread for the congregation and visitors. One of the best things about visiting different mosques for *iftar*, also known as 'mosque hopping', was that we got to meet so many Muslims from so many different backgrounds – Pakistanis, Bengalis, Moroccans, Algerians, Somalis, Nigerians, Caribbean, English and Irish reverts. I never tired of hearing how different sisters had come to embrace Islam and, with each account, my faith increased ten-fold. Ramadhan is a special time for all Muslims who take the time to immerse themselves in it – but your first Ramadhan is unlike any other.

Sara shared her feelings about Ramadhan with me: 'I *loved* the fasting. I was on such a high from that! I loved waking up early in the morning while it was still dark; having that discipline to get up and eat something while the rest of the world was sleeping, knowing that you were setting out to do something really special for the day and that there were Muslims all over the world that were doing this: a silent solidarity.'

Another pleasure was learning Arabic, which, for many, was their first serious attempt at learning a foreign language. As the language in which the Qur'an was revealed and the language in which Islamic scholarship has traditionally been carried out, Arabic is central to the Muslim heritage. Many reverts and returnees are eager to learn it so that they can interact with Islamic texts for themselves, without the need for clumsy translations that try, in vain, to convey the essence of the original.

The Badge of Belonging

The *hijab* deserves a special mention because of its centrality to how we saw ourselves as new

Muslim women. Because covering oneself is a religious obligation and an act of worship, I have spoken to countless sisters who measure the strength of their *deen*, their level of *iman*, their spiritual fitness, by their *hijab*.

> 'I always thought that women in *hijab* were beautiful, I really respected them. I couldn't wait to be like that.'
> Nadia

After coming back to London and taking my *shahadah*, I was fortunate to land a job as a receptionist and administrator at a community college in Forest Gate, in the East End of London. That job was perfect for me because it was in the evenings after my university classes and it was very people-oriented, which I really enjoyed. Also, because of the multicultural area we were in and the open-minded attitude of the management, I had no problems praying at work or wearing my headwrap. The regular income came in handy too, of course. I also liked the vibe of the area – the London Borough of Newham in general has a very diverse population – English, Asian, African, Caribbean and immigrants of all shades mingle on its main streets and shopping areas, creating quite a unique buzz. As I progressed from colourful headwraps to little scarves, to longer lengths of material, to the gown-like *abayah*, then on to the *jilbab* (the voluminous outer garment sometimes known as a *burqa*) and the *niqab* (the face veil), my bosses remained unfazed, supporting me through every stage.

Hijab was like a badge of belonging, a new thing that we were exploring, experimenting with, making our own. At that time, I was a veritable fabric junkie, first looking for the thick, stiff material that makes a good headwrap and then the lighter, flowing fabric that makes the best *hijabs*. The shops on Green Street became my favourite stores for fabric. There was always a large variety available and the prices were very competitive. No one could argue with £1.50 a yard!

For many of us, wearing the *hijab* made us feel totally different from how we used to be. It was accompanied by a heightened spiritual awareness and a strengthened identity as a Muslim.

'When I walked out of the house with *hijab* on, I felt beautiful in the eyes of Allah. I felt protected, shielded – I just felt like somebody was watching over me.'
Nadia

Companions on the Journey

> 'Whenever you were [at the *masjid*], someone would help you with a *surah*, or a *du'a* – everyone was helping each other with their *deen*, learning. The atmosphere was very supportive and helpful because everyone was in the same boat.' Umm Muhammad

After taking my *shahadah*, I was surrounded by a close-knit group of other reverts (my friend Sandra being one of them) and 'returnees', one of whom was Sandra's Egyptian friend, Hanah. And we all embarked on this most exciting of journeys together. We had become very close by this time and, when not attending lectures, spent most of our days together. Almost every evening without fail, I would leave my flat in the high-rise and walk down the main road to Sandra's place in the university halls of residence. How well I remember the high that I was on then! I would ring the buzzer and, knowing it was me, Sandra would come to the gate to let me in. Dressed in her long skirts and loose shirts with a headwrap now expertly tied about her head, she would strike a pose at the gate, her smile wide, and cry, '*Asalaamu alaikum,* baby girl!'

Striking a similar pose, I would reply, '*Wa alaikum salaam,* honey child!'

'You OK?' she would ask, to which I would

reply, '*Alhamdulillah*, I'm cool!'

And then it was time to enter into 'the zone'.

'The zone' was our own private space where we ate the tastiest food (we never had to make do with student grub while at 'Sandra's Kitchen', as we had dubbed her student digs!), and indulged in passionate discussion and rowdy debates about Islam and all its aspects, often staying up until the wee hours, praying the dawn prayer before falling into makeshift beds, painfully aware that we all had a ten-o'clock start!

Even when we were on vacation, we would still be together, often travelling across London to attend Islamic talks and, in Ramadhan, we would try to pray *tarawih* (the long prayers that take place every night during that month) at a different mosque each evening. As our *deen* progressed, we encouraged each other in our first attempts to wear the *hijab* and would give advice about which materials made the lightest, coolest *abayahs* with the best flow. We talked about everything: our pasts, our families, the *hijab*, the Qur'an, the Prophet Muhammad (s) and anything else that was on our minds. That closeness, born of a common experience, was intense. It seemed to me at that time that we were living in a kind of bubble, where the *deen* was the central focus of our lives, with every-thing revolving around that – and only those already inside the bubble could really understand.

'You feel like you're part of something, you're part of the *ummah* [Muslim nation] now and you have your place. You are united by something bigger – the worship of Allah – and you're all doing it together.'
Safwa

Some of the sisters, like Claire and Aliyah, had come to the *deen* with their partners and this gave their relationships a new depth. I asked Aliyah about her relationship with Ahmad when they were both new Muslims. She told me, 'Our relationship at that time was good. When I look back, I think that was definitely the best time in my marriage – we were very happy, very contented. It definitely brought us closer – we shared so much.'

Claire described to me her new Islamic lifestyle with Gareth: 'Having a flat together really put in place our Islamic identity, our Islamic relationship. It was our own space; there were no inhibitions about what my image-conscious friends would think. We had a shelf of Islamic books, a place where we always prayed . . . We learnt a lot together and we were really striving to have knowledge of specific things. We used to sit together a lot and read Sahih Bukhari or the collection of the Forty Hadith, and we would read the Qur'an every day – that was really nice.'

Some of us found ourselves in vibrant communities, many of them full of fellow reverts. Along the way, we met some truly remarkable people whose influence was to last even as they moved on.

Jameela told me about her greatest role models as a new Muslim: 'Living in Assiyah and Siraj's house was definitely the best part [of my life as a new Muslim] – the house was filled with *deen*, morning, noon and night. During the day, the house was filled with sisters and brothers and Qur'an, there was an abundance of food, you just took what you wanted – it was a real open house. The whole purpose of their house was to spread and teach Islam, and most of the people that I have now known for years, I met there. These were people who always had time for everyone: their time was everybody else's. I have never seen another two people like them. They were like parents to me, as if they had replaced my own family.'

Umm Muhammad, too, remembers Siraj and Assiyah and she described to me the effect that their deaths, quite soon after each other, had on the fledgling community.

'When Assiyah died, that was a blow to the community. I think everyone was shaken up by that for at least nine months. It was one of the first deaths in our community and it was someone we all knew, loved and respected. When her husband died, about a year or so later, that was another blow. It was our first time experiencing death from a Muslim point of view – that this was their Hereafter starting.'

I have often heard other sisters speak of Assiyah as one of the pivotal people in their learning and sense of belonging as new Muslims. They speak of her with fondness and respect.

In my job, I was always meeting people from around the world because they would come into the college to enrol for English classes. I felt blessed to meet and converse with so many people from different backgrounds and I particularly appreciated meeting so many Muslims. Now that I had taken my *shahadah*, I felt a definite kinship with the Pakistanis, Bengalis, Algerians, Somalis, Albanians and West Africans I would see on a regular basis. I remember that my face would glow with pleasure every time I was asked if I was a Muslim. It felt so good to reply in the affirmative, confident and sure of myself. And I have to say, the Muslims, by and large, warmed to me and we were always pleased to call out the Islamic greeting of peace:

*'Asalaamu alaikum warahmatullahi
   wabarakatuhu.'*
*'Peace be unto you and the mercy and blessings
   of Allah.'*

No longer did we only associate with members of our own race, age or class or our intellectual equals – the beliefs that we shared with fellow Muslims outweighed all those considerations and broke down many barriers.

As Aliyah put it, 'There was this great friendliness from everybody – I didn't feel like they were being fake or anything. You were just Muslim, you believed in what they believed in. You know in the film *Malcolm X* when he talks about when he went to 'Umrah with all the people, no matter what colour they were? That was what it seemed to me then. As soon as you'd meet someone, they would put their arms out and hug you, and that was something you never really got before Islam.'

'To me, it was just brilliant: there were so many sisters, and they were young, and they were Chinese, Black, White, Asian, all together, and I was really overwhelmed by it. Everyone was fresh to the *deen* and very enthusiastic. I was just amazed by the whole experience.' Rabia

Whereas before Islam, I had had little time for other races, I now found myself growing close to Arabs, Asians, Whites and all kinds of mixed races, as so many of us did. I shed many of my pro-Black ideas, and my strong aversion to mixed marriages became a thing of the past. The sheer plethora of mixed marriages that I encountered on a regular basis was fascinating. We would sometimes compete to see who could site the most unlikely mix: was it Nigerian and Egyptian, Irish and Arab, Algerian and Jamaican, Somali and Pakistani or Chinese and Ghanaian? But there were always more examples of cross-cultural marriages than we could name.

Being a part of this Muslim community was a precious part of our new experience. Sometimes, this was all the more so because our families and friends didn't understand or accept our new way of life. The loneliness and isolation that we felt was alleviated by the warmth of the new family we had found – the Muslim family.

A Whole New Vibe

For centuries, in every time and in every place, mankind has asked questions about the meaning of life. And, in our society of instant gratification and material ease, even when all one's dreams have come true and all one's wishes have been granted, there is always that gnawing feeling, that nagging question – *is this all there is?* It is as if the need of the human soul is so deep that no amount of good times and enjoyment will ever fill it completely. So, sometimes, the man or woman who 'has everything' cries alone at night in despair or seeks comfort in a pill, in a bottle or a fine white powder, anything to quench that insatiable thirst for something meaningful, something real.

> 'Worshipping Allah made me feel like I had found what I was looking for. I found I had a direction where before I had no direction. Before I came to the *deen*, I had no direction whatsoever, I would get up in the morning and feel so depressed it was unbelievable.'
> Aziza

But we had found something that gave meaning to every waking moment, something that made our lives purposeful and focused. Some of us were pleased to have left the slavish following of society's whims.

In a way, we had taken a very strong stand against the prevailing culture. We had said, 'No, I am not going to live my life according to your trends and dictates. I am not going to lose myself in your enjoyments and distractions. I am not going to dress according to your fashions. I am a Muslim and I worship Allah, not *Vogue* or the *Sunday Times*.'

'When I first started covering,' Sara told me, 'a university friend of mine said, "I can't tell you how much I respect you for what you've chosen to do." I think she saw us as young, female, qualified, with so many things before us – the world was our oyster. And in a way, I was making a complete U-turn, saying, "This is not what I want." '

'To me, the fact that you were not submitting to society, the fact that you were not just doing things that everybody else was doing because they were doing it – that felt good. Especially coming up to sixteen, going off to college and not doing what everyone else was doing, not dressing the way everyone else was dressing, and doing what the *deen* says, purely for the sake of Allah, that gave me a real buzz . . .' Begum

For many of us the days, weeks and months that followed the *shahadah* were among the best days. Everything was new and exciting. There was so much to learn, explore and discover. It was the start of an epic journey into the rest of our lives, and our optimism, much like the optimism of youth, was not marred by disappointment, disillusionment or despair. Having opened the door to the treasure house, we were eager to delight in its wonders, and we did, with our minds, with our bodies, with our very souls.

4

BEING A NEW MUSLIM – THE PROBLEMS AND THE CHALLENGES

Do people think that they will be left alone because they say: 'We believe,' and will not be tested? Surah al-'Ankabut 29:2

Coming to Islam is often a positive, uplifting, even exhilarating experience. As the previous chapter showed, you can feel like a new person who has just understood 'what it's all about'. There is so much to learn and, if you are like many who are new to Islam, you are filled with a passion to know more and more about the *deen*, the faith you have embraced. And with this new knowledge comes a new way of life: new friends, new clothes, new pastimes, new ambitions and a new outlook on life. Some find this transition fairly smooth. However, for most, becoming a Muslim also involves facing many, many challenges. It is as if your whole world has been turned upside down and, in a way, it has. Things are no longer as they were, there is a new set of values, priorities, loyalties, and adjusting to these can be painful.

Family Values

Often the hardest thing to deal with as a new Muslim is the reaction of one's family. It is rarely a positive one. Once, in my headwrap phase, I spoke to my paternal aunt about the changes I had made to my lifestyle. By that time I was no longer eating pork, drinking alcohol or going out clubbing. I had also taken to praying, in my own way, in the darkened living room on the thirteenth floor of our tower-block flat. I found it necessary to communicate with God (who I thought of as The Higher Being) regularly, while exploring my spiritual side – a side of me that had been, up until that point, completely under-developed. For me, it was enough that I had started to 'clean up' my life. I was never intending to make a firm commitment to any faith, not even to Islam. Although at the time, the lifestyle espoused by Muslims appealed to me with its emphasis on self-discipline and closing the doors to temptation, I had never actually considered becoming a Muslim officially. My aunt had her reservations and was quite sceptical, but she listened all the same. But when my father heard on the family grapevine that I was becoming involved with Islam, he called me long distance and I could tell that he was upset. I kicked myself for even mentioning anything to anybody in my family – I should have known that the news would make its way back to him, albeit in a mutated form via my grandmother.

My dad didn't waste any time in demanding to know what was going on: 'What's this I hear about you becoming a Muslim?' I just laughed it off, assuring him that I didn't actually want to become a Muslim; I was just 'doing a few Muslim things'. And I was telling the truth. I didn't want to become a Muslim, although I had to admit that it seemed like a very 'good', safe way of life. My dad didn't see it that way. As a self-avowed atheist, I think he had hoped that I would avoid entanglements with any religious doctrine. In fact, he said that he thought he had raised me better than that, that I had grown into an independent, free-spirited young woman and now, here I was, humbling my spirit in subservience to an imagined deity. To this day, I believe I heard tears in his voice and it still saddens me to think of his pain.

Trying to reassure him, I said, 'Dad, it's not like I've become a Jehovah's Witness or anything!'

Needless to say, that did not comfort him at all. For him, it must have been like a slap in the face: I was turning my back on a bright future and all the hopes he'd had for me, rejecting everything he held dear and it must have hurt him, just as it hurt me to disappoint him.

My father's reaction was by no means unusual. Yasmin shared her experience with me.

'At first my family just thought it was a big joke. "Oh, it's just a phase she's going through, next week it will be something else." Then it was, "How dare you change your religion?" Then it was the sly comments about becoming dowdy, frumpy, God rendering your heart and not your garments. I wasn't wearing *abayah* [the wide dress-like garment worn over everyday clothes]. But I had started to wear really baggy clothing, loose clothing . . . I remember my brother – who had also become a Muslim – saying to me, "Mum says she doesn't want any more Muslims in the house," so I said, "Fine, I'm moving out." I was nineteen.'

'Before coming to the *deen*, my life had started changing anyway. I had stopped smoking, I had stopped drinking, stopped raving, stopped all sorts of things. So my life was taking a turn and I didn't realize what turn it was taking until Islam came to me and I thought, This is what Allah had been preparing me for.'
Aziza

In my case, my conversion seemed to come out of the blue. My student lifestyle did not allow for regular contact with my family, due to a combination of time and money issues – living as an overseas student in London doesn't give you much freedom in that department. As a result, my family members were never really privy to the thought processes or experiences that led me to choose Islam as a way of life – they never saw the gradual change. Unsurprisingly perhaps, in a family that comprises Jews (my maternal aunt and her family), Christians (my Scottish ancestors), followers of African traditional religion (my Zulu family) and an atheist (my father), religion was not a favourite topic of conversation. And so, no one ever asked me why I had decided to change my life, what I now believed in, whether I was happy. It was never discussed. Of course, 'issues' were discussed – the role of women in Islam, covering, Afghanistan, Palestine – but never the very things that were driving me, the beliefs I had embraced. Perhaps that was the only way for my family to cope with this Muslim who was so different to the girl they had known. And although, with time, their love and acceptance managed to transcend their initial shock and misgivings, at the time of my conversion I often felt very isolated and misunderstood.

Mei's father was devastated when she finally told him that she had become a Muslim.

'I didn't tell my parents that I was a Muslim until a year after taking my *shahadah*,' she told me. 'Although I wasn't wearing *hijab*, when I came back home after university, my parents knew there was something different about me. One day my dad said, "Are you happy? What's wrong with you? Why are you so sad?"

'I said, "Nothing, I'm not sad, I'm all right."

'And he said, "No, tell me. You've got something to tell me, something's changed."

'So I said, "I'm a Muslim." And he went mad. He was so hurt and upset – he couldn't believe it. But I was so relieved. I didn't like lying to my parents – it had made me feel ill. But now I was happy. I thought, I've told them now, that's it. I knew I had to do what I had to do. I knew that if I didn't take my *shahadah*, if I didn't become a Muslim, that would be even worse. It was like Allah had superiority over my parents. I tried to change that but I couldn't. God was in my heart from when I was young – if you took that away, it was like taking my life away.'

I wanted to know how she had managed to live in the house after that.

'There was turmoil in that house – it was a nightmare. They knew I was praying then and my dad would make it very difficult for me to pray. I kept my *hijab* in my bag and my dad found it and threw it in the bin, threw it away.'

And during that time, her parents offered to sell the business and move away where no one knew them, so that she could give up her Islam without losing face. They offered her money, love, anything she wanted, 'but I wouldn't touch it because I knew it was a bribe. I couldn't pray, I couldn't practise Islam, I felt ill, I wasn't happy – it just felt very uncomfortable.

'In the end, it was so bad, I told my mum I had to leave. And she agreed. I had already packed my bags and my brother took me to the station and that was it: I left. It was a very sad day. But before I left, my father said to me, "You think if you have children, that we will accept you? No, I won't accept you, even with the children." And I will never forget that.'

My mother and sister reacted differently to my father. When my little sister came to see me when I had my register office marriage, she was quite shocked by the change in me, mainly my appearance. Where were the plucked eyebrows, full make-up, slick hairstyle and skimpy clothes she knew? She looked down at my feet and shook her head. I was wearing peep-toe mules with socks – white socks.

'Aysh,' she said, using a favourite Zimbabwean

expression of disbelief, 'now you've broken all the rules.'

But she didn't judge me. She asked questions about everything – and I was happy to answer her, hoping, as all reverts do, that she too would see the beauty and truth of Islam and consider converting. I think that one of the hardest things for new Muslims to bear is their families' indifference, scorn or even hatred of the *deen*. The home becomes a battleground and loyalties can be sorely tried.

I think my mother, more than anything, was happy that I had 'found God'. Having returned to the Church herself, I think she was relieved that, although we had been raised in a godless environment, I had acknowledged my Lord and was living my life to worship Him. More than anyone else in my family, she understood the spiritual dimension to my conversion.

But even women from Muslim backgrounds are not safe from family pressures. My generation of sisters who came back to the religion of their birth no longer wanted to practise Islam according to tradition, or culture or community expectations; they wanted pure Islam, the true Islam, an Islam free from cultural interpretations and deviations. I would often be surprised, as someone who was brought up to have a lot of respect for my African culture, to find Asian

Muslims, Pakistanis and Bengalis ridiculing their own cultures. It was only when I understood that, often, when culture is mistaken for religion and charged with religious zeal, it leads to such aberrations as forced marriages, honour killings and female genital mutilation, all of which are often, if not always, incorrectly attributed to Islam.

> 'Back when I was twelve, there was a lot of hardship because, at that time, there were not very many practising Muslims at all. So [when we started practising pure Islam] we basically took on the community, we took on the family, the relatives and friends – everybody, as far as the religion went. To them, this was a new religion we had found.' Begum

Indeed in many communities, the line between the traditional culture and Islam is extremely blurred. This results in cultural norms, which are often skewed in favour of one sex, social class or economic group, being perpetuated and enforced, usually at the expense of true Islamic principles. I will never forget the time I was invited to do bridal henna for a young Bengali girl in North London. In the Bengali culture, the *mehndi* night is a big affair with all the family, male and female, gathering to eat, socialize and greet the bride. The application of the henna itself is quite a minor part of the whole event, as I was to discover! The bride was very tense, at times laughing wildly with her sisters and friends and at others sullen, pouting or close to tears. We did our best to calm her nerves as she tried to get her elaborate red sari to cover her midriff, because 'Mum will make a fuss'. Imagine my horror when I discovered that she had been promised to the son of her late father's best friend, a young man she didn't know and didn't want to marry. I found it hard to imagine what the scene would be on her wedding night – alone with a man she doesn't want, may not even like, and probably longing for the one she loves but can never have. It was not the fact that her marriage had been arranged that bothered me. Like most of my sisters, my marriage was 'arranged' (more on that later). But what did bother me was the fact that all the rights that this young woman had under Islam had been stripped from her by the demands of her Bengali culture: the right to see and meet her suitor, to refuse him if he did not appeal to her emotionally and physically, the right to accept or refuse him for no reason at all . . . It almost broke my heart. But what did I expect? Although born and bred as Muslims, her family didn't really follow the faith and she couldn't help expressing admiration for the way in which my young henna assistant,

Sadia, and I treated each other with friendship and respect, how we always exchanged greetings of peace ('*Asalaamu alaikum*'), how we often mentioned the name of Allah, the way we covered and our manners in general.

That whole evening, which ended with the police being called to deal with a brat of a 'little' brother who was abusing his mother and sister, crystallized my objections to traditional culture being treated as inviolable. Unfortunately, even in the West, the horrific reality is that those who reject such cultural beliefs or call for them to adapt and change – in extreme cases – pay with their lives.

A Changing Lifestyle

Becoming a Muslim in your youth often means becoming a social pariah, especially if you are actually trying to live by Islamic Law, the *Shari'ah*. It means that you are always 'taking a rain check' when your non-Muslim friends are getting ready to go out to a party, bar or club. Even a seemingly innocuous place like a restaurant poses almost insurmountable challenges. Will men and women be together there? Will they be serving alcohol? Will the meat be *halal*? Will the music be blasting and will they all want to dance? Will I feel strange in my *hijab*?

Will I be compromising my *deen*? These are the questions that haunt any social occasion, particularly where non-Muslim family and friends are involved.

I remember the time when accompanying my flatmate Efua to her relatives' house for a party to welcome her new baby left me feeling embarrassed and uncomfortable. It was mid-afternoon and time to pray *'Asr*. I found myself a little corner in the otherwise jam-packed house to lay down my mat and pray. But, as I bent over into the position of *ruku'*, I felt a body brush past me and I stiffened. I became aware of someone standing on the stairs behind me and my face burnt with embarrassment. I couldn't concentrate on my prayer after that. Also, I found that everyone was looking at me like I had just dropped from another planet because I was wearing a *hijab*. I was the odd one out, the one who was no fun, the one who was *different*.

'I noticed that people broke away from me because I wasn't talking like they were, because I wasn't into what they were doing, because I wasn't like them any more. Because I was trying to follow the *deen*, I was boring to them.' Sadiqa

In the end, outings with my non-Muslim friends became a rarity and I began spending more and more time in 'Sandra's Kitchen', with Muslims who, like me, were either reverts or 'returnees' to the faith. That, in itself, brought its own conflicts, as my old friends thought I was changing, growing away from them. But what could I do? I wanted to immerse myself in this new faith that was unfolding before my eyes. There were so many topics to debate, so many questions to ask, so many attitudes to re-examine, and I was completely wrapped up in it all.

'When I came to the *deen*, it wasn't a conscious decision that I wanted to practise. It was as though I woke up one day and my heart had changed. I wasn't looking for anything, but Allah just chose to guide me. Because it happened so quickly, I was very lonely because I had to cut everybody out of my life. My family had thrown me out, emotionally and physically, and my friends were all non-Muslims. I felt like I had been born again, but I had to start everything from scratch: find a new community, find new friends, new clothes . . . and I was very lonely. I had no one, I had nothing, and all that was keeping me going was Allah, nothing else.' Ghaniyah

One of the choices that Sara had to make was between practising her *deen* and competing in basketball tournaments, an activity that she adored.

'Sport was the one thing that I could not envisage giving up,' she told me. 'I had played basketball since I was fourteen and it had always been a big part of my life, keeping fit and relieving tension. I loved the whole social aspect of it as well. I could not imagine eliminating that part of my life. But, *alhamdulillah*, that passion for it faded and, in a way, that was replaced by a passion for walking – in parks, fields, anywhere.

'And as I became more spiritually aware, I started to appreciate everything: the rain, the sky, the trees, all the different shades of green, all the things that Allah has given us.'

Aside from the social aspect, it is not uncommon for reverts' friends to have other misgivings too. After all, they have often been through thick and thin together, sharing hair-raising stunts, mad escapades and dodgy make-up. This is the girl who slept over at their house, who they snuck out with, who lied to their parents to cover their tracks, who bluffed their way into nightclubs and danced the night away, wearing borrowed high heels. And now she's a *Muslim*? She's covering up? She's not drinking, raving, not interested in men? Can she really have changed *that* much? And just who, or what, is she changing into?

'After I started covering, I spent some time with a sporting friend from my neighbourhood. We were chatting away when she suddenly said, "You're just the same! Telling the same jokes and everything!" She was really surprised.' Sara

Being aware of or even imagining your friends' scorn is humiliating. But how do you convince an old acquaintance of the honour and beauty of your new way of life when she is looking at you with pity and probably thinking, Poor girl, look at her. Why did she have to go and throw herself away like that?

'I felt really depressed about it, especially when I would see people from the area where I grew up. They would look me up and down and say, "What, you? You became Muslim, *you*?"' Zubeida

I will never forget my embarrassment at meeting an old school friend on a sunny morning at an East London tube station. She and I had been party buddies at school and I had not seen her since after our O-Level year. So for her to see me for the first time in years in a sombre black *hijab* and *abayah* with my make-up-less face, a little tired-looking from an early start, was almost more than I could bear. I didn't want the word to reach the 'bush telegraph', for my old friends in Zimbabwe to hear how I had become so dowdy and awkward, so different to the girl they all knew. It could have been my own sense of insecurity, but I was loath to meet anyone from my past for a long time afterwards. And although you know that what you are doing is right and that what you believe is the truth, the feeling of being looked down upon and sneered at stings like no other. There was no way that I could reach out to all who knew me and explain how or why I felt compelled to embrace Islam, so in a sense, I retreated. I felt most comfortable around those who needed no explanations – no justifications.

Claire told me how she gradually withdrew from her friends, afraid of their criticism and unsure of her own ability to live up to her *shahadah*.

'I didn't really communicate to my friends where I was coming from very well,' she said. 'That was partly because I knew that they would think that I had become Muslim because of Gareth, as he had been the one telling me about Islam. That was hard enough for me to come to terms with, without having to explain to other people that, yes, it was partly because of him, but it could not and will never be totally about him. I was afraid of what they would think of me and

I was afraid of affirming that difference with everyone, just in case I couldn't live up to it myself. I doubted my own ability to embrace certain things. I became very distant from all my friends. I didn't really tell them much about it because I felt that was the way I needed to do it. I don't really think I could have done it any other way.'

Another area of conflict for me and many of the sisters I spoke to was 'free-mixing'. This is the term Muslims often use to describe a situation where men and women who are not related mix socially. Within the family unit, relations are free between men and women who are either married or are related and cannot marry. These relations are clarified in the Qur'an, in Surah an-Nisa:

> Forbidden to you [for marriage] are: your mothers, your daughters, your sisters, your father's sisters, your mother's sisters, your brother's daughters, your sister's daughters, your foster mother who gave you suck, your foster milk-suckling sisters, your wives' mothers, your step daughters under your guardianship, born of your wives to whom you have gone in – but there is no sin on you if you have not gone in them [to marry their daughters], – the wives of your sons who [spring] from your own loins,

and two sisters in wedlock at the same time, except for what has already passed; verily, Allah is Oft-Forgiving, Most Merciful.

Surah An-Nisa 4:23

Inversely, this means that a Muslim woman does not cover or observe *hijab* in the company of her father, sons, brothers, paternal and maternal uncles, etc. She will wear her ordinary clothes, make-up and perfume and share a relaxed and informal relationship with these men who are known as her *maharem*.

However, relationships between unrelated men and women are governed by a moral code that involves observing *hijab*, lowering the gaze (both men and women, although men are commanded with it first in the Qur'an), not being alone together, not having physical contact and generally behaving in a respectful and business-like manner whenever there is contact. In our lives, this often takes place in the context of business transactions, studying, shopping, among others. However, we make great efforts to keep this contact to a minimum. Many non-Muslims and even some Muslims find the idea of separation between the sexes unnatural and cannot understand it.

At this point, it may be helpful to remember that, as Muslims, we live by a different moral code from the society we live in. It is the morality that is outlined in the Qur'an and part of that morality is the seriousness of adultery: *zina*. For the practising Muslim, this is something terribly heinous and is to be avoided at all costs.

I would like you now to picture this scenario: a group of friends, men and women, is on a night out. The women are dressed to kill, and have their dancing shoes on. The alcohol is flowing and all the guys are showing off, eager to make a good impression. When they meet, hugs and kisses are exchanged. Maybe one hug between friends lasts a little longer than usual – is it the softness of her hair or the aftershave he is wearing? But it is nothing, they are just friends. Besides, they both have long-term partners whom they love and respect very much. The friendly banter lifts everyone's spirits and there are a few flirtatious encounters. One woman, sparkling and witty, has the men eating out of her hand. The men are loving it, especially her good friend – he just loves locking horns with her: she is such a challenge, unlike his partner who seems less interesting by comparison. Now it is just the two of them, going head to head. Everyone else watches their exchange as sparks fly. His girl-friend sinks into her seat, embarrassed and ashamed that she can't hold his attention in that way. Her boyfriend senses his own inadequacy –

she never has that sparkle in her eye when they talk. And so the evening goes on – everyone dances with everyone else, alcohol fuzzes the brain and sensations take over. What will happen at the end of the night? Will the 'good friends' go home together? Will his girlfriend cry in the car on the way home, angry at being upstaged by another woman, powerless in the face of his denials? Will her boyfriend call her a 'little tart' and slap her face, furious at her for making a fool of him? Or maybe nothing will happen, nothing out of the ordinary. Maybe it will be just a regular night out. Or maybe not.

This is just one such scenario and to many it will seem like nothing more than a harmless and fairly normal interaction between the sexes. However, very often, where there are men and women, the seeds of desire are sown. Some seeds die before they can take root, others manage to produce shoots before they too fade; others grow into fully fledged blooms.

The media knows this all too well. In countless films, novels, songs and poems, the theme of adultery is explored and exploited. I think it would be fair to say that the language and imagery of adultery is a part of our society, whether we like it or not, and the popular media neither condemns it nor warns against it. Instead it glamorizes it and the people who fall into it:

the ladies' man, the heartbreaker, the Don Juan, the Lothario, what are they after all but serial adulterers, to put it bluntly? The fact that there are not as many admiring descriptions for women who have many sexual partners is an indication of the way in which our society works, even in this era of gender equality.

However, for Muslims, adultery does not have a glamorous image at all: it is a major sin and anything that is likely to lead to it is avoided or restricted – and this includes 'free-mixing'.

But how does the new Muslim, who has been 'free-mixing' all her life, adjust to this separation from her ex-boyfriend and male friends? The issue of 'free-mixing' was not a particularly hard one for me, not because I did not have guys that I had been close to, but because I could appreciate the reasoning behind it. I had seen for myself the consequences of those mixed environments, had shared the pain of a friend crushed by her best friend's betrayal, and the turmoil of a platonic friend's sudden and unwelcome declarations of love. So I could appreciate the safeguard of staying away from those situations altogether.

However, not everyone found it that easy.

'It was hard because most of my friends were guys,' Yasmin told me. 'After a while I started to pull away from them and they were still trying to hold on and that was hard with the ones I was really close to. With the girlfriends, I was glad to get rid of them!'

Born into a Muslim Somali family, Suad found starting to practise very difficult, both in terms of free-mixing and in terms of family pressures. She expressed as much to me when she said, 'It was hard telling all my Muslim guy friends, "Oh, I can't talk to you any more, it's *haram*, I can't do that." And I cut everyone off, male and female – anyone I thought could influence me in the slightest. I didn't phone them any more, I completely cut off. But I couldn't cut my sister off, the sister who lived in the same house as me, and who was continuously saying, "You're so extreme. I don't understand why you need to do that." I could fight off those who weren't family, but when it's your sister and your cousins who are on your case like hawks, you can't even walk away.'

Other sisters had to deal with having non-Muslim boyfriends or partners when they came to the *deen*. Some had been high-school sweethearts, others married for many years, but becoming Muslim meant they had to make some very hard choices. Muslim women can only marry Muslim men as is stated in the Qur'an:

O you who believe! When believing women come to you as emigrants, examine them, Allah knows best as to their Faith, then if you ascertain that they are true believers, send them not back to the disbelievers, they are not lawful (wives) for the disbelievers nor are the disbelievers lawful (husbands) for them . . .
Surah al-Mumtahanah 60:10

Because they did not want to be 'living in sin', this ruling meant that the women had effectively to choose between their partners and their Islam – it was a simple, though hard, choice: the *deen* had to come first.

This may seem like an impossible choice to make, especially if the relationship in question is a good one. But there is a way of understanding it: imagine that you were an alcoholic or a smoker and decided to quit. Your partner, on the other hand, carried on drinking heavily or chain-smoking. Can you imagine the difficulty of weaning yourself off a way of life that still flows through your veins, that calls to you and still has a hold on you, while the one you love and live with is still living that lifestyle and all that goes with it? It would be near impossible to quit and save your relationship at the same time. That is how it is with Islam. As a new Muslim, you want to live an Islamic life, from the moment you wake up to pray *Fajr* to the moment you go to bed at night. But having a non-Muslim partner means being confronted with your old lifestyle on a daily basis and being exposed to all its tests and trials, its *fitan*, be it bad language, free-mixing, drink, drugs or just the smell of a bacon sandwich. So, facing this stark choice, many women separated from their partners. I asked Umm Safwan how she could bear to stop seeing her boyfriend of five years.

'Allah gave me strength, that is all I can say!' was her answer. 'I felt that I couldn't be with a disbeliever any more. If I was, what would be the point of me coming to the *deen*? I might as well just keep doing what I was doing before and thinking that I was a Muslim – just kidding myself.' In her case, her boyfriend was so curious about this religion that had, in effect, stolen his girlfriend, that he went to the mosque to find out for himself what it was all about. He sub-sequently became a Muslim too; as did his sister and his mother, and today he and Umm Safwan are married with four children.

A New Look

Based on the sisters who were interviewed for this book and my own experience, the *hijab* is, without doubt, one of the most difficult aspects of Islam for new Muslim women. It entails an overhaul of so many things: the way you see yourself, the way others see you and how they treat you as a result. For some, myself included, the *hijab* was something that came fairly naturally, although I began with a headwrap and worked my way up to covering fully. Others eased themselves in by starting with a hat, a bandana or, as in Halima's case, a snood: 'It was winter and I started off with a snood, do you remember snoods? But then I thought, OK, it's getting warmer now – I can't wear a snood all the time! So I got a scarf from Covent Garden and I started wrapping it . . . and I was like that for ages. Then I got to the stage where I thought, OK, I can do this now.'

Yasmin had her own experience of covering: 'A challenge for me was the covering of the head. Covering of the body? Hey, no big deal. Covering of the hair? Man, I used to pay good money for my hair! Back then, £40 was a lot of money just to have your hair relaxed and blowdried and I used to pay that money – and I wanted people to see that hair! It took me about six months to wear the hat. So I went from the hat to the *hijab*.'

There is a certain amount of self-effacement that must take place when adopting the *hijab*. Islam is a religion of peace and submission to the

Creator and this humility is something that should be manifest on the body of the believer. Part of the purpose of the *hijab* is to stop the believers from displaying themselves, their clothes, their bodies, and it is precisely this aspect that makes it difficult for reverts who, like Aliyah, were into fashion and 'looking good'. As she said to me candidly, 'I think the *hijab* was what I found really hard because I had always loved my clothes! That was partly because I was coming to the mosque and then going back to my non-Muslim family and I felt slightly ashamed of the *hijab*. When I put it on, I always felt so hot, even on the coldest day, like everyone was looking. Then eventually I just grew to love it. But it didn't come straight away, it did take a while.'

So, for many sisters, the *hijab* was a challenge! I myself found it ugly when I first saw it all those years ago in Egypt. But after actually trying it on, I felt I could live with it and, eventually, I actually felt proud to wear it. The other outer garments, such as the *abayah* and the *jilbab* were a different story altogether! Yasmin had a lot to say about the wide dresses and overcoats that were to be worn over our clothing.

'I'm sorry, but I thought the *abayah* was so ugly. I just thought, Oh my gosh, I'm going to look like some little Turkish granny! Oh no, I can't do it! I dress modestly, my clothes are loose, you can't see the shape of my body – all this rubbish. It was an issue. But then I started reading and studying more and I realized that, at the end of the day, this was the least I could do. Allah guided me to Islam, to me that was something important. I wasn't one to show off my body in the first place so I didn't see why it was becoming such an issue to put on an overgarment to go outside. If you were cold, you would put a coat on to go outside so why can't you, every time you go outside, put your coat on?'

We all had to contend with the *abayah* that was de rigueur about five, ten years ago, namely a wide gown with shoulder pads, gathered sleeves and big gold buttons down the front. They were really the only ones available in the Islamic shops all over East London and I hated them. Amid fits of laughter, Claire made clear her feelings towards those *abayahs*: 'Ughh, they were nasty! You put it on and you're really trying, you're trying to fight your desires and be pious and say, "No, it's not as bad as you think," but it's actually worse. This thing has two pleats down the back – this is like maternity wear gone wrong!'

I vowed I would never wear one of those *abayahs* and, happily, by the time I was ready to wear an outer garment, we had found a wonderful sister from Bradford who made sleek, streamlined *abayahs* that fit more like wide-flowing dresses, and without a padded shoulder in sight. It was seeing her *abayahs*, which we called *jilbabs* then, that convinced me that I could cover more without looking like a frump. I didn't feel that wanting to look neat, smart (and half decent!) conflicted with my faith in the slightest.

For some of the sisters I spoke to, the *hijab* was quite simply alien to who they were at the time, what they were all about. As Halima explained to me, 'It was just opposite to what I was doing, my personality, my lifestyle. I was at college, in the second year, just discovering myself basically. I had just moved away from my family and I was my own person and so the covering thing was the opposite of what I was about. *Masha Allah*, I started with the headwrap and then the whole of the body. How people saw me in the community was how I was at college. Some sisters would say, "We get round the corner from the mosque and we put everything on." Well I can't do that, to me that's hypocrisy – as you see me is as I am.'

As Claire, the former Riot Grrrl, admits, '*Hijab* was absolutely, painfully, terribly difficult for me. I think if I had met someone, a really good mentor, that would have helped me. But unfortunately, I didn't. So I rebelled for a long time. When I did start wearing my *hijab*, it was very progressive: baggy jeans, little scarf, bit by bit, and *now*, I love my *hijab*!'

Another aspect of starting to wear *hijab* is how people look at you differently. By this I don't just mean men – that is completely understandable. In fact, one of the best things about wearing *hijab* is the sense of relief at not being viewed as a sexual object. But aside from that, there are some people who assume that you are some sort of alien without a voice or a mind of your own. And the most pervading belief of all, particularly when people have known you before Islam, is that you are somehow less than the person you once were. Before I fully embraced Islam I had become quite friendly with one of the secretaries at my university and would often stop by her office for a laugh and a chat. However, when I started replacing my Afro-print headwraps with the *hijab*, a black one at that, she had great difficulty accepting it. When mentioning the change in me, she would often begin her sentences, 'Oh, but you used to be so . . .' Vibrant, colourful, full of life, fun – these were all things that, for her, I was no longer. I tried in vain to explain my reasons for covering, but she just could not deal with it. She could not see past the exterior – could not see the happy, confident me beneath the dark fabric.

It was then that I came to an important realization: our society teaches us to be obsessed with appearance. As long as someone is beautiful, thin, wealthy, fun-loving or talented, we are happy to accept him or her at face value. We are not ever taught to look for – or care about – what lies beneath the surface. So, my secretary friend could bemoan the death of the free-spirited girl she knew without ever having to think about the insecurity, the vanity, the arrogance and the turmoil that were also part of that girl. This superficial, misguided view is most acutely exposed by society's obsession with celebrity. No matter how self-obsessed, ego-tistical, vain, greedy, vapid and shallow an individual 'celeb' may be, no matter that most of what we are shown is nothing more than clever PR and fake images of perfection peddled to enhance their celebrity status. As long as they look beautiful and smile for the cameras all is well and the audience is satisfied. And we waste our time, fantasizing, reading about every outfit, award and extravagant gift that these 'beautiful people' exchange, while sniggering about their bad hair days, the divorces, the drug overdoses and all the other sordid evidence that shows us that 'they are only human after all'. They may be a waste of space, but at least they beautify that space! And on this scale, the Muslim cannot compete: no matter how intelligent, talented, kind, generous or honest she is, she doesn't 'look the part' and that is some-thing she will not be forgiven for.

Suad found that, when she began practising, she began to gain weight: 'That was a result of my lifestyle change and not feeling the need to dress up any more. There was no image to keep up any more.' Her family would not let her forget it: 'My family used to say, "Since she started practising, she just let herself go. The *abayah* wasn't fitting her, she was fitting it . . ."' All this had a very negative effect on her self-esteem and only made her feel resentful towards her *hijab* and *abayah*.

But for some, the *hijab* is not the problem per se. It is that the *hijab* is a symbol of a particular identity; an identity that they have trouble conforming to. By the time I had come back from Guinea, I had been wearing the headwrap for a good six months – I felt comfortable with it: it covered my hair, it looked good (and that was still important to me!), it wasn't too 'extreme' and it fitted in with my African identity. Imagine my surprise when the sisters who I would often see in the prayer room began asking me when I was going to start wearing a 'proper *hijab*'. I was, quite frankly, insulted. Who said that their version of *hijab* was better than mine? So I would proudly declare that this is how we wear *hijab* in Africa, that I was not going any further than this. The sisters would then smile doubtfully, not sure what to make of my full-on Black nationalist attitude. But for me, the *hijab* that covered what Allah says it should cover was too alien, too foreign, too un-African. It wasn't *me*.

Claire felt the same way: 'I didn't want to wear *hijab* and I didn't wear *hijab* for a long time, and I tried to force myself to be who I was before, but my soul couldn't feel happy with it. But then at the same time, I couldn't enter totally into something else.'

The issue of identity is a complex one. The 'old me' was secure, a known entity, I had been comfortable with her. Now I was changing and a part of me resisted that change. I battled with myself, torn between what I knew was right and what my desires were calling me to. This was not an everyday thing, mind you, most days were good days. But there were bad days, days when it all seemed too much, as if the ideal that I was striving for was too lofty and well beyond my reach.

The following lines of poetry are a good indication of my confused feelings at that time.

Immerse myself in yards and yards of headscarf
Trying to hide my pain in the dark.
I don't know when this feeling of empti-mess
    started.
I must concede
That during *Eid*,

The feeling of elation began to recede.
And now I find myself crying, dressed in black
Begging for some of what I had to come back.
Forget what science says, the world is flat!
I can see it stretching for miles and miles
Of greyness and a chilling absence of smiles.
Even as I write, my face is set,
It's harder to stretch these lips these days.
In what way is this a hell of my own making?
Is it my fault for half-baking my theories?
For not setting the timer to allow my soul to
　　heal?
For pushing myself too hard towards an
　　impossible ideal?
This is blatantly the way I feel,
And even my bright purple jacket
Doesn't make the brightness
Real.

Thankfully, the low points were few and far between because I was blessed to come to the *deen* with Sandra, Hanah and our close-knit group of new Muslims and returnees. That meant that we all had similar issues with what lay ahead and what we were leaving behind. So, by and large, we had a lot of support. Other sisters, however, did not have such a good support network. Some were the only reverts in a group of born Muslims, Muslims who could not understand the ache of an old love, the pull of a throbbing bass line, the temptations of summer. For them the struggles of adapting to this new way of life were a secret and lonely affair. For other sisters, the pace of change was too much: there was too much to give up too fast and too much to implement in a short space of time. That was the situation in which Halima found herself.

'When I came to the *deen*, I saw how other sisters were practising and very early on, I felt under a lot of pressure. I felt inadequate because all it was about in those days was "you can't do this", "you can't do that", "give away all your clothes", etc. So very early on, I felt that pressure and I nearly came away because I thought to myself, I don't doubt the religion but I doubt whether I can commit, and that was after just three months of being Muslim. Then somebody said, "Why are you doing that? You don't have to." And I said to myself, I'm going at my own pace. And I've done that all along . . . I've got to find my own way.'

A New Belief

Islam is a *deen*, a way of life, precisely because it is so much more than just a religion. As such, it encompasses a complete belief, social, economic and political system. But aside from all the lifestyle changes that took place when my friends and I turned to Islam, there was also the upheaval of our belief systems to consider. For many who had previously been religious, it was a small leap towards *tawheed* – belief in Islamic monotheism. For others, like myself, it seemed like a moon-step. Having laughed and joked my way through years of religious education classes at school, I suddenly had to contend with the notion that the prophets really existed, that the Qur'an was revelation, divine and perfect, that the Prophet Muhammad (s)'s sayings had been recorded and were meant to be followed.

I remember finding the whole idea of the *ghayb*, the unseen, particularly difficult to accept, and, for a long time, I just didn't think about Heaven or Hell, angels or *jinn*. It was a leap of faith that was too far for me at that time. Not having grown up within a religious context, I found the idea of being accountable for one's actions and having to answer to God quite daunting. It was only as my knowledge of the intellectual and scientific proofs for the Qur'an and the Sunnah grew that I was able to trust, on reasoned faith, that the unseen world of spirits and angels was a reality. As a scholar from the past put it, the Qur'an presents mankind with rational proofs of its truth and authenticity and, based on these proofs, the reader can then accept those things that cannot be proven. That was how it was for me.

But by far the greatest trial for me and many others was actualizing what is really the essence of Islam – submission. To become a Muslim is to become one who submits to the will of Allah. That means ego out, arrogance out, pride out: the self is brought to heel.

Sara's long road to where she is now was paved with resistance: 'I was resisting full submission. I was happy with the way I was living my life – I had always been very active, outgoing, I liked going out, seeing art-house films, visiting galleries, going to nice restaurants, I liked my fashions . . . And that was very much what my dad wanted for me – to be worldly, to speak different languages, to have a good education, to excel in my field – and because I loved and respected him, I wanted to live up to that.'

After spending our whole lives rebelling against some authority or other, we had chosen to submit to the highest authority of all – Allah – and sometimes it burnt like fire. How to explain the agony of wanting something so badly it hurts, even though you know that it is not allowed and has been forbidden for very good reasons? As Allah says:

Jihad is ordained for you though you dislike it, and it may be that you dislike a thing which is good for you and that you like a thing which is bad for you. Allah knows but you do not know.

Surah al-Baqarah 2:216

Although this verse speaks of the physical *jihad* that the Prophet (s) and his Companions were ordered with, it holds true for *jihadunnafs*, the fight against the self and the desires. This is the first battle that everyone must wage, the battle in which one struggles against one's baser instincts and aspires to something greater, nobler and purer. No one said the battle would be quick or easily won, but it is a battle that we all face. I struggled with it then and continue to struggle now, every day of my life, and will, *insha Allah*, keep fighting until I die.

For everyone coming to Islam from the life of *jahiliyyah*, revert or returnee, there are painful moments and sacrifices to be made. But in all our hearts is the memory of those who were the first to hear the message of the Prophet (s) and embrace Islam. Believing in the One God in a land ruled by idol worship and ancestral tribal law, the new Muslims were stripped of their wealth, driven from their homes, beaten, tortured and killed – but they did not give up their faith.

One story that sticks in my head is that of Sumayyah (r), one of the female companions of the Prophet (s). After days of being tortured on the burning sands of the Arabian desert, she was killed by Abu Jahal who, incensed at her refusal to renege on her Islam, stabbed her with a spear in her private parts. She is honoured by all Muslims as being the first ever martyr in Islam and her courage and conviction is a source of inspiration for us.

And something that has continually surprised and touched me is the unshakeable conviction of every one of the sisters I spoke to that the pain, tears and heartache have all been worth it – not one of them would take back their *shahadah* if ever they had their time again. They are prepared to go through all the trials and tribulations to achieve their goal: to hold on to their *deen*, to hold it close to their hearts, for its beauty to permeate their lives, their bodies and their souls and so gain the pleasure of their Lord and His Love and to, one day, see the beauty of His Face.

Part Two
Living Islam

5

COVERING OUR BEAUTY

Yesterday, we were walking down the street looking like most other women do – with our hair done to perfection, outfit carefully selected for maximum impact, perfume wafting in our wake, hips swinging, heads turning: queen of the street. Then, in a matter of days and weeks, Islam came into our lives and changed everything. Now, we revisit those same streets clad from head to toe in all-enveloping black, with only our eyes showing. Which paths brought us here?

First Steps

In the beginning, covering myself with the head-wrap and loose clothes was a tonic. I wanted and needed to free myself from my reliance on my looks. I wanted to test myself, to see whether I had the courage to get by on the strength of my personality, character and deeds. It was not a decision that I took lightly – though at the time I could not have known what that initial desire to cover up would lead me to. I suppose, after having considered my modus operandi to date and having seen that there was a better, albeit more difficult, alternative, I would not have been able to carry on as before. How could I have any self-respect if I found myself, once again, batting my eyelashes or deliberately choosing to wear a pair of trousers because they made me look 'absolutely ravishing'? Indeed, I remember thinking to myself, You've grown to rely on your looks in this way for so long – how much respect do you really have for yourself? I had long thought the practice of judging women according to their measurements totally unacceptable (which is why I was dead against beauty contests!) but hadn't we, in our own way, been part of such a system?

Beautiful women the world over have an unfair advantage and an easy ticket to social success: guest-list nightclub entry, free drinks, a constant stream of admirers. Of course, for any young woman just coming to terms with her feminine power, this can be very exciting. You feel as if the whole world is at your feet, if only you can make friends with the 'right people' and hang out in the 'right places'. But hadn't I seen those same girls, time and again, become complacent? Lazy? *Boring?* It was as if, now that they knew how far they could go with their looks alone, they didn't feel the need to develop their intellect, their sense of humour, their ambition – to have a personality and a mind of their own!

Although my case had not been that extreme, I knew that I was ready to make a change. And so, on the day after I got back from Egypt, I took a length of cloth and wrapped it around my head. This was by no means the first time I had done this – I had often worn headwraps when I was performing, at traditional Zimbabwean performances and with our band, as well as at other times, particularly when I was having a 'bad hair day'! But this time it was different somehow. I was not wearing this piece of cloth to make a cultural statement – 'I'm Black and I'm proud' – I was doing it to curb a certain part of me, and to carve out a little private space for myself, even if it was only my hair that was covered.

So on that day, I took my first tentative steps towards covering. And I admit, it was miserable. No one was looking at me, there was no flirtation, nothing – I felt completely invisible. That lasted for about half a day. Then something inside me just clicked. I thought, Good, don't look, don't compare me with your latest squeeze, don't try and guess my measurements – my body is my own business.

And I have had that feeling ever since. And that feeling is one reflected time and again by women who choose to cover themselves and make their bodies their own private space.

Journeys of Transition

It was only after a few months of wearing a head-wrap that I considered wearing a 'conventional' *khimar*, the headscarf that covers the hair, neck and chest. I think one of the reasons was that I was still getting unwanted attention from guys who thought my headwrap meant that I was a 'conscious Black sistah' and therefore still 'available'. I realized that my headwraps were not fulfilling their function as I had intended them to. But more importantly, through our increased study of the *deen*, Sandra and I had come to realize that the *hijab* was a religious obligation, an integral part of our submission and an important act of worship.

'The *taqwa* – the fear and reverence of Allah – is why you are doing it mainly. Allah has told us to do this and it is a must for us. It's like having to eat and sleep . . .' Umm Safwan

The covering of the Muslim woman is referred to in the Qur'an, in Surah an-Nur:

> And tell the believing women to lower their gaze, and protect their private parts and not to show off their adornment except that which is apparent, and to draw their veils all over *Juyubihinna* [i.e. their bodies, necks and bosoms, etc.], and not to reveal their adornment . . .
> Surah an-Nur 24:31

And in Surah al-Ahzab, Allah says:

> O Prophet! Tell your wives and your daughters and the women of the believers to draw their cloaks [veils] all over their bodies. That will be better, that they should be known [as free respectable women] so as not to be annoyed. And Allah is Ever OftForgiving, Most Merciful.
> Surah al-Ahzab 33:59

Aisha, wife of the Prophet (s) and a prominent scholar in her own right, remarked in a *hadith* in Sahih Bukhari, that when the women of Madinah, the Ansar, heard these verses, they tore their wrappers (scarves) and covered their heads and faces with them.

Indeed, the *hijab* is mentioned in the Qur'an,

181

in the *hadith* and it was practised by the earliest generations of Muslims. It is not merely a relic of Bedouin culture that has somehow infiltrated the Muslim mainstream – the *hijab* is Islamic.

Based on these and numerous other evidences, we learnt that our outer clothing had to fulfil certain criteria. These were:

- It should cover the whole body, except for the face and hands. (Some Islamic scholars consider it obligatory to cover the face.)
- It should not be tight-fitting so as to show the shape of the wearer
- It should not be see-through
- It should not be brightly coloured
- It should not be specifically men's clothing
- It should not be specifically the clothing of non-Muslims
- It should not be ostentatious or showy

There are also guidelines on Muslim men's clothing. These are:

- It should cover the area between the navel and the knee
- It should not be tight-fitting in this area
- It should not be see-through in this area
- It should not be specifically women's clothing

- It should not be specifically the clothing of non-Muslims
- It should not be ostentatious or showy
- It should not be silk
- The lower garment should be raised above the ankle

In addition to this, men are not permitted to wear gold, and are commanded to allow their beards to grow, in accordance with the *Sunnah*, the way of the Prophet (s). Women, on the other hand, are not expected to keep their beards!

I remember the day that my friend Sandra and I decided to give those lace-trimmed *hijabs* a try, in her room on campus. Gingerly, we held the triangular pieces of cloth over our heads and brought the two ends together under our chins. We then fastened them with safety pins and looked nervously at our reflections in the mirror. And do you know, it was as if, because we had so wanted to start wearing the *hijab*, Allah had put light in our faces. We didn't look funny or dowdy or plain – we looked beautiful. I was reminded of the Egyptian lady who had set the whole ball rolling and I smiled. We both breathed a huge sigh of relief – '*Alhamdulillah*' – and went to visit Hanah on the other end of campus, pleased as punch.

However, not everyone found their first outing

with the *hijab* as positive as we did. Sara told me about her first attempt at wearing the *hijab*: 'I was in Central London and I felt very self-conscious. I had wrapped my scarf, Jackie-O-style, tightly around my face and neck and had chosen clothes that covered my curves. I was acutely aware that no one was looking at me, that I had a different kind of presence, just with that little scarf. From a distance, I saw a girl who had known me at school and was used to my cool and trendy image – I really tried to avoid her as much as I could – I even crossed the road!'

I was fortunate in that I was not a lone warrior, facing the strangeness of this new look on my own. I had sisters around me to encourage and strengthen me and it was not very long before I had a wide selection of *hijabs*, made from many different kinds of fabric. I mixed and matched them with what I wore and they became very much a part of me.

Changing Outside, Changing Inside

None of us started covering ourselves without experiencing certain changes in ourselves and the way we related to those around us.

The first effect that the *hijab*, the headscarf, seemed to have on us was to encourage modesty – in dress and in conduct. After a lifetime spent showing off our clothes and our bodies, we suddenly felt shy to flaunt ourselves in public. The *hijab* reminded us of the standards of behaviour that were expected of us as Muslims and, more specifically, as Muslim women. We became more aware of upholding Islamic manners – trying not to be rude or to lie, to be kind and generous. When it came to the opposite sex, we no longer felt comfortable having conversations that were too personal or familiar and the *hijab* made flirting a definite no-no. Although we were only wearing scarves at this point, we grew to feel less comfortable about showing the other parts of our body and, consequently, our style of dress began to change. It just didn't feel right to wear the *hijab* with a pair of hipsters!

We became acutely aware that we could now be identified as Muslims and, as such, were representatives of the faith wherever we went. So we would ask ourselves whether what we wanted to do or where we wanted to go was appropriate for a Muslim. And we figured that hanging out at the Students' Union bar just might be one of those things that was a tad inappropriate!

The *hijab* also gave us a sense of pride in our Islam. We were happy to be recognized as Muslims and, while others may have thought us dowdy or plain, we felt beautiful in the eyes of Allah.

'The *hijab* is about saying who you are and what you're about, although I didn't see it like that at the time. But now, I really want to have that identity, to show that I am a Muslim as opposed to blending in with this society.' Claire

But we were not the only ones affected by our decision to cover. Because we were sending such a clear message to the outside world – 'I do not want to be bothered, I do not want to be approached sexually, I am off limits for you' – men could not help but change the way they related to us. They would no longer observe our movements, watch the way we walked, size us up or compare us. The old ways of relating to women's bodies were no longer applicable because our bodies were not on display.

This endowed our interaction with men with a new level of respect and courtesy, however begrudgingly it was granted. We were clearly no longer sexual objects – we had to be treated differently.

'As a Muslim woman, I feel protected by my *hijab*, protected from the way men can look at you. I feel I have more respect this way, because they aren't going to look at me and comment on how big my bum is or how big my chest is.' Rabia

To the *Hijab* . . . and Beyond

In the summer of that year, Sandra announced that she wanted to start wearing an *abayah* – the wide gown worn over one's clothes, which we called a *jilbab*. Although, in the Qur'an, Allah instructs the believing women to wear an outer garment over their clothes, I was shocked – did she really want to wear that sack every day? Not me, I assured her. But still, I went with her to a sister in Stratford who had made *abayahs* for our friends. She was a very sweet sister from Bradford, of mixed Pakistani and English parentage. I have already described how we dreaded the shoulder-padded, gold-buttoned *abayahs*. Well, hers were a lifetime away from those.

Often made from a heavy but fairly thin fabric, they fitted like wide, flowing dresses, having a seam under the bust and one straight down the front. When Sandra tried hers on, I knew that I wanted one straightaway. And indeed, I used to spend many happy hours in the fabric shops on Green Street, selecting fabric for a new *abayah* and a *hijab* to match. My collection grew to include different colours – brown, black, navy blue, cream. By this time, we had progressed to wearing our *abayahs* with larger *hijabs*, ones that covered our chests with an elegant sweep of fabric, pinned on the shoulder and falling into a triangle at the back (see diagram on page 191). Not long after us, Hanah started wearing the *abayah* as well and we were like the Three Musketeers, going everywhere together and swapping tips on where to get the best fabrics and how to hem them.

Now, wearing the *abayah* is different from simply donning a scarf. For many, the *abayah* is a logical extension of a growing Islamic awareness and an increase in faith. But once you decide to cover your clothes, it is as if there is no going back – you have passed the point of no return. And in other people's eyes, you are different too – you're on a different level. Those guys who still spoke to you when you wore the *hijab* no longer feel as comfortable chatting to you. Non-Muslim women, too, keep their distance. In their minds, you look like a nun and you are a world apart from them.

'When I started wearing the *abayah*, I began to see that there is a wall of incomprehension between us and non-Muslim women: we are unknown to them, we are not on a par with them ... They don't know why we cover, whether we're doing it for ourselves, whether our partner made us do it ... to them, it probably smacks of lack of confidence, of shyness.'
Sara

Not that we noticed – we were far too busy exploring and creating our Islamic identity to worry about what other people thought of the way we dressed. I think the *abayah* also confirmed to those who had known me before Islam that I was serious, that this was not a phase I was going through and that I wouldn't be seeing them at the 'Flava' R'n'B session at the Students' Union!

And then I was introduced to the half-*jilbab* (see diagram on page 191), the form of covering that was brought to Western shores by the Somali women who came to seek refuge from the civil war in their country. I would see them every day while at work, sweeping into the college entrance with their big blue, green, pink and mustard-coloured half-*jilbabs* framing their faces. And one day, one of them offered to make one for me. When she brought it in to college a couple of days later, I slipped it on over the bandana-style headpiece and swung round. It rose up around me like a cloud before settling back down in purple folds – and I fell in love. It was wide, airy and streamed behind me when I walked – it skimmed over my shoulders and my shape was indiscernible. I remember thinking, This is more like it . . . this is the real deal. And so, after that, I would wear a half-*jilbab* whenever I could. My Sudanese flatmate, Hayat, and I were in agreement that this was a much more complete way of covering.

So imagine my horror when Hayat showed me the full-*jilbab* (see diagram opposite) she had had made! I was shocked and repelled – it was so big, so black, so *extreme*! Fortunately, Hayat was the kind of person who knew her own mind and she didn't let my ignorant reaction stop her wearing her full-*jilbab*. Right then, I decided that I wouldn't be seen dead in one. Famous last words.

Of course, Allah knew better than I did. He knew that I was going to meet a sister called Umm Tasneem, who herself wore a *jilbab and* a *niqab*, which covered her face. He knew that we were going to get along very well and He had decreed that I was going to spend the weekend at her house one April Bank Holiday. We were getting ready to go to the *Jumu'ah* prayer at mid-day when she asked me about wearing *jilbab*. I assured her that I would never do any such thing. She suggested I try it on. I did. I looked in the little mirror by the coat stand. I looked at the folds that fell either side of my face, all the way to the floor, I felt the air move in the space between my body and the fabric. And I turned to her, my face bright with surprise and pleasure, and said, 'Make me one too!' And, with that, another vow bit the dust.

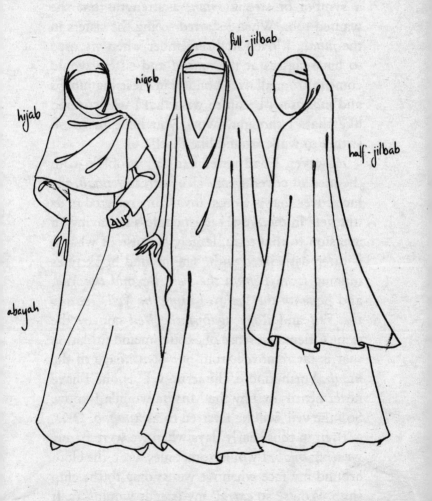

hijab

niqab

full-jilbab

half-jilbab

abayah

However, not everyone had an initial aversion to the *jilbab*. Sara told me how it seemed to her a symbol of strong *iman*, a strength that she wanted too: 'When I started seeing the sisters in the *jilbab*, I loved it! I remember when we used to have classes at the *masjid* and sisters would come in from all over London in these big *jilbabs* and *niqabs* – I began to wish that I was covered like that. I thought, Wow, you have to be so strong to walk around like that!'

However, I had never had any problem with the idea of covering my face with the *niqab*, the face cover that is almost invariably referred to as 'the veil' in the West. I must confess to having an aversion to that term, largely because of what it is often associated with. The myriad book titles ranging from *Behind the Veil*, *Beyond the Veil*, and *Beneath the Veil* to *Lifting the Veil*, *Tearing the Veil* and *Rage against the Veil* convey the same Orientalist sense of exoticism and titillation that is far removed from our own image of the *niqab*. Furthermore, the term 'veil' is one I have never heard used by the Muslim women I know. So, 'the veil' will be referred to as a *niqab*, OK?

Even in those early days when we were barely wearing *hijab*, I would sometimes wrap the cloth around my face when we were going to the chip shop. 'You're so *extra*!' my friends would say. It was only while in my *abayah* and big *hijab* phase

192

that I got the urge to cover my face again. I started wrapping my *hijab* around the lower part of my face and pinning it there, on the way home from work. I enjoyed the feeling of anonymity it offered. I liked the fact that people couldn't see my face, that I was a mystery to them. I had begun to feel uncomfortable with the fact that anyone, any man, could see my face – I felt that, although they didn't have a right to it, they were still able to take a curious look whenever they wanted to.

'Niqab was nice – you felt protected from the outside world. It was a mental thing. You just felt like there was a covering, that Allah was protecting you because you're doing what you should be doing and He was pleased with you.' Mei

I think that, around this time, I came to the realization that wearing the *niqab* was the least I could do as thanks to Allah who had done so much for me. It was on an afternoon that I remember as if it were yesterday: the buzz of busy streets of Whitechapel, the thought of my new marriage and wonderful husband, all the years that Allah had protected me from every danger, the good life He had given me, the blessing of guidance, of good friends, of security, and now, love – all these things were rushing through my mind. The *niqab* was not something I disliked – in fact, I quite liked it; it was not difficult for me to wear it – I was living in the East End, after all, and my husband was supportive.

Wearing the *niqab*, choosing to cover in that way, seemed the least I could do to thank my Lord, to show my gratitude, to enact my submission. I didn't have time to waste on petty concerns – I had been given this chance to do something better, and I decided to take it. And, at that moment, other people's opinions, their hang-ups and points of view, faded into the background; my eyes were fixed on the pleasure of Allah.

And then, on the same Bank Holiday weekend during which I first tried on a *jilbab*, I attended the Friday prayer at a mosque where the majority of women covered in *jilbabs* and *niqabs*. At one point, during the sermon, the *khutbah*, I looked around me and was struck by the beauty of the sisters around me. At that moment it seemed to me so natural that we should want to cover that beauty, to protect it, to keep it private. Some people are appalled when they see beautiful women covering themselves – but I wasn't. Instead, I felt proud to be covering like them.

But I needed a *niqab* that suited me, that fitted in with my lifestyle. So, as soon as I could, I commissioned Bintu, a Guinean sister who had become a good friend, to get one like hers made for me – neat and tidy, in one single layer, in very light cotton. And that was how it began. Because the handmade *niqab* was so unobtrusive, I felt comfortable wearing it with my big scarves and *abayah* and, later, with my *jilbabs*. Again, I found my employers at the tertiary college on Green Street supportive and helpful – I had no problem wearing the *niqab* at work. I dread to think what my contact at the temp office thought when she came in to see how I was getting on at work. They had put me on their books as a smartly dressed young lady with a neat white headwrap, only to find a woman in a diaphanous half-*jilbab* and a *niqab* flipped up to perch on top of her head, busy working the phones in the office. But, to give her credit, if she was surprised, she didn't show it.

The students were gently curious; the Muslim men lowering their gaze and becoming shy when they had to speak to me, the Muslim women admiring my decision. One of the lecturers, a wiry Englishman who used the centre from time to time, asked me, 'So how come you're in *purdah* now?'

I was greatly amused by his expression – I wouldn't quite call working in such a busy environment as an administrator *purdah*!

'I don't even know what that is!' I said to him, explaining that I merely wanted to cover more and felt that my face was my private space, a space I didn't feel like sharing any more. He considered my response, jerked his chin and shrugged his shoulders, and went in to class.

So, I began to wear the *niqab*. My husband was chuffed and Umm Tasneem and other friends were pleased. But, inevitably, not everyone approved. Some thought that it was an unnecessary step, that I was going overboard. In fact, my friends Hanah and Sandra were not particularly impressed. But in the mini bubble that is the East End, I felt comfortable and confident – Bengali women were often seen around with *niqab* on so I didn't stick out like a sore thumb. And, more importantly, I felt right with my Lord.

Covering More and Showing Less

How can I explain that impulse to cover more? There are many feelings that contribute to wanting to 'step up a gear': wanting to do more to please Allah is definitely one of the main ones. Deciding to take that step is also a result of higher *iman*, of deeper faith and of a stronger spiritual commitment. For some, it is as if the *hijab* has a domino effect and, indeed, you do become more aware of yourself once you start covering. And when you see someone covered more than you, you become aware of how exposed you are. You experience an increased awareness of your own body and the desire to make more of yourself private, to cover it, to protect it. All of a sudden, you feel sorry for your arms and legs, so exposed; you wish your body and clothes were protected by the silky folds of the *abayah*, shielding your movements.

Wanting to wear the *jilbab* and *niqab* is driven by that same instinct to cover more and show less. And if you felt sorry for your arms and legs before wearing the *abayah*, you feel even more keenly aware of your face, arguably the most attractive part of you, being on display. Knowing that the female companions and wives of the Prophet (s), the best women of creation, used to cover their faces is also an incentive. At that point, the various obstacles and restrictions that come with wearing the *niqab* literally wash over you because, when your *iman* is high, you are immune to the difficulties, thinking only of the pleasure and reward of your Lord.

The *Hijab* – Liberating or Oppressive?

But how is it that we desired a thing that so many consider to be the ultimate symbol of oppression? How could the *hijab* ever be liberating?

As a woman in this society, as in most others, one grows to expect certain things: to be judged by one's appearance, to have fashion trends dictate one's style and ideal body shape, to get both welcome and unwelcome attention from men, among other things. There is the woman who enjoys all of these things, considering them an essential part of her femininity – many of us felt this way too. But then, there comes a time when the charm begins to wear off – the constant preening and maintenance becomes tedious, the rush to acquire the latest Manolo Blahniks or dress from Ghost seems empty and futile, the seasonal shift towards and away from the hourglass figure and heroin chic begins to sour and appear as it really is: shallow and meaningless. And you begin to wonder, Am I not more than the sum of my parts? What will be the consequences if I drop out of this race? What about when my body starts to change – from age, illness or pregnancy? It is from these and other concerns that covering, with the *hijab* and everything else, liberates the Muslim woman.

Birds in Gilded Cages

In our society, as in so many, women are judged by their appearance in a way that men are not.

But the covered woman cannot be judged on her appearance because nothing personal about her can be seen. She has, in effect, taken her looks out of the equation. She does not feel the need to live up to society's changing expectations of women's bodies. Nor is she a victim of the various pressures to conform to the latest looks or project a 'cool' image. So whoever relates to her must relate to what she has presented – be it what she says, does or thinks. It was for this reason that Ghaniyah said to me, 'If you go for a job and they can't judge you on anything except for the piece of paper in front of them [your CV] and what you're saying, you know their decision will not be based on your looks. THAT is liberation!'

'Who I am extends beyond my image and I don't want to be judged by my image any more.' Sara

The Meat Market

It is natural for men to want to look at women: we are beautiful, after all! And many women find it flattering and fun sometimes. But undoubtedly, there are other times when it is unnecessary and bothersome. Stares, wolf whistles, catcalls, comments, phone-number missiles, advances – there is a thin line between flattery and sexual harassment.

'Sometimes I watch a guy walk past a girl and he'll turn back and look at her legs or her chest and I just think, I would hate that to happen to me. It doesn't appeal to me, it's not flattering, I can't understand how that can make a woman happy. To me, it's nicer when a Muslim brother passes by me and looks down. To me, that is more respectful than someone whistling at my legs.' Rabia

The covered woman is not available for this type of exchange. She is clearly not interested in men's advances, nor in being seen as attractive or sexy – she retains ultimate control of her body and how it is seen by others.

The Body Beautiful

The pressure on women and girls to look a certain way is immense and leads to all sorts of hang-ups and crises. Eating disorders such as over-eating, excessive dieting, bulimia and anorexia are some of the effects of this pressure. Dissatisfaction with our bodies can result in low self-confidence and increased anxiety about body shape.

Because the covered Muslim woman is not judged by her physical appearance, she does not define herself by it. As a result, her sense of self is not wrapped up in her looks. This makes her free from the angst over physical appearance and everything that goes with it.

> 'Initially, I felt like I had found my space and a certain degree of anonymity. By that I mean the sexual parts of the body being anonymous because I don't want my body to be used by anybody – I want it to be my own and to give it to who I want to give it to.' Hajar

The Beauty Within

In our society, women are subtly encouraged to pay attention to superficial concerns – looks, appearance, physical attractiveness – and the vanity and narcissism that accompany them. While many people are obsessed with outward appearances, the covered woman is taught by Islam to cultivate a beauty that is far more than skin deep – that of her character, manners and morals. Thus, she is liberated from wasting her time and energy on achieving outward beauty, knowing that it is what is in her heart that will make her truly beautiful.

And When It Isn't Liberating?

Perhaps the reader wonders whether wearing the *jilbab* and *niqab* is always liberating, whether there are never any difficulties in being covered, from head to toe, every day, in black fabric.

> 'It is oppressive when it is really hot – and no one can say that it is liberating in that moment. You're thinking, You know what? I would just like to take everything off and sit out here with the sun touching my skin.'
> Hajar

One of the most frequent comments that one gets is, 'Aren't you hot in that thing?' and certainly one of the hardest things about wearing full *hijab* is physical discomfort – most commonly, the heat. I remember reading about a sister in *hijab* who was asked whether she wasn't hot wearing it. Her response was blunt: 'The heat of the Hell-fire is hotter.'

Blunt, harsh maybe, but totally apt. I only wish I had the courage to give that response whenever somebody asked me that question.

And although the heat of Saudi Arabia and other countries where women cover traditionally is much fiercer than anything England can offer, we can still find it a little hot sometimes under those layers of black cloth. I have always dealt with this inconvenience by making sure that I am dressed lightly underneath, in natural, breathable fabrics, with a small, light scarf. The fabric of the *jilbab* itself is also crucial – *jilbabs* from the Gulf are made from very light materials, so light that, sometimes, you feel like you have nothing on over your clothes at all.

> 'I found it hard to wear it, to manage it – getting in and out of the car, it was a struggle – you have to get used to it and get used to the extra bits of material here and there.' Mei

Another thing that makes wearing the full *hijab* difficult is the reaction that one often gets from non-Muslims. When I started dressing like a Muslim and not a 'conscious Black sistah', I suddenly found myself being defined by others – others' views of Islam, of Muslims and of me as a Muslim woman. It was strange for me to hear myself defined in those terms – 'Muslim woman' – because I knew all the images and preconceptions that went with that description. And I knew that I didn't fit that image and that I had no intention of ever doing so. The *hijab*, the *jilbab* and especially the *niqab* can provoke extremely virulent responses from the public. It is as if, once you put on the *niqab*, you cease to have a human identity. I know that the *niqab* is a shock to the system for most people in non-Muslim societies – we are used to seeing so much personal information about people around us, being able to tell their race, their age, their physique and their attractiveness. The *niqab* gives none of this information. What does the non-Muslim see when he or she sees us in the street? A relic of a bygone age? A lingering symbol of oppression in a liberated world? A religious fanatic? A terrorist or terrorist's aide? An outsider, immigrant, interloper?

This attitude was particularly galling for Hajar, having been a fairly big player in the record industry prior to coming back to her Islam: 'Before, I was somebody they wanted to know, somebody they needed to know. It was like, "I can get into this place if I know her, I can get that record deal if I know her, I can get into that party if I'm with her." And suddenly, I was an outcast: I was rejected, I was insulted, overnight. And I just thought, Were I to take this stuff off, you would come running back to me . . . That really bothered me.'

It seems to me that, once you cover your face with the *niqab*, you are no longer seen as an individual – you become a symbol. I say this because, for the first time, people talk about you or insult you right in front of your face, something that never happened when your nose and mouth were visible. Many people no longer make eye contact, extend a friendly hello or start up casual conversation. A part of me understands why – I am so obviously different from them, what if I misunderstand them, what if I can't understand them, what would they talk to me about, what is there to say? I also know that I have gone through times of avoiding eye contact, for fear of being rejected, have kept my mouth shut, for fear of making a fool of myself. If you allow it to, wearing the *niqab* can be a very isolating experience – there are no more friendly strangers on the high street. It is up to you to reach out and break the ice. And, sometimes, it takes extra guts to be who you want to be and do what you want to do, regardless of what people around you expect. It is easy to allow other people's reactions to alter your personality while you are amongst them, making you withdrawn where you used to be outgoing, making you fearful where once you were brave, making you a shell of who you really are. This is something that, in this society, one has to consciously resist.

'My *hijab* is detached from my body – it doesn't feel like it affects my personality in any way because I will do anything I want to do, I go anywhere I want. I will go out with a group of non-Muslims who are all wearing jeans and trainers and I'm not fazed at all.' Hajar

I often feel that, as a covered Muslim woman, I have so many attitudes to confront, so many false images to dispel. I know that people are surprised when they hear me speak English or

French, when I express an opinion, when I talk in a friendly way to their child, that I drive a road-hogging car, that I am university-educated, that I work, that I love to travel – that I don't fit into the common stereotypes that they hold of women like me. I often feel under pressure not to make a mistake – in my car, with change in a shop, with disciplining my child – lest people attribute it to the fact that I am covered and therefore incapable. And these are things that I have often heard sisters talk about. But when I make the effort to talk to a stranger, risking a rebuttal, and we exchange pleasantries, I leave that encounter feeling buoyed, feeling that I have connected with another human being and, just maybe, given her something to think about. Perhaps I have even made a small dent in that wall of prejudice and suspicion? And so I make a point of walking tall, speaking confidently and smiling with my eyes – anything to project an image beyond what they see of me, demanding that they relate to me and not to my *niqab*.

> 'I'll never forget attending a horse show with my son who really loves horses. It was in Avignon, in France but it could just as easily have been Texas! Everyone was wearing leather chaps and cowboy hats! I just said to my family, "Right, everyone, act natural!" And everyone was really friendly.' Hajar

Sometimes, however, people surprise me with their lack of preconceptions. I will not forget seeing a young female doctor when I had fractured my toe. She asked me how I had injured it and I told her that I was doing kickboxing and had hurt my toe while practising on my husband. She just smiled. And I pictured the scene from her angle: this bouncy woman in black, sitting cross-legged on the high hospital bed, chatting about kickboxing. After mulling the scene over in my head, I asked her, 'Do you find it strange to hear that from a woman dressed like me?'

She smiled knowingly and shook her head, saying, 'In this job, you learn not to assume anything about people.'

Suffice to say that there are certain things that make wearing the *niqab* difficult. This then prompts the question: 'Why don't you just take it off?' I asked sisters this question, challenging them to give me an answer that would make sense and answer that question once and for all.

'I don't take it off because of my faith,' Hajar told me. 'All my reasons for wearing it would no longer be valid if other people's reactions or the heat of the sun made me take it off. I would feel a bit shallow. When you want integrity, you have to stick with it all the way – you can't sell out.'

Also, it had never occurred to me that bearing the hardships of wearing the *niqab*, or any aspect of the *deen* for that matter, was akin to working by a code of ethics in an unethical business environment. During the apartheid years, there were companies that refused to deal with South Africa or any firm with interests in South Africa. The cynics scoffed at their decision, citing the business they were missing out on and offering many other spurious arguments to support their reasons for abandoning the boycott. But I am sure most people with a conscience would agree that it was better not to sell out the ideals of a free and non-racial South Africa to the demands of the pound and the dollar. It is strange that no one ever pities vegetarians when they can't indulge in a pepper steak, or vegans when they can't have an ice-cream, or organic food consumers when they have to pay more for their food. They are respected for standing by their principles. Everyone assumes that they made a rational choice and they are largely admired for that.

'I think the belief and faith behind it is stronger than those little problems that you come across. Everything has got its difficulties and the thing with the *jilbab* and *niqab* is, it's not something you think about every morning – it's part of you. It's like second nature – the thought of taking it off or lifting it up becomes strange.' Rabia

But although the practising Muslim woman who has chosen to dress and live the way she does suffers some degree of inconvenience due to her principles, she is never given the same respect. It is assumed that there was no rationale behind it. Sometimes, what she does is hard – but she doesn't give up. She is strong against the opposition, patient with the trials, striving constantly. There are only degrees of difference between her and an eco-warrior – I only wish that people would give her some credit for knowing her own mind.

Arabian Princesses

People make all sorts of assumptions about why the Muslim woman covers herself. We must either be thoroughly bewitching beauties or be as 'ugly as Hell'. To those who assume we must be very attractive to want to cover ourselves, we are exotic, mysterious, even erotic to the more bizarre amongst them. These people allow their imaginations to run wild, fuelled no doubt by fantasies of harems and sensual Eastern women. They would be disappointed to know that the woman they see as an Arabian princess swathed in veils was born Jane Smith from Pimlico. We are not exotic, sensual beings that have flown in from the desert on a magic carpet, although I prefer that assumption to the alternative, for obvious reasons! To those who think, or pretend to think, that we dress the way we do because we are ugly, overweight or otherwise ashamed of our bodies, we are figures of fun, good for teasing – the favourite insult being 'Ninja!' This particular attitude can also be expressed by spitting, swearing or actual physical assault. I remember one day when Umm Tasneem and I were walking home with the babies in their prams, some kids threw some eggs at us from their flat window. One of the eggs narrowly missed my baby's face, smashing on the pram hood. I was terribly shaken, knowing that if the brutes had found their target, my baby's face would not be what it is today.

Almost every sister who wears a *niqab* has a similar story to tell. However, after several incidents, one becomes desensitized to the insults and sometimes barbaric cruelty of some of the perpetrators who, unfortunately, are often youngsters. Like most people, they fear what they do not know.

However, while we may find hostility when we step outside our front doors, we also encounter curiosity. The majority of non-Muslims have never actually met with or spoken to a Muslim woman, especially not one who dresses and lives as we do. So there are always questions: what are we really like under our flowing garments? Do we ever take them off? Are we just the same as them? Many people wonder what it would be like to take a peek 'behind the veil'.

Beneath the Layers

All around us, every day, through every medium available, we are bombarded by images of impossibly beautiful women telling us that we can find happiness in a designer dress, a new fad diet or a bottle of peroxide – because we're worth it! From the catwalk to the high street, from the television to the internet, stick-thin, Botoxed celebrities with hair extensions and implants are sold to us as the ideal of woman-hood. So, in an image-conscious society where women and girls alike experience the pressure to live up to the latest trends in beauty, where does that leave the Muslim woman, who is covered from head to toe: the woman who has, in effect, opted out of the fashion show? Do Muslim women who cover their beauty have anxieties about fashion, weight and ageing? Or, because they are secure from the appraising gaze, do they blossom in other ways, ways that are not dependent on the way they look?

One of the most commonly held notions about the *hijab* is that it turns women into desexualized beings, dowdy and unattractive. Some people think that the *hijab* is an institution that strips the woman of her femininity, her 'right' to adorn and display her body, thus rendering her dull and unkempt, like a butterfly that has lost its wings. When I first started covering, my non-Muslim friends couldn't understand why I still bothered to try new hairstyles, buy make-up or update my wardrobe – 'What's the point?' they asked. 'You're just going to cover it anyway.'

Out With the Halter Necks!

If there is one practice that almost every woman new to the *deen*, whether born Muslim or revert, can relate to, it is the ritual of throwing away one's old clothes upon entering the *deen*. There is no law that commands this, no *hadith* that encourages it and yet, time and again, new Muslim sisters throw out the clothes of their previous lives, hotpants, stilettos and all. And it usually doesn't stop with the party clothes; anything that is remotely fashionable finds its way to the local charity shop. It's like an exorcism, purging all the memories of our non-Islamic past, our *jahiliyyah*.

'I think we thought that, once you start practising, you're meant to age about sixty years! Chuck away all your clothes, yeah, I did that along with many others.'
Jameela

212

'New Muslim Tramp' (NMT) Syndrome

Admittedly, starting to cover did have an effect on the way many of us dressed underneath. It was as if we felt that, as Muslim women, our clothing should be longer, wider, darker, in a word, frumpier. I refer to this trend as the 'New Muslim Tramp' phenomenon. The New Muslim Tramp is characterized by a devastating lack of style beneath her outer garments (*hijab*, *abayah*, *jilbab*, etc.), often in direct contrast to the way she dressed before Islam. This can include wearing mismatched clothes, a husband's tracksuit bottoms or tatty clothes that don't fit properly.

It would appear that this 'New Muslim Tramp' persona is a Western trend – and that could be the root of the problem. Whereas before, we might have selected outfits based on their sex appeal, this is Islam now and Muslims are commanded to be modest in general, and even amongst other women, halter necks and miniskirts don't really cut it! So sometimes, the clothes that we wore before we became Muslim really were unsuitable to be worn in a gathering of sisters.

But, oh how we lamented the rash decision to throw them all away when we got married! How that slinky backless number would have been appreciated now, within the realms of the *halal* – the lawful!

> 'I did throw away the stuff I thought was not quite appropriate, but then I regretted it because you can still wear that sort of thing in front of your husband!' Sadiqa

There is not only an issue with the type of clothing we used to wear; there is often a new (mis)understanding of what a Muslim woman should look like. There is this feeling that, now you are Muslim, you have to, in the words of Umm Safwan, 'go grubby and forget about life'. That includes no longer wearing nice clothes, doing your hair, wearing make-up, and anything else that could be considered 'worldly adornment'.

> 'There *are* some sisters who don't care what they look like, who don't care about what they wear . . . No, it's not an Islamic thing but I think, with a lot of sisters, when they start wearing *hijab*, they become lazy.' Ghaniyah

This image is certainly one that many outsiders hold of us. But this attitude is, again, a Western revert complex. In the majority of Muslim societies and Muslim countries, from Pakistan to

Somalia, from Malaysia to Saudi Arabia, women have perfected the art of looking good, albeit under their Islamic covering: they wear the embroidered saris; the gold-trimmed Pakistani suits, *shalwar kameez*; the bejewelled *lenghas* with their full skirts; the hand-dyed *boubous*, the kaftans of West Africa; the translucent Somali *dira'* and *gogorat*, the embroidered underskirt. They decorate their hands and feet with the dye of the henna powder, they line their eyes with kohl, they perfume their clothes with *bukhoor*, a fragrant incense, and decorate their limbs with gold and silver. But us poor Western reverts knew nothing of these mysterious arts – all we knew was that we had become religious and that the religious woman had no business wasting her time with such frivolities.

Hajar told me about the difference between Western sisters and their counterparts in Saudi Arabia: 'We are frumpy here, compared to them, and they do look down on us for that. They think we are old bags.'

This new attitude to clothing and looking good was something that I couldn't understand when I moved to a new community of reverts, after getting married. Before that, at my henna party, I had invited my friends from university, mostly born Muslims, and they all really made an effort and they looked gorgeous! They all

215

wore jewellery and their clothes shone in silks and satins. The little hall that Sandra, Hanah and Hayat had decorated was a riot of jewel colours and laughter, skirts swirling in time to the *duff*, the hand drum that we played as we sang. We had a wonderful time, just us girls, *masha Allah*, and it was one of the best nights of my life.

Fast forward to my *waleemah*, the celebration that is meant to announce the new couple to the community. Mine took place in my new community of revert sisters and I was really taken aback: many of these sisters didn't take off their *jilbabs*, let alone dress up to the nines! There was no jewellery, no make-up, no effort to mark the occasion as different from an Islamic talk. The only ones dressed up were Umm Tasneem (we were celebrating our *waleemahs* together), my old friends from university, my family and I! It was quite depressing actually and I couldn't understand it. Rabia told me that she had been just as puzzled: 'From the Pakistani culture, it's important to look nice at weddings and other celebrations and I found it strange when I would go to weddings and I would be the only one dressed up.'

Ghaniyah told me about her experiences with NMT syndrome: 'You take your *hijab* off and everyone looks at you like you're Joan Collins and you're like, "This is me dressed down!" I've been to weddings where I have looked more dressed up than the flipping bride!'

However, there is another possible reason for the New Muslim Tramp phenomenon: the fact that deep down there is that little voice that says, 'Why bother? No one can see you anyway!' After all, this is no longer *jahiliyyah*, the time before Islam, where every garment had to be chosen with care because there were men out there with appreciative eyes if the outfit worked and women ready with a swift put-down if it didn't! So we dressed to re-affirm ourselves and we dressed for others, aware that we would be judged on that. And that attention and affirmation was all part of the game – it made all the time and money spent worth it. We gladly suffered the sting of the leg wax, the tug of the tweezers, the pinch of the pointy-toed shoes, and the cold of the miniskirt on a winter night. Whoever said, '*Il faut souffrir pour être belle*' (the French saying that means 'one must suffer to be beautiful') must have been talking to us! All that effort was worth its weight in catcalls, wolf whistles and corny chat-up lines.

So what is the point of all that if no one, no man, is going to *see* it?

'Why did I used to make so much effort in *jahiliyyah*? We say that it's not to draw men's attention, that it's just because we want to, but it's not really: a lot of the time, it's to impress other women as well.' Safwa

217

For the most part, the sisters in our community and in most places where Muslims are practising, are very down-to-earth; there is no posing, no preening, no showing off your latest acquisition – this will not score any points. So there is no image to keep up – no one is watching to see whether you wore that trouser suit to the last wedding or whether your accessories match your outfit. Many of us were happy to be spared all that stress. However, that down-to-earth, laid-back atmosphere can also impact 'negatively' on the woman who is used to the cut and thrust of the high-street catwalk fashion show. For her, it's a case of no image, no effort!

I had a very lively discussion with Suad and Assiyah about why we dressed the way that we did in *jahiliyyah* and our attitude to dressing now.

Assiyah: 'Compared to how I was in *jahiliyyah*, I feel like I've let myself go. A part of me feels like it is a waste of time to look good around women.'

Na'ima: 'When you dressed up in *jahiliyyah*, who were you really dressing up for?'

Assiyah: 'The men, of course!'

Na'ima: 'You're not just saying that, are you? Was it really men?'

Assiyah: 'Definitely, and other women too.'

Suad: 'Basically, it was to impress everyone! To

be honest, I wanted everyone, from the old to the young, from the male to the female, even for the dog to turn its head! I wanted *everyone* to recognize that I was the queen that day!'

This is the issue that sisters had to come to terms with when they started covering. Would they really let themselves go because there was no appreciative audience any more? I found that I had a chance to see whether what I had always maintained was true – that I really did dress well for my own sake and not for other people's approval. And because I had always maintained that stance with ferocity (although I don't think I really believed it 100 per cent at the time!), I had a point to prove. I was determined the *hijab* was not going to turn *me* into a frump!

'I know a lot of Muslim women say, "I used to wear that but I can't be bothered, what's the point?" I have never understood that concept of being practising and not bothering any more. To me, I think I should look better. After all, you're still a woman and you're still beautiful, *masha Allah*. Now I'm not saying that you should be dolled up from head to toe but it doesn't mean that you have to wear your tracksuit bottoms and your husband's socks all day! I don't think there should be this sudden change: "I'm practising now, I'm going to look like a tramp."' Rabia

While most sisters either regretted or laughed about their abysmal dress sense when they were new Muslims, I found that Aliyah had a different take on the issue, a viewpoint that I hadn't considered.

'When I first became Muslim,' she told me, 'my attitude to clothes didn't change because I refused to wear the *abayah* and stuff. I was still wearing my French Connection dresses and putting my *hijab* on with them. But once I put on the *abayah*, I thought, These things have got to go – it's as if I'm trying to hold onto that and I don't want that. So I got rid of them. And then I became quite frumpy. I think I spent so many years trying to beautify myself, I would spend hours waxing my legs, doing my eyebrows, all this kind of rubbish. I felt like Islam wasn't about that any more. You were beautiful no matter what you looked like. So I didn't think I had to make as much effort as I used to in *jahiliyyah*. And I enjoyed not having to do all that! I felt liberated by that.'

Undercover Beauties

However, other sisters maintained their standards, from *jahiliyyah*, through *hijab*, *jilbab* and *niqab*.

'Throwing out my clothes was one thing I never did and I'm glad I didn't, *masha Allah*. I consider myself a stylish person and I think that we are the same as other women in that respect.' Sadiqa

Today, there has been a seismic shift in the attitudes that contributed to NMT syndrome, to the point where, now, new Muslim sisters are advised *not* to throw away all their nice clothes, not to make the same mistake that we all made. Sharifah, who only became Muslim a few months ago remembered *her* attempt to get rid of her clothes: 'I was going to take all my clothes to the charity shop but my sister came by, bright and early, got my clothes, put them in boxes and put them in her shed. When I saw that I said, "How dare you do that? This is my decision to do this, this is what I want to do." As far as I was concerned, she was interfering in my life. But then afterwards, I talked to the sisters about it and they told me I didn't have to abandon my wardrobe. They all said, "Hellooo! Keep hold of your clothes, girl!"'

Over the past few years, I believe there has been a renaissance of sorts in our little community, as far as the sisters are concerned. I will never forget a fundraising dinner I held at my house a couple of years ago. I called it a Princess

Night, and everyone had to come dressed up as a princess – and there were no children allowed. Prior to that night, I had never seen so many sisters out without their children, looking so beautiful and relaxed. We ate, talked and laughed, while one of the sisters did makeovers upstairs. One sister said, 'It is so lovely to see all the sisters looking so nice – we don't often get a chance to dress up, do we?'

And then, things began to change. All of a sudden, sisters started to get dressed up to go to each other's houses, wearing a touch of make-up, maybe some jewellery, all of this under their outer garments. *Eids*, weddings and other celebrations became, as they are in other communities, a celebration of the different cultures in our community – Chinese *cheongsam*, *kurta* pyjamas, hooded *jalabiyyah* and the hot favourites – the traditional Somali *dira'* from Dubai – were all procured for the day and worn with henna patterns, bangles, dangly earrings, strappy sandals, hair jewels and body shimmer powder. We began to have regular beauty days at different locations around London. These served the dual purpose of allowing the sisters a break and time to pamper themselves in private and supporting those amongst us who were freelance beauty therapists, hair stylists and henna artists. Other sisters began to trade in silver jewellery, attractive underwear and health and beauty products, all of these finding a ready market amongst sisters who now wanted to look after themselves as they had done before, if not better. Today, there are many fitness and leisure activities available for sisters, ranging from aerobics and circuit training to kickboxing and swimming. There is even a well-attended Muslim gym, with brothers' days and sisters' days. It is my fervent hope that the days of the New Muslim Tramp are well and truly over.

However, this renaissance has been tempered by various factors. Sisters are still cautious of going to extremes with their clothes and make-up, aware that they are only material things, after all. Also, certainly in my community, there has always been a strong desire to avoid competition between ourselves and judging each other according to how good we look or how much of an effort we have made. These factors have stopped things from going too far, from becoming that same pressure to look a certain way and wear certain things that we all experienced in *jahiliyyah*. As I once said to Zubeida, 'We felt oppressed by the whole "keep your *abayah* on all the time" thing because we wanted to look nice. But there are some sisters who don't want to or can't dress up for every function. They may feel that the pressure to take off their *abayah* and wear an amazing outfit is an oppression in itself.' So the trend hasn't taken over our lives – we haven't become fashion victims and we don't vamp it up at every soirée – but we no longer feel the need to apologize for looking good amongst our sisters when we want to.

However, many people cannot get their head around the fact that we cover on the outside and look good on the inside. It is not uncommon for a sister to find herself the object of incredulous scrutiny over the halter-neck top, hipster trousers or pretty underwear she is buying.

> 'I think people feel that Muslim women don't wear fashionable clothes, that they don't like to do their hair, wear make-up. Sometimes, you go into a shop and they're looking at what you're picking up to buy as though, "Hold on a minute, what's she doing with that? Why's she picking up that skirt, that top?" It can be quite annoying sometimes.' Umm Muhammad

I have also found it interesting to hear the younger generation of girls who cover, those who grew up with Islam, talking about their attitudes to looking good. Sixteen-year-old Rumaysah has been covering her face for several years and I wanted to know how she suddenly became a pro' with the glitter eye shadow and ceramic straighteners!

She told me, 'I think, as you get older, you become more aware of your appearance and you try out different things. I liked fashion when I was younger but it was more my mum who would get out what I was going to wear. Now, I normally go to the shops by myself and choose my clothes, although I will still ask her opinion on certain things. But my mum's quite hip, quite on the ball when it comes to fashion.'

And since clothes are frequently one of the battlegrounds between Muslim teens and their parents, I wanted to know how her mother, Umm Muhammad, who had been very fashion conscious herself, felt about her daughter's growing fashion sense. I was quite surprised to hear that she was all for it.

'I always used to tell Rumaysah to wear more fashionable clothes,' she told me, 'but she wouldn't wear them – she wouldn't wear earrings, she wouldn't do her hair, she didn't want to wear nice clothes. I would say that when she was younger, she was timid, even around the sisters. But as she's got older, she's grown more confident and she's aware of looking nice. And that's fine because it's under her outer garment anyway.'

It would appear that, even as a teenager who has grown up covering, the *hijab* has not stifled Rumaysah and her peers' growing self-awareness and sense of style.

My *Hijab*, Myself

Wearing *hijab* forces you to look at your self-image, your motivations and intentions with a critical eye. As the Muslim woman is not meant to show off her adornments, this can lead to a crisis of intention: if I don't show off my adornments, is there any point having any? And while, at the beginning of our Islam, we wrestled with this question, most of us came to the conclusion that looking good and maintaining oneself had to be a matter of self-respect and of taking care of one's appearance, no matter who could or couldn't see us. So now, we truly do dress for ourselves and not to seek outside approval. Nowadays, when I speak to sisters about how they feel about themselves and their looks underneath the *hijab*, I get a very positive vibe. None of us feels any tension whatsoever between covering on the outside and looking good on the inside. It is as if, beneath the layers, the multi-coloured wings are unfolding, unfurling, and the sisters are taking flight.

For those of us who have chosen to live according to the laws of Allah, revert and born Muslim, the *hijab* means many things to us: it is our covering, our reminder, our comforter, our shield, our liberator, a symbol of our servitude to our Lord. It is not an unwelcome burden, it is not

226

an aberration, it is not a symbol of our oppression: it is a fundamental part of our identity as Muslim women. And those who would work so hard to 'free us' from it would do well to listen to the voices of those they seek to liberate – for one woman's liberation, however well intentioned, could well be another woman's incarceration.

6

LOVE AND MARRIAGE, MUSLIM-STYLE

About nine months after taking my *shahadah* and entering Islam, I met a man and married, Muslim-style. Ever since my stay in Guinea, the subject of marriage had never been far from my mind and, in Sandra's kitchen, we spent many hours discussing it. The foundations of an Islamic marriage, the rights and responsibilities it entailed, how to negotiate meetings with brothers, what kinds of questions to ask, what to do if he started 'acting up' – we covered it all, with earnestness, candour and a fair bit of shrieking laughter.

We were all unmarried then and of course didn't really know what to expect. But after several unsuccessful meetings, I had sworn off brothers, vowing not to give marriage another thought, making hazy plans to travel the world instead. And then one of our acquaintances from university told me about a brother that he had grown up with. According to the description – practising African revert brother, beard, running his mum's firm, educated, cool, responsible – he sounded closer to perfect than anyone else I had met. I agreed to arrange a meeting between him and my *wali*, my guardian, an imam at Regent's Park mosque, who took him through the preliminary round of questions. Happily, he made it through to the next round and, after ringing me at work, we had a chaperoned meeting at the mosque. I knew I wanted to marry him three days later.

On Love and Marriage

The Prophet (s) said, 'When a servant of Allah marries, He has completed half of his religion. Let him then fear and revere Allah with regards to the other half.' *Hasan li-ghayrihi hadith* reported by at-Tabarani

Ever since my sojourn in Guinea, I had been aware that marriage was an integral part of the Islamic way of life. As I said earlier, everyone I met had been trying to match me with someone they knew. In a way, I understood why. I looked around me and saw husbands and wives, children and grandparents, uncles and nieces –

all joined by the bonds of family. And I realized then that marriage was one the of most important foundations for all of that. Through it, families were joined together in kinship, new families were formed, a new generation nurtured, the older generation taken care of. I could well imagine how lonely it would be to try to live an Islamic life alone, with no one to wake me in the morning to pray, no one to open the fast with, no one to remind me about Allah when I was feeling down, to share the joys and tribulations of raising a Muslim family.

On a personal level, marriage provides a haven in which love, affection and companionship can flourish, free from constraints. This is the ideal that Allah speaks of when He says:

> And among His Signs is this, that He created for you wives from among yourselves, that you may find repose in them, and He has put between you affection and mercy. Verily, in that are indeed signs for a people who reflect.
> Surah Ar-Rum 30:21

Because physical intimacy is something that is freely available in our society – through pre-marital and casual relationships, cohabitation and one-night stands – many people today believe that the benefits of marriage are few

LOVE AND MARRIAGE, MUSLIM-STYLE

compared with the responsibilities it entails. Not so for the Muslim. In many ways, getting married represents a kind of freedom for us. Within marriage, so many things that were once forbidden become lawful, encouraged. As a young man and woman, you can now interact with each other, freely and without limits, you can let down your guard, remove your *hijab*, laugh and cry, go out or stay home. In short, you can now share everything with one special person. What's more, the 'pleasures of the flesh' are yours for the taking. Indeed, one of the express aims of an Islamic marriage is to allow the followers of the faith to satisfy their desires in a way and in an arena that is lawful (*halal*) and actually brings rewards, in this life in the form of pleasure and offspring and in the next in the form of the reward from Allah.

Marriage is thus designed to protect the individual from the unlawful and from the various ills that result from either frustrated sexual desire or sexual promiscuity.

Unlike other faiths, monasticism has no elevated status in Islam. In fact, the Prophet (s) castigated those who sought to become more pious by staying away from sexual relationships with women, saying, 'Marriage is a *sunnah* [tradition] of mine and whoever does not follow my *sunnah* is not of my followers.'

So, it was clear that marriage was something I was not going to be able to avoid. Not that I wanted to – I was excited at the prospect of meeting someone and sharing my time, my *deen* and my life with him.

Expecting the Unexpected

I remember clearly that in the very earliest days of my Islam, none of us wanted to marry a brother who was a 'strict, practising Muslim': 'What, and have him tell me that everything is *haram* [forbidden] all the time? No fear!' Those were the days when it was common to hear statements like, 'My wedding is *blatantly* going to be *haram*!' That meant that men and women wouldn't be separated, that the bride wouldn't be covered properly and that there would be a great big party afterwards, with everyone doing the Electric Slide! This reflects where our understanding of Islam was at that time. As we learnt more and became more committed spiritually, our priorities changed. We no longer wanted one of those *da'eef* (weak) brothers – we wanted someone strong in the *deen*, someone who would encourage us to learn more and do more, someone who wanted to 'live Islam' as much as we did.

> 'I was looking for someone with good *deen* who liked to learn, go to classes — someone who would establish an Islamic household. A household where *deen* would be at the forefront, where Islam would be practised and not just spoken about, not just on a Friday. Islam is a way of life and that was what I wanted: an Islamic way of life. I wanted to *live* Islam.'
> Umm Muhammad

Like most Muslims, I based my ideas of the ideal Muslim husband on the Prophet (s) himself. As I mentioned earlier, I was enchanted by Muhammad (s), the family man.

He was a fine example of Muslim manhood, one who balanced religious and worldly affairs perfectly. While, on the one hand, he would be teaching the Muslims about their *deen*, attending to their affairs, judging between them, as well as receiving the revelation, he would cry in his *salah* and stay up all night in prayer, so much so that his feet would be swollen. I also loved the way he was described in the *hadiths* reported by his wife Aisha: how he would place his lips where hers had touched the cup when drinking milk, how they would playfully race each other, how he would tease her and she him. I learnt that he was extremely mild and patient, helping in the house, serving his family and mending his own shoes. It was quite a hard act to follow.

More than anything, I was in love with the idea of marrying a Muslim – a man with the humility to prostrate to his Lord five times a day, someone who embodied the lofty ideals of the Islamic personality. I expected him to be honest, generous, kind and responsible. I wanted someone who would fear Allah in public and in private, someone able to admit when they were wrong and ready to accept advice from others, especially his wife!

So, in many respects, I had quite high expectations of any potential partner, expecting him to be far superior to all the playboys we had known before Islam, in *jahiliyyah*. And it certainly was a relief to know that, for the most part, only those brothers seriously interested in getting married would dare enquire about a sister in *hijab*! Having had a serious relationship in *jahiliyyah*, Hajar said, 'I had really high expectations of my Muslim marriage – I went to my meeting with my husband with two and a half pages of questions. And he had been through enquiry upon enquiry before it even got to that meeting stage.'

I also expected my husband to fulfil his role as provider. In a *hadith*, the Prophet (s) said that the woman's right is to be fed as her husband feeds himself, to be clothed as he clothes himself and to be housed as he houses himself.

But my personal ambitions did not fade even as my desire to marry grew. Ever since my teenage years, in the 'big house in the suburbs of Harare' phase of my life, I had always hoped to have my own business, earning just as much if not more money than my husband. Now that I was Muslim, I still intended to earn my own money (though at that stage, I was not yet sure how) but I also knew that, according to the laws of Allah, it is the man's duty to look after his family, financially and otherwise. The benefits of marriage were confirmed to me when I realized that whatever I earnt, as a woman, I could keep for myself, put aside and spend more or less as I pleased. I could see definite advantages in that set-up!

It was never my intention to settle for less than what Allah had granted me and this had to be reciprocated by a shift in my own priorities. I, like most other Muslims, expected to marry someone who was ready to start a family. There is such great emphasis on having children in the *deen* that it is rare to find a practising Muslim man who shies away from the responsibility of being a father. In my mind, marriage and children went hand in hand.

Previously, I had seen myself as a career woman first, having children but employing a nanny or maid to look after them, enabling me to pursue my career. But Islam made me look at my future role as a wife and mother differently. I decided that I would want to bring up my children myself. I knew, as do many working mothers, that the demands of raising children, running a home and having a career would spread me very thinly. I didn't want to have to juggle multiple roles and responsibilities. And I didn't want to miss out on those precious moments bonding with my baby, seeing those first steps, hearing his first words, shaping his character. When the time came, I wanted to truly throw myself into motherhood and for my child to have the stability of a constant maternal presence at home. I felt, as Islam teaches, that all that would be far more valuable than any extra money I would be bringing in from a job outside the home. So the traditional Islamic set-up of husband going out to work and wife looking after the children at home appealed to me, so long as I would be able to maintain some sort of outside interest, and perhaps earn a little money on the side.

'I don't expect to be provided for totally but, in the *deen*, that is what the husband is supposed to do. If you restrict that aspect, then it's like making him less of a man, less than what Allah has ordained that he should be doing.' Sharifah

But there was a part of me, the wayward part no doubt, that felt compromised and 'resigned' to marrying that 'good Muslim'. I would say to myself, What do you think comes with all that worship and piety? Sure, you'll get a man who is good and kind, a man who prays and fasts but, face it, he's going to be dead boring.

I don't know where that idea came from, but I had this image of a practising Muslim man as staid and old-fashioned with no sense of humour. Would he be constantly telling me to fear Allah, to stop laughing, that this or that thing was *haram* – forbidden? Somehow, I didn't think the kind of fun, frolics and romance that one is taught to expect from a relationship in the West had a place in an Islamic marriage.

And worse still, there was a darker side to my expectations. A part of me was afraid, very afraid, that I would have the kind of Muslim husband one hears about in all the horror stories. I was afraid that he would turn out to be a monster, keeping me locked in the house, forbidding me from seeing my friends and family, crushing me into being the kind of wife, the kind of woman he thought I should be. I was afraid of being trapped in a marriage that offered me security, stability and protection with one hand and robbed me of my individuality, personality and freedom to grow with the other.

'You Married After One Meeting?!'

Once Sandra, Hanah and I started thinking seriously about getting married, the Islamic system of 'courting' was something we grew to know very well. It was not uncommon for a brother to see a sister and then send his friend's wife to ask, 'Sister, are you looking to get married?' That was normally accompanied by furtive glances at the young hopeful, blushes and titters if he looked like a suitable candidate, stifled guffaws and elbow-nudging if he didn't. Sometimes, it might reach a stage where the potential couple would meet, in the company of a chaperone, and then, amongst her sisters once more, the woman would share all the gory details. Unless it looked like he could actually be 'the one', in which case, things were taken much more seriously. Then, books on the subject of marriage would be devoured, lists of questions drawn up, advice sought from 'veterans' and fierce discussions held about how to tell if he was the 'real deal'.

So how exactly *do* two practising Muslims end up meeting each other and, eventually, getting married in the Western context? How it usually works is that a woman, for example, will decide that she has come to the stage where she is ready to get married. She will then tell her parents, family and friends that she is 'looking to get married' and will discuss her criteria.

> If one comes to you seeking marriage, and you are satisfied with his *deen* and character, then marry him otherwise a *fitnah* and great destruction will become rampant on the earth.'
> *Hadith* of the Prophet (s), reported by Imam at-Tirmidhi, hasan

Her criteria could include primarily the level of *deen* she is looking for, type of character, personality and looks, as well as his educational and cultural background – anything that she thinks will help her family and friends to find a good match. Both men and women were advised by the Prophet (s) to look for partners who are religious, whose Islam is strong. This means that the practising Muslim woman will look for a man with good character, who is noble and kind, generous and patient, a man who fears Allah, who prays, fasts and obeys his Lord in public and in private.

Then, people will either suggest potential partners or start asking around. So it could be that the girl's brother has a friend, or that her friend has a brother, who would make an ideal match. This stage is normally followed by a period of investigation. On behalf of the girl, the family and friends will observe the man in question in his 'natural surroundings', getting a feel for his character and how he relates to others. They will also ask other people who know him and get references from them.

If the brother checks out with all concerned, the girl's father or guardian may approach him or his parents. Then, if he is interested and the guardian and family are satisfied, the young people will have a chaperoned meeting. And, as Muslims are also encouraged to marry someone whom they find physically appealing, this meeting gives them a chance to see whether they are attracted to each other. They will also have the chance to discuss the things that are important to them and ask any questions they might have. In fact, the potential couple may have any number of meetings, depending on the circumstances. However, Muslims are always advised not to have too many meetings before actually getting married. There are a number of good reasons for this. One of them is that, according to Islamic law, the two people concerned are still not *halal* (lawful) for each other – they are not allowed to spend social time together or be alone together – officially, they are just like any other Muslim man and woman who are not related. Clearly, when meetings take place, there is an element of socializing and this needs to be kept to a minimum, thus reducing the chances of inappropriate behaviour. It is not unheard of for a normally practising couple to fall into *zina* (unlawful sexual intercourse) because excessive contact led them into temptation. At such moments, the senses take control, and all the rules, warnings and consequences are forgotten. And no practising Muslim wants to lose control of himself or herself in that way.

Choosing your partner based on your emotional response to him or her sounds normal and positive to most people. But emotions like love and lust have a way of painting pictures, of furnishing fantasies and creating illusions. The man or woman you fall in love or lust with is not necessarily the most honest, trustworthy, generous, kind and responsible one – and is not necessarily good marriage material. So, by keeping the emotions at bay, one is able to assess a person in a sane, rational way; one can see clearly their good points and bad points, and consequently one is able to make a sensible choice. But sometimes, of course, you know that there is absolutely no point in even considering having a second meeting – there is no spark at all!

My friends and I were fortunate because we had the pick of the bunch when we were looking to get married. When we were approached by brothers, we either accepted or turned them away at will. It was so unlike the stereotype of the Muslim girl being pushed into an arranged marriage. Part of this was due to the fact that, as reverts, we operated fairly independently. Although my friend Sandra and I both shared a guardian, because he wasn't a family member, he couldn't force us or prevent us from doing what we felt was right. Also, we didn't have strong family influences and so were quite autonomous in our dealings. I had always thought that was a good thing – you know, independent young women, making their own way. That is, until I started seeing examples of that very autonomy going terribly wrong. In the community that I moved to, the majority of girls' families, being either non-Muslim or non-practising, were not involved in their decisions. So I witnessed sisters marrying brothers without checking them out fully. I saw them getting taken in by appearances. I saw them giving up their rights – to the dowry they wanted, to a contract, to maintenance – because they didn't have the knowledge (or the guts) to insist on what was rightfully theirs. And that made me think seriously about the role of the family in an Islamic marriage and just how well it can work to protect you.

In almost all societies outside of the West, marriage has always been a family affair, rather than an individual one. This means that families take an active part in helping their children choose a partner. And why not? After all, a marriage is a joining of two families as well as two individuals. So I wanted to discuss the issue of 'looking to get married' with someone who had that Islamic family set-up around her – my friend, Rabia.

She told me, 'I have the bonus of my family. I know that the brother will be completely checked out, he will have to fulfil certain conditions, he will have to prove himself as a responsible man. I never worry about that side of things because I know my dad will take care of it. For me, I just need to discuss *deen*, his personality, what his plans are for the future, and things like that. I feel very fortunate that I have that family support and also that I am less approachable for brothers, less vulnerable. Some of them wouldn't even get past my dad!'

I wanted to know whether it didn't irritate her that her father could vet her suitors. She seemed surprised at the question and laughed.

'A brother who is unemployed, living at home with his family, someone with no prospects or qualifications, new to the *deen*, he would know that there is no point! Because he knows that the first thing my dad is going to ask him is, "Have you got a job? How are you going to support my daughter?" And I want someone who has answers to those questions!'

Unlike the 'arranged marriages' of some cultures, my union was not planned while I was in the womb or to a cousin 'back home'. And unlike the public's perception, my 'arranged marriage' was neither forced on me nor conducted without my involvement. I saw my husband-to-be and he saw me, albeit while wearing my *hijab*. We discussed various issues and developed a liking for each other and a desire to marry.

Indeed, the main difference between a culturally arranged marriage and an Islamic one is the element of choice. Historically, throughout the world, children were betrothed to each other, sometimes from birth, and would often only meet each other on the wedding night, after the ceremonies had taken place. Marriages were contracted in order to secure thrones, join powerful families, strengthen lineages, improve family ties, and dowries were paid to the families. In all of this, the young people involved were expected to submit to their families' decisions, mere pawns in a larger game. Even today, in Asian and other families, arranged marriages are often akin to forced marriages, with family and societal pressures ensuring that the children accept their parents' choice of partner without question.

The correct Islamic version of the 'arranged marriage' is quite different. According to the *sunnah* of the Prophet (s), a marriage that does not have the consent of the man *and* the woman is not considered valid. And *no one* is authorized to contract a marriage on behalf of their child. In addition, the couple have to meet and see whether they like each other. The *mahr* (dowry) is a gift that the man gives his bride-to-be as part of the marriage. Unlike in many other cultures, this gift belongs to her and not to her family.

Therefore, the true Islamic 'arranged marriage' is halfway between the restrictive, manipulative forced marriage and the free-mixing, dating, cohabiting world.

I have always thought that there are many advantages to looking for a husband the Islamic way. Anyone who has spent years building a relationship, only for the man to turn around and say that he's 'not ready for a commitment' will appreciate the beautiful simplicity of a man who talks straight: if he's ready to get married, he approaches you, if he isn't, he stays away.

Whenever I tell people about my own 'arranged marriage', they express surprise, incredulity and more than a touch of envy: 'You mean you were never alone with him? You never held his hand? You knew you wanted to marry him three days after meeting him?' I asked Hajar about the advantage of marrying the Islamic way and she said, 'Cutting out all the crap! All the rubbish of pretending, making out that you're someone else, trying to please someone, living up to their expectations.'

That is not to say that the Islamic way is without its own problems and peculiarities. There is always the chance that the brother could present a false picture of himself, pretending to be pious and God-fearing when he is really a fiendish monster, hell-bent on destroying your life! Obviously, it is crucial to make sure that you and your family have thoroughly researched potential husbands and their backgrounds.

It can also happen that, after fulfilling all the criteria, the man just doesn't have what it takes in the looks department. That can be quite a worry, as physical attraction is considered an important criterion!

'One of my biggest worries was what he was going to look like – was I going to like him? Was I going to fancy him? I was very concerned that the person was not going to "do it" for me.' Safwa

In the *Shari'ah*, Allah has set out rules and guidelines for all our affairs, in our *deen* and our worldly life. There are thus guidelines for looking for a good husband or wife the Islamic way.

LOVE AND MARRIAGE, MUSLIM-STYLE

Not only do the following guidelines conform to the *Shari'ah* but they are also tried and tested: they are based on my and my sisters' experiences.

- Have a pure intention. Make your intention to get married for the sake of Allah, to fulfil what He has commanded and to worship Him more. If you have questionable intentions, like trying to get a British passport, getting someone into the country or breaking up someone's marriage, don't expect Allah's blessings in your union!

- Know your rights and responsibilities. As a Muslim, you must learn about something before doing it – make sure you learn about Islamic marriage and what it entails. Understand your rights and his rights and be prepared, at least mentally, to fulfil those rights!

- Keep your family on side. Try not to alienate your family (be they Muslims or not) as their support is important. Even if they are not able to take part in the selection process, try to involve them in the wedding celebrations and other occasions if you can. Having a strong family behind you is also an added incentive for the brother to take the whole process seriously and respect your decisions.

- Do your homework. Think of marriage as an investment. If you had £100, 000 to invest in a particular company, you would do your research thoroughly, looking into the characters of the directors, their past records, their references, their reputations. Similarly, when looking to marry someone, you must value yourself as much if not far more. Take the time to check the brother out thoroughly, ask around, get your friends to ask around, ask his friends, his teachers, other people he deals with – even if it takes a while. Never be hasty when taking this type of decision.

- Keep it clean. Be mindful of not approaching *zina*, sexual relations outside of marriage. Don't let your guard down completely, don't spend hours on the phone and do not see him privately. Not only is it not allowed, but you could find yourself in a very compromising situation if the chemistry between the two of you is too potent!

- Be honest. Tell the truth about what you have to offer and what you expect from your husband. Encourage him to be honest with you about his expectations – never assume that he will want to travel the world and stay in expensive hotels every weekend – or that he won't. Muslim men are not all the same and neither are Muslim women. If you are the kind of woman who will want to stay at home full-time, make that clear. If you expect to work or continue your studies, make that clear also. If you marry under false pretences, this will cause a lot of friction. The last thing you want is to marry someone who is expecting to marry Mrs Cleaver, housewife par excellence, and finding that she is really Martha Stewart, business tycoon extraordinaire!

- Don't sell yourself short. Be realistic about your contract and your *mahr* (dowry). If there are conditions that you want in your contract that are in accordance with Islamic law, do not feel shy about including them. Don't demand an impossible *mahr*, as the Prophet (s) has advised against this. On the other hand, don't undervalue yourself. The dowry is a right that you have and no one should limit that. It doesn't hurt for the man to sweat a little in order to win you – just don't go asking for the riches of Arabia if your sweetheart-to-be drives a bus!

- Pray your *Istikharah*, the prayer that is recommended when seeking Allah's assistance with a decision. Once you have decided either way, pray the two *raka'at* (units of the prayer) and make the supplication of *Istikhara* for Allah to facilitate your chosen path. If the marriage will not be good for you or your *deen*, you will find that obstacles will be put in your path and you will know that he is not the right one for you.

After deciding that I wanted to marry my husband (three days after meeting him!) I prayed

Salat ul-Istikhara and waited for some sort of sign. The next day I rang my mother to tell her about my intentions. Now, my mother had always said she didn't want to hear any talk of marriage before I turned twenty-seven so, as I was only twenty-two, I was understandably nervous. But she said to me, 'You know what? I don't know why, but I've got a good feeling about this one.' And I took that as a good sign, if ever I saw one!

- Trust in Allah. Know that, if you are sincere and obey Allah and keep to His commands, He will bless you and give you success in your marriage. Don't worry excessively about what might happen or what the future holds – trust that Allah will protect you and keep in close contact with Him through remembrance of Him, supplicating and doing good deeds.

The vast majority of my sisters had Islamic 'arranged marriages' and lived to tell the tale. Umm Tasneem met and married her husband in the space of one week and her story is one that never fails to delight Muslims and surprise non-Muslims. Her daughter from her previous marriage was six years old at the time and, after several unsuccessful meetings with unsuitable brothers, she had all but given up when she was told about a new brother to the community: he was a student at an Islamic university, was running a small business, had a gentle nature, and was looking for a wife. All his references were glowing and she realized that she was going to *have* to meet him! Well, she did end up meeting him and, when she asked him how he felt about looking after another man's child, he said the words that she had been longing to hear, words that no other man had mentioned: that, as the *hadith* says, the man who looks after an orphan will be close to the Prophet (s) in Paradise. They were words that melted her heart and, just as others had told her she would, she knew immediately that she wanted to marry him. Her daughter, who had been unhappy with all the other men her mum had met, insisted that she *had* to marry him because he was 'the one'. And, in fact, the brother in question was so sure that she was the right one for him that he was prepared to marry her without even seeing her face! However, he did see it for a brief moment and, one week later, they were married. Six years and a few more children down the line, her face still lights up when she tells her story.

A Love Like No Other

Discussing the subject of love with a group of sisters is an interesting experience, made all the more poignant by the fact that, to the outside world, we appear not to enjoy 'those types' of emotions. After all, when was the last time you saw a Muslim couple, the woman in *niqab* and the husband with a big beard and white robe, holding hands, hugging or, dare I say it, *kissing* in public? Right, you just never see it. So it wouldn't surprise me if the overall impression of a traditional Islamic marriage is one of domination and submission, rules and regulations, can'ts and don'ts, duty and sufferance. How can there be space for passion, romance, intimacy and love in such a dry, arranged union?

When we came to Islam, most of us hadn't purged ourselves of all the ideas and traditions we were brought up with. One of the most pervading ideas in Western popular culture, disseminated through films, books and music, is simple: 'love makes the world go around'. From an early age, through fairy tales and other childhood experiences, girls are taught to wait and prepare for 'the love of your life'. We all believed in 'love at first sight' at one time, that 'love conquers all' and the importance of finding 'your one true love'. A cursory glance at any pop chart from any era will confirm the centrality of love to the Western world view. So what about love and romance when one comes to Islam?

Although it may share similar characteristics such as tenderness, romance and intimacy, Islamic love is different from love in *jahiliyyah*, the 'time of ignorance' before Islam. In essence, Islamic love is based on loving for Allah's sake and that means loving what Allah loves about a person: their *iman*, their submission; their *taqwa*, their Islamic manners; good character and strong *deen*. These aspects of a person take precedence over other more material or worldly attributes.

During a very moving evening of debate, confession and laughter, Ghaniyah told me, 'The difference between the love in Islam and the love in *jahiliyyah* is that in Islam, you love for the sake of Allah, whereas in *jahiliyyah*, you love solely because your heart and your desires are attracted to that person.'

Claire added money, status, privilege and sex, but, in the heightened mood, Ghaniyah was on a roll and continued: 'Someone who looks like Brad Pitt, someone very rich or [said in her best Lahori accent] someone who's a doctor or an engineer or pilot or whoever pleases your parents.' There were laughs of acknowledgement and agreement from the other women.

'In *jahiliyyah*, all sorts of factors influence you – parental ambition, values you've been raised with. In my case, that would have been qualifications, good career prospects, probably intellectual or academic training in something, shallow things, really. It was very difficult for me to come out of that way of thinking when I first started practising. As my faith and understanding of Islam increased, I learnt to put my trust in Allah. I stopped being so caught up in image and looks and realized that what was beautiful in a man was his degree of servitude to Allah. When I first had a meeting with my husband, he had none of the things that I would have looked for in *jahiliyyah* but instead he had another set of values and characteristics that were far more beautiful to me now-that I had learnt to love what Allah loves.' Sara

Loving for the sake of Allah is superior in many ways to loving for other, more selfish reasons. Firstly, loving for Allah's sake does not fluctuate according to your own whims and desires – it is constant, as long as the other person is also striving to please Allah. Secondly, that love is the kind of love that will compel a person to give their partner their rights, even if they don't particularly feel like it.

As Allah says:

Live with them in kindness; even if you dislike
them, perhaps you dislike something in which
Allah has placed much good.
Surah An-Nisa; 19

'If he fears Allah, if he worships Allah in the way that
he is supposed to, he's going to treat you well, knowing that you are Allah's slave and he's Allah's slave.
Allah is going to ask him about how he treated you
and how you were a wife to him, so it all goes back
to Allah.' Ghaniyah

Often, people make a distinction between 'love
marriages' and 'arranged marriages', as if the
two are opposites. By the time I was on the verge
of getting married myself, I knew that this was
not the case. Most people believe that love grows
from shared interests, spending time together and
physical intimacy. While these things can serve to
increase love, as Muslims, we believe that love is
like a seed that Allah al-Wadood (The Loving)
plants in the heart. So, it is Allah that brings the
hearts together and puts love there. And that is
how we have faith that we will have loving
marriages, even though, from the outside, it
seems as though we have done nothing to make
that love grow. But all the pure intentions, the
whispered wishes in prostration, the striving to
obey Allah together, even the most tender touch

– these are the things that bring the blessing of love between two Muslims.

My Nikah

After much to-ing and fro-ing about the date – first Ramadhan, then September, then August, then April, then finally February – I awoke on the morning of my *nikah* – my wedding day – bubbling with excitement. My dear flatmate Hayat had prepared a special breakfast for me – cereal with fresh strawberries and orange juice in a delicate fluted glass. I had had a new khaki-coloured *abayah* made for the day and wore it with a dark aubergine-coloured Chinese silk brocade scarf. However, in comparison with traditional preparations for a Muslim wedding, mine were quite sparse: I had had a henna party the week before and a Sudanese sister had decorated my hands and feet with dark henna patterns. There was no sitting around being per-fumed with fragrant incense, *bukhoor*, for hours on end, there was no steam bath, no sugaring of arms and legs to remove the hairs that grow there, there was no huge family gathering, no great pots of food being cooked, no relatives from all over England and around the world. It was a quiet and simple affair. I married my husband in the basement of an Islamic bookshop, squeezed between the books of Sahih Bukhari on one side and the computer on the other. That was my *nikah*.

Wedding

The *nikah* is the simple ceremony that solemnizes the Muslim marriage. The groom and the woman's guardian are there, together with the bride and sometimes friends and other family members. The marriage contract is presented and witnessed. The *mahr* – the dowry – is stated and witnessed. And that's it.

Compared to the traditional Western wedding, the Islamic *nikah* is short on ceremony and expense.

The marriage contract is similar to a pre-nuptial agreement. In it, the woman makes certain conditions that her husband must agree to and sign before the marriage takes place. These may include stipulations on working, re-marriage, leaving the country – in short, any condition that the woman wants to ensure is respected and carried out. Non-fulfilment of marriage contract conditions is grounds for divorce in Islamic law.

The dowry, *mahr*, is similar to the dowries and *lobola* of other cultures, except that it is presented to the bride and not to her family. She can stipulate as much (or as little) as she likes, financial or otherwise. Some examples of *mahr* include knowledge of the Qur'an or any other aspect of the *deen* (which will be taught to her), money, gold and jewellery, books, clothes, household items or travel. In Umm Tasneem's case, part of her *mahr* was a trip to Saudi Arabia on 'Umrah, the minor pilgrimage.

While the *nikah* is usually a quiet, private affair, the *waleemah*, the wedding celebration that follows it, is the total opposite. Its purpose is to announce publicly that the two people are now married and it is a time for celebration and joy, at which food is served and the women and children sing and play the *duff*, the hand drum, amongst themselves.

I remember the first time I went to a *waleemah*. All the sisters had been planning what they were going to wear for weeks and, in the end, the colour of the night was pink: pink trouser suits, pink and red *shalwar kameez*, pink and gold embroidered petticoats, *gogorat*, and pink saris. The sisters glowed with goodwill and carefully applied make-up, their ears twinkling, their arms and fingers weighed down with gold and silver – everyone had gone all out. After eating the delicious North African food, the bride went to change, as is the tradition at Algerian and Moroccan weddings. We organized the little girls to escort her up the stairs while we lined up in two rows, ready to receive her. She came up the stairs, her head covered by the hood of her embroidered Moroccan *jalabiyyah*. A sister pranced up with her, playing the hand drum and, as soon as she entered the room, we began singing her special song, the song we had written for her, with her name as the refrain. She had to twirl around in the centre a few times before taking her seat on the cushion prepared especially for her. Then we sang, told stories, gave her advice, danced and sang some more, until late into the night. Even today, that sister smiles at the memory of her *waleemah* – that day of sisterhood, joy and laughter that marked her entry into married life.

7

THE OTHER SIDE OF THE *NIKAH*

So you're married. Here you are, two virtual strangers, alone together for the first time. Is there any way to describe the nerves, the shyness, the tentative thrill of anticipation that character-ize those first days and nights? While 'newlywed nerves' are virtually unheard of in the West today, the early days of an Islamic marriage are full of exploration and discovery, excitement and wonder: you are two individuals getting to know each other, spiritually, mentally and physically. Often, you and your husband will begin living together, although it is not uncommon for this stage to be delayed until you find a new home to share. For many newlyweds, that 'grace period' is quite wonderful. You can behave more like friends and lovers than husband and wife because you can do everything you want together but don't have the pressures of being thrust into each other's space and all the responsibilities that go with that. It is a time to get used to each other, to get to know each other properly, to go for walks, to go on 'dates', to be young lovers – a blissful time of discovery.

Wedding celebrations and 'dating' are all very well, but sooner or later, the post-'honeymoon' period is going to have to begin. As converts, my friends and I knew from all our research that an Islamic marriage consists of rights and responsibilities and, as these are literally God-given, they are to be taken seriously.

So just what kind of deal were we getting here?

Rights and Roles in Marriage

Any discussion of rights and roles is pointless if one doesn't take into account the fact that, in the eyes of Allah, men and women are equal. They receive the same reward for their good deeds and the same punishment for their bad deeds. Indeed, it was because Umm Salamah, one of the Prophet (s)'s wives, asked him why Allah always referred to men in the Qur'an that He revealed the verse,

> Never will I allow to be lost the work of any of you, be he male or female. You are [members] one of another.
> Surah Aali Imran 3:195

261

and also the verse,

> Verily, the Muslims, men and women,
> the believers, men and women, the men and the
> women who are obedient, the men and women
> who are truthful ... Allah has prepared for
> them forgiveness and a great reward.
> Surah Al-Ahzab 33:35

The Muslim woman is not exempt from any of the acts of worship – praying, fasting, studying the *deen*, attending the mosque, paying *zakah* (the compulsory charity) – except where there is a physical hardship that is particular to women, such as pregnancy, menses or postpartum bleeding. Just as the man is expected to study the *deen*, she too is obliged to learn as much as she can, strive to perfect her prayer, remain sincere and do good deeds – the standard that is expected of women is no different to that expected of men. Unlike in other faiths, there has never been any debate in Islam about women possessing souls or being responsible for the 'fall of man' or, for that matter, being inherently evil and prone to sin. This is something that not many people are aware of but it is certainly something that has always given me great solace.

Although spiritually, men and women are equal, they fulfil different social functions in Islam and have different roles. Therefore, they sometimes have different rights from each other. Within an Islamic marriage, the role and responsibilities of the man are quite distinct from those of the woman. This means that the *rights* of husband and wife are also distinct from one another, as a way of complementing the different role that each of them fulfils.

In addition to the rights that every woman has under Islamic law, such as the right to her own property, wealth and legal identity, the rights of the wife include being treated well and having all her needs taken care of, being fed, clothed and housed as her husband feeds, clothes and houses himself. She has the right to a physical relationship and to have children. She is responsible for raising the children and running the household and, on the Day of Reckoning, she will be questioned by Allah about that.

Each of you is a shepherd and each of you is responsible for his flock. The leader is a shepherd and is responsible for his flock; a man is the shepherd of his family and is responsible for his flock; a woman is the shepherd in the house of her husband and is responsible for her flock; a servant is the shepherd of his master's wealth and is responsible for it. Each of you is a shepherd and is responsible for his flock.

Hadith reported in Sahih al-Bukhari

In Islam, every social grouping has a head, male or female, someone responsible for the care of the others, be it the state, the mosque, a business or a household. And while that head is encouraged to consult with the other members of the group, the final decision rests with him or her and he or she is answerable to Allah for that. For example, a woman running a business will be answerable for the treatment of her staff, for the honest dealings of the business and the sound management of the finances.

The Islamic family unit is headed by the husband. Although he is by no means the sole guardian of the spiritual, physical and financial well-being of all within it, it is he who has the ultimate responsibility and he will be questioned by Allah concerning it.

The husband has the right to have his needs looked after in his home – the cooking and cleaning and the mending of clothes. These wifely duties seemed quite old-fashioned to me, but I soon learnt that the Islamic attitude to what is now derogatorily known as 'women's work' is quite different to the one I had grown up with. The woman's care of her husband and family makes the home into a haven of peace and tranquillity, a welcome break from the stress of the outside world. Taking care of her husband's needs is something a woman is rewarded for just as her husband is rewarded for taking care of her. Therefore, there is absolutely no stigma attached to these duties in Islam, particularly if they are performed with the correct intention. And I reasoned thus: The poor man has been out working all day to pay for everything that I need and want, is it too much to have a meal ready for him when he comes home? To look after our lovely home? To care for our beautiful clothes? It didn't seem too tall an order. In addition, just like his wife, the husband has the right to a physical relationship and to have children.

But the husband has another right: his wife must obey him in all that is good and all that does not contradict the *Shari'ah.*

To *obey*?

Obey, like what – like a child? An underling? A *slave*? Obey who?

I'm not going to lie for one minute: that last one was the only one that made me pause for thought! It took every bit of my *iman* – my faith – not to pack it in right there and then. It was so contrary to what I had been brought up with, what I had been taught, what I wanted to do! I did not have a mother like Mei's who told her, 'When you get married, you're going to have to leave us and follow your husband: *obey your husband . . .*'

I had never received such advice and I didn't

want to. It was utterly alien to everything that I was about.

> If a woman prays her five daily prayers, fasts her month [of Ramadhan], obeys her husband and guards her chastity, then it will be said to her: 'Enter Paradise by whichever gate you wish'.
> *Hadith* of the Prophet (s) reported by Ahmad and at-Tabarani

So, how did I work through it? With difficulty: with much soul-searching, reading, trying to understand and, in the end, submission. I had to keep reminding myself of the statement of Allah:

> . . . and it may be that you dislike a thing which is good for you and that you like a thing which is bad for you. Allah knows but you do not know.
> Surah Al-Baqarah 2:216

And I also realized how very important it was to have a husband who truly feared Allah, someone who wouldn't become a mini despot, a tyrant bent on ruling his home with an iron fist. And, in my youthful paranoia, I also made sure that my husband-to-be knew that I was not about to put up with any nonsense: I wouldn't be ordered around or talked down to. And even though he never showed the slightest sign of being like that, I wasn't taking any chances. I warned him practically every time I spoke to him until, one day, he told me he had 'got the message, OK?' I took the hint.

Oppressor/Oppressed

It would appear that there is something in the image of a bearded man walking with a covered woman that provokes thoughts of repression and submission, of the powerful and the powerless: 'I bet he made her wear that thing!' Woe betide that woman if she dares fall behind her husband for any reason: 'See, he makes her walk behind him, he does, ten paces behind!' And if she is carrying the shopping and he is holding the child: 'Treats her like a donkey, doesn't he?' And if he is holding the shopping and she is holding the child: 'Bet she never gets a break – all they do is breed!' It is as if any action, no matter how insignificant, can be interpreted as confirmation of whatever views the person already holds. It is the story of 'The Miller and his Donkey' on a daily basis!

As Claire told me, 'People believe that, in Islam, the man is in charge of everything – that the Muslim woman doesn't choose anything, she is just told what to do, that she has no ideas of her own, no plans of her own, no life of her own.' All this from the mouth of a sister with rebellious Celtic blood running through her veins – it could only have been said with tongue firmly in cheek. But is there really life beyond the rights and roles of marriage?

Beyond Rights

The Islamic marriage is so much more than just rights and responsibilities – these are merely its founding principles. Typically, the rights are the first to be put in place, before love, romance and friendship blossom, and the last to go, sometimes long after the love has gone. But beyond the duties and obligations, lies a haven, just like other marriages in other cultures and religions. And although love between Muslims is guided and moulded by the *Shari'ah*, it is as tender, sweet and passionate as any other, just as our Prophet (s) showed us when he said, 'The believers who are most complete in faith are those with the best manners and the best among them are those who are best [in treatment] to their women.'

As Ghaniyah told me, 'In terms of this worldly life, my husband is my protector, he's my best friend, my advisor, my punch bag, my bank! Someone I learn with; when things go wrong, someone I talk to . . . Our husbands are our best friends, and though we like our female friends and we're happy to do our own thing for part of the day, we find our husbands indispensable, because Allah has blessed us.'

> 'All I can say is my husband looks like they just freed him from the Taliban — he looks like an Afghan, through and through! But he is the gentlest, most loving, wonderful person on the face of this earth, *masha Allah*. I wish everybody could have a husband like him . . . just don't take my one!' Begum

And if I had thought that the Muslim husband would be proud and aloof, above doing what he considers 'women's work', I found that the true Muslim man, the one worthy of respect, is not afraid to humble himself or get his hands dirty! As Sara told me, 'When I was pregnant I was sick constantly. My husband was very supportive, he wasn't repulsed by me and that is how it should be, they *should* be supportive in that role!'

I asked sisters what their views were on romance. Does it exist in a Muslim marriage? And just what do Muslim men know about it? Layla told me, 'Of course there is romance — you can teach a Muslim man to be romantic, you can show him how to do it.'

It is worth noting that, as reverts from Western backgrounds, our idea of romance is particularly

Western – flowers, chocolate, perfume, that sort of thing. Sara too had always had this idea until marrying an Arab man made her re-examine her understanding of romance: 'Western culture encourages that sort of romance,' she told me. 'You see it on the television, you hear it in the music, a specific type of romance. But if [non-Western men] haven't been exposed to that, if they've never seen an example of it from their culture or from their parents then I think they really have no idea. And you do have to show them.'

So how did she cope with the culture shock?

'Well, I was exposed to many cultures when I was growing up and I knew when I entered the marriage that there were going to be some cultural conflicts. For example, if he buys me a pair of shoes, he's really happy – that's his way of showing his love, whereas I see romance in a Western context – "When you see flowers, you should think of me!"'

And so, in spite of what I saw then as an insurmountable hurdle, I have experienced and witnessed Islamic marriages that transcend the issue of obeying one's husband, of the man being the head of the house. These are unions that are loving, secure, supportive and honest. In the best tradition of a leader, the husbands respect their wives, their opinions and their feelings; they work together as a team, helping and supporting each other.

And so I began to understand that the Muslim husband is like any leader – if he is corrupt, he will use whatever he can to abuse his position. But if he is a good leader, and he loves and fears Allah, he will be all his wife wants and needs him to be – and all that Allah *demands* him to be!

And so, after much soul-searching and struggle, I found an equilibrium between doing what Allah has asked of me and safeguarding my own sense of self. For although I had been commanded with compliance to my husband's wishes, I had been blessed with a mind of my own, a voice, tact, the *deen* as a safeguard against tyranny and a man who feared Allah more than he sought to rule his home with an iron fist.

Stepford Wives

It was some years into my marriage that I happened to see the original version of *The Stepford Wives*. I remember being profoundly affected by it: I was left feeling vulnerable and afraid. 'Is that what men really want?' I asked my friends. 'Would my husband exchange me for a robot if he could?' The idea that, secretly, every man would give up his wife's personality, talent and individuality for a docile and submissive wife whose greatest pleasure was seeing her husband's contented face reflected in a perfectly polished floor chilled me. With my own history of wrestling with the rights and wrongs of the Islamic husband–wife relationship, my unease was understandable. I saw the Stepford Wife as a shell of a woman: one without her own personality, opinions, interests or motivations.

But, as we have seen, there are aspects of the Stepford Wife persona that we, as Muslim wives, are encouraged to aspire to: obeying our husbands, taking good care of them and our children, looking after our homes, taking care of ourselves and looking nice. So that prompted me to ask the question: isn't the ideal Muslim wife in actual fact a Stepford Wife? And indeed, in her dedication to her children, home and husband (not necessarily in that order), doesn't the ideal Muslim wife rival the wives of Stepford? If she does not work outside the home, she will invest a lot of time and energy in her housekeeping, her cooking, cleaning and decorating, as well as nurturing the children, playing with them and teaching them. However, looking after her home is not the reason for the Muslim woman's existence. She was created to worship her Lord and, while she can achieve this through her work in the home, there are a myriad other ways that she can fulfil the purpose of her creation. And, I had to ask myself, wouldn't every man love to come home to a sparkling house, a hot meal, a beautiful wife and happy, compliant children every night? And if not every night, which might become a bit too tiresome, at least *once in a while*? Indeed, what woman wouldn't want to have a husband who would find all her jokes funny, want to 'talk about us' whenever she liked, always pick up his socks, buy her anything she wanted – a Stepford Husband? Show me the woman who would say no!

Undoubtedly, there are men out there, Muslim and non-Muslim, that dream of turning their spouses into Stepford Wives. She's easier, more pliable, less difficult – less like a 'real woman'. But for most men, it is one of those idle fantasies. Because the reality is that, for most men, a Stepford Wife would bore them to tears after a couple of weeks.

'My husband deliberately set out looking for a wife with personality, someone mature, someone he could bounce around ideas with, someone who will push him in certain ways.' Hajar

What's more, for the Muslim man, there is an added dimension. The strong, confident Muslim man, while not saying no to a little compliance from his wife, a little pampering and a regular hot meal, wants a Khadijah or an Aisha. These two great women, wives of the Prophet (s), are amongst the Mothers of the Believers, the best women of creation. Yes, they were good Muslim wives but they are also the strongest proof I have found against the ideal of a Muslim wife as a Stepford Wife. Khadijah was a successful businesswoman, older than the Prophet (s), who hired him to look after her caravans. Seeing that he was trustworthy and hardworking, she asked *him* to marry *her*. And when the Prophet (s) first received the revelation, who did he run to? Khadijah. Who was the first person to accept Islam and believe in the Messenger (s)? Khadijah. Who took the Prophet (s) to Waraqah? Who explained the signs of prophethood to him? Khadijah. This was not a Stepford Wife, acting under a docile, robotic programme. And then, of course, there was Aisha, the scholar, the interpreter of Islamic law, the poet, the doctor. She who refused to thank the Prophet (s) when Allah revealed her innocence of the adultery she had been accused of, thanking Allah instead. She challenged him, she teased him and she beguiled him. And, when Muhammad (s) was asked who was the most beloved to him, he answered without hesitation, 'Aisha.'

Therein lies one of the crucial differences

between the two types of wife. The Stepford Wife is programmed to have no individual personality. Nowhere in Islamic literature is it indicated that this is expected of the Muslim wife – the different characters of the wives of the Prophet and the female companions are testament to that fact.

Also, the Muslim woman is encouraged to study her *deen*, to be educated and to know about her rights and the rights of others. And knowing about these rights should give her the confidence to defend them. This is not part of the Stepford Wife's programming.

> 'Although the Muslim wife *is* encouraged to look after her husband, her children and her home, there is a great emphasis placed on her education and study. Many sisters I know, who weren't into education, have gone into serious study – initially religious and then other than that – because of this. They developed a love and understanding of learning – you don't find that in Stepford Wives.' Hajar

Indeed, the confident, upstanding Muslim man has been encouraged by the Prophet (s) to marry and cherish the strong righteous woman so that she can help him in the affairs of the Hereafter, learning with him, teaching him, reminding him and helping him to obey Allah.

So we concluded that, while there are aspects

of the Stepford Wife that we as Muslim wives should try to adopt, the *deen* does not compel us to be mindless, robotic domestic technicians. In short, the ideal Muslim wife is *not* a Stepford Wife – not unless she happens to have a Stepford Husband, of course!

Don't Mention the 'S' Word

But surely there is something missing here? We've discussed the Islamic marriage in detail – the duties, the benefits, the responsibilities, romance – and yet we have not mentioned sex!

In the Western world, sex is a commodity, openly marketed, bought and sold. Advertisers use it, singers sing about it, film-makers film it, actors act it, psychologists study it, writers write about it and everyone reads about it – and nobody gets as much of it as they claim! This is the essence of a sexually open society.

If one were to believe the mass media, there is no longer any concept of restraint, abstention, taboo or shame – there is a complete moral void. Where once, for better or for worse, religion, culture, family and community regulated human sexual behaviour, there is now a vacuum. And that vacuum is being filled by the interests of industry and capital – sex sells, like never before. It would appear that, in this day and age, only paedophilia has not gained media acceptance. But aside from that, is there any sexual practice that is not encouraged, accepted or, at the very least, tolerated by this society? From pornography to sodomy, from group sex to sado-masochism, there are magazines, videos and sex shops to cater for every taste.

In light of all this, anyone would be forgiven for thinking that Muslims are uptight about sex. After all, Muslim women cover, free-mixing is not allowed, men have to lower their gaze and we are warned in the strongest terms from discussing our sexual lives publicly. So, what exactly does Islam teach about sex? Is it something shameful, dirty, reserved solely for procreation, and even then, with one's eyes shut, in the dark?

No. Islam, the religion, considers sex to be something wonderful, an expression of love and intimacy between two people. It is important here to focus on what Islam says, not on what Muslims do. So whether some Muslims feel ashamed of sex is neither here nor there – what is important is the kind of attitude that the *deen* encourages Muslims to have.

According to the *hadith* literature, sex can be an act of worship if performed with the right intention. It is something healthy and beneficial, resulting in physical pleasure and procreation, adding to the numbers of the Muslims. It is something that human beings desire and there is no shame in that desire. It is, after all, the way Allah created us. We are thus encouraged to fulfil that desire within the limits set by Allah. This means that sexual pleasure is to be enjoyed within the context of marriage. Allah says in the Qur'an:

> Your women are a place of cultivation for you, so come to your place of cultivation however you wish, and put forth [righteousness] for yourselves . . .
> Surah al-Baqarah 2:223

Within marriage, there are few limits to how couples pleasure each other. Some of these limits include the prohibition of anal intercourse and sex during menses, although any other form of intimacy that avoids the woman's private area is allowed at this time. Both the man and the woman have the right to sexual pleasure and are encouraged to have a loving relationship: the woman is strongly advised not to constantly resort to the old 'I've got a headache' routine and to be as compliant as possible when her husband approaches her. This makes a lot of sense when one considers the negative effect of sexually frustrated men on the loose in the wider society. The husband, in turn, is advised to practise foreplay, to make sure that his wife is satisfied and is not allowed to practise *coitus interruptus* (withdrawal) without her consent, for fear that her pleasure will be compromised – sexually frustrated women being no less dangerous to the wider society! In fact, one of the great scholars of the past, Ibn Qudamah, said, 'It is recommended for the man to caress and fondle his wife prior to intercourse in order to arouse her so that she will get as much pleasure from intercourse as he does . . . And, if he climaxes before her, it is disliked for him to pull out until she climaxes . . . because that would otherwise cause her harm and prevent her from fulfilling her desire.' How different was this Islamic scholar's understanding from so many religious men the world over who considered desire, especially a woman's desire, shameful and dirty!

Indeed, during the time of the Prophet (s), the Muslims discussed sexual matters – from sexual positions to wet dreams – and this was never discouraged. The Prophet (s) always gave frank answers, dispelling many misconceptions.

Therefore, the Muslim attitude to sex is simple: it is something wholesome and natural that has its time and its place. Sex between two people is an intimate, private affair that belongs to the private sphere, within marriage, not on the public stage.

Marry Two, Three or Four

After about two months of marriage, I considered asking my husband to take another wife. Now it was not that I didn't love my husband – quite the opposite. But, in those first few months of married life, when I had the flat to myself and only saw him every other day, I grew to love my own company, my own space. I cherished the time I could afford to lavish on my friends, who often visited. I enjoyed the thrill of seeing him again after our separation – it kept our relationship fresh. But, more importantly, I had met a sister that I had grown very close to and I genuinely believed that marrying my husband would make her happy – and that was what I wanted for her. I was prepared (mentally, at least) to 'share' my husband with her because I loved her for the sake of Allah. But my husband wasn't interested and, after we began living together, the idea receded from my mind. But that feeling of space and sisterly love is one I have never forgotten.

Could it be that what is seen as possibly the most oppressive aspect of Islam is actually liberating for some women? The subject of polygamy is one fraught with assumptions, misunderstandings and very strong emotions, amongst Muslims and non-Muslims alike. However, it would come as a surprise to many Westerners to discover that polygamy is not a solely 'Islamic institution'. Not only have men in most world cultures been allowed and encouraged to take more than one wife, but polygamy was known historically amongst the Jews and Christians, and was practised by prophets and followers alike. Even today, in many societies and, if we are honest, even in our own, 'unofficial polygamy' is widespread. The desire for conquest, the sexual advances, the one-night stands, the visits to prostitutes, the flings and long-term affairs that characterize most societies are examples of this. Whether due to an innate polygamous nature or to social conditioning, it would certainly seem that, although some women are trying hard to catch up, men are more driven sexually, less hindered by biological processes (menstruation, pregnancy, childbirth, breast-feeding, a more complex arousal process and more elusive orgasms) and more willing to consider having sex with someone other than the woman they love.

Islamic law, the *Shari'ah*, recognizes this aspect of the male nature and, instead of pretending that it doesn't exist, creates a framework that forces the man to take responsibility for his sexual urges. For when Allah asserted women's rights within marriage in the Qur'an, they were not just for the first wife, but for every wife. Under Islamic law, a man cannot 'enjoy' a woman without being legally obligated to her: he has to approach and be vetted by her family or her guardian, he has to pay her the *mahr* (dowry), he has to marry her and make their union public, he has to provide for her, he has to acknowledge their children and she becomes one of his legal heirs. In addition, the man is restricted to a maximum of four wives, wives who have to be treated and maintained in the same manner, who have the right to be housed separately, who have the same rights to time and attention as each other, who have the same status, and whose children are all recognized as legitimate and inherit from him. A cursory glance at the status of the mistress and her children in our society will show that there is a big difference between an extra-marital affair and a second marriage. While the second wife is considered equal to the first in every way, the majority of mistresses and their children are never acknowledged. It is these children who are viewed as illegitimate, who never get to have their dad at their school play or sports day. They have no rights, he is not responsible for them – they are the 'dirty secrets'.

But if polygamy is all about keeping the man's sexual urges in check, what does it offer women?

After Khadijah's death, the Prophet Muhammad (s) married several times. However, contrary to the image popular amongst non-Muslims of the insatiable oriental sultan surrounded by nubile concubines, most of the Prophet (s)'s wives were war widows and divorcees, some with children from previous marriages. This *sunnah* highlights an aspect of polygamy that few are aware of: that it ensures that widows, divorcees and older women are all able to find love and security in a marriage, while having time to take care of their other responsibilities.

It has often occurred to me that the polygamous system is one that is ideally suited to a certain type of woman: the woman who is busy with her studies or career, whose friends and family play a big part in her life, the woman with children from a previous relationship, the older woman who just doesn't want a man around all the time because she enjoys her own company.

'Polygamy is in favour of the woman,' Umm Muhammad stated emphatically, 'because when the husband spends his time between his wives, they have more time for their children and for themselves. After all, when was the last time many women did something for themselves: painted their toenails, had a manicure? They also have time for their Lord, and that is very important. While her husband is away, the woman has time to read Qur'an, listen to a tape of Islamic knowledge, look over her study notes in peace.'

'I'm glad I am not a single wife. I have always been a very independent person – I like my own space and, this way, I have space for myself and when my husband comes back, he appreciates me, he's glad to see me.' Aziza

Another positive aspect of polygamy that sisters mentioned was the extra support that a 'co-wife' can often provide, particularly in places where the extended family is no longer present or near by.

'My co-wife and I are really close. We're there for each other – if she wants to go out, our husband and I will have the children. We want fairness for each other.' Aziza

Wives can help each other out, sharing child-care if one has to work or study, cooking for each other if one is sick or has just had a baby, learning and studying the *deen* together. Indeed, there are many instances of co-wives building a strong family unit, of having lasting friendships and treating each other as sisters in Islam, wanting for each other what they want for themselves. There are also wives that get along with each other, independent of their husbands. These are women that find that they have a lot in common, who genuinely like each other as individuals.

> 'She's my sister in Islam and that's the most important thing. The *deen* comes first.' Aziza

That is not to say that it is ever easy to learn that your husband is considering taking another wife. The emotions hit you like a ton of bricks because the bottom line is this: as far as you are concerned, he is yours and you don't want to share him. It is not easy for most couples to work through this stage and those who don't manage to come to a mutual understanding either abandon the whole idea or go their separate ways. But there are many who manage to get past this stage and it is often their *iman* that helps them through. And they find that they get through the various trials and tribulations and emerge from the experience stronger and wiser, as individuals and as a family.

Polygamy is not obligatory, it is an option, a choice. No one can be forced to enter a polygamous marriage or to stay in one. And for many women, if given the choice between having the honoured status of a wife or the potential humiliation of being the mistress, the co-wife role wins hands down.

Hitting the Rocks – When Things Go Wrong

When we were first learning about the *deen*, we believed that all marital problems would be avoided, as long as we kept to the Qur'an and *Sunnah*. As the *deen* provides guidance on everything, all we needed to do was stick to the guidance and we wouldn't go far wrong. But life is rarely that simple. Even amongst the most devout Muslims, there are marital problems, some temporary and fixable, others more permanent.

Conflict Resolution

Although marriage is a wonderful and fulfilling institution, like most other things that are worth anything, it has its share of tests and trials. An Islamic marriage may run into the same problems as any other marriage – personality clashes, failure to appreciate each other, stress, financial worries, amongst other issues. But Islamic marriages can have their own particular problems too, typically, failure of the spouses to give each other their rights, spouses becoming weak spiritually or leaving the *deen* completely. All these issues have a detrimental effect on the husband and wife, as well as any children they may have. You cease to feel good about each other, the love starts to seep away and it becomes harder and harder to give the person their basic rights, let alone show love and affection.

The *Sunnah* is replete with advice on how to deal with hardships and tests – mechanisms that will stop the individual from losing patience with their situation. Patience is one of the hardest characteristics to have but one of the noblest. It was a quality shared by all the prophets and it is a quality that is often praised in the Qur'an. The Muslim couple *must* have patience with each other and with the challenges that they face. Having patience means staying within the bounds of Allah's laws and not transgressing them in desperation, doing forbidden things out of anger or a need for revenge.

The Prophet (s) advised the Muslim men thus: 'Let not a believing man hate a believing woman; if he dislikes a characteristic in her, he would be pleased by other characteristics.' Obviously, the same applies to the Muslim woman. We are thus advised to overlook and cover each other's faults and make excuses for each other.

As Muslims, men and women, we are also encouraged to look at ourselves first when confronted with a trial, to see what we might have done to bring it on, either in terms of how we have behaved towards the other person or how we may have been negligent with regards to our *deen* and our relationship with Allah.

As Allah says:

> Allah will never change the condition of a people until they change what is in themselves.
> Surah al-Israh 17:31

Knowing this makes it possible to focus on something we can directly change – ourselves – instead of focusing on something that we are not in control of – the other person's behaviour.

Indeed, the *Shari'ah* gives the best advice on dealing with marital problems and that is for the husband and wife to return to their Lord. Often, such difficulties, and the way we respond to them, are a direct result of lack of *iman*, of weakened faith. By increasing in *dhikr* (remembrance of Allah), in *du'a* (supplications and prayers), in good deeds and seeking forgiveness, we grow close to Allah. And when we re-focus on Allah rather than that person, we either find that Allah makes that person change, or we change or the situation itself fades in significance.

There are also other steps that can be taken as a couple to resolve differences – couples talking over their problems, advising each other, even admonishing each other, particularly if the problem is *deen*-related. They may also seek arbitration from family members or someone well versed in Islamic knowledge. It also helps to know the Islamic position on the conflict at hand. However, this last usually only has an effect when both spouses actually want to obey His laws.

What's Love Got To Do With It?

My father once gave me an analogy of a relationship, an analogy so true and so apt that I tell it to everyone when the topic of relationships comes up. No one has found fault in it yet.

A relationship is like a bank account. All the loving moments, the gifts, kind words and fun times are the deposits. All the arguments, disappointments and hurt are the withdrawals. In the Islamic context, the deposits include fulfilling each other's rights. The withdrawals are times when those rights are withheld. If there are enough deposits, the love account remains in the black and the withdrawals can be borne with patience. So the good times make up for the bad times and make them easy to forgive and to be forgotten. If, however, the withdrawals begin to outnumber the deposits, the account goes into overdraft, into the red. If that continues and the account reaches a stage where there are only withdrawals and no deposits to make up for them, the account becomes bankrupt. When a relationship reaches that stage, it is hard to come back from the edge. Because of all the hardship, the tender feelings and respect have been spent, leaving nothing but resentment and disappointment. And when it reaches that stage, just what has love got to do with it?

Once, at a gathering at my home, I heard a sister quoting that line and I didn't understand what she meant. I asked her to explain. In essence, she said, 'When you're not being given your rights and you're not being respected, when your husband is just taking liberties, what has love got to do with it?' At times like these, what does it matter if you still 'love' him? Should you stick around, holding onto love, when everything else is gone?

> 'I couldn't say that I fell out of love . . . I don't think love came into it. Even now, I love him for the sake of Allah because he's a Muslim . . . it's just that he's become such a *weak* Muslim and that's not what I want for myself. It's very hard to stay with someone when they are disobeying Allah. It almost makes them totally against what you believe in.' Aliyah

The sisters I spoke to about this all agreed that

it isn't necessarily love that will make couples treat each other fairly, it is the *deen* – obeying the command of Allah. Therefore a marriage with love and no *deen* is a risky one – how will the husband behave if he falls out of love, or if he falls in love with someone else? There are no boundaries, no rules, no minimum requirements, nothing that he has to fulfil even if he is not in love with his wife. The same applies to the woman – the *deen* is what will make her treat her husband well, even if she no longer loves him.

'For me, it's not love but the *deen* that conquers everything. Yes, every man and woman wants to love and be loved but I can't live with love and no *deen*. It wouldn't be nice to live with *deen* and no love but that would probably be easier. At least if a man has *deen*, he will love for the sake of Allah, he will respect and honour you and give you your rights at least.'
Umm Muhammad

However, some sisters responded differently. Hajar, for example, said, 'Love is absolutely necessary in a marriage. To me, if there isn't any love then there won't be a marriage. I have to love my husband, otherwise it would be an incomplete marriage.' But she too found *deen* an indispensable part of the marriage structure.

'You need both love and *deen* because the *deen*

is the structure. I think that that is the downfall of many a marriage today – that lack of structure. The husband wants to be the wife and the wife wants to be the husband and then eventually, no one wants to be either! Nobody really knows what their roles are – it is so much easier when you know what your role is and what his role is. We might need to come away from the structure from time to time, but we will always refer back to it and return to it eventually.'

And yet, it all sounds so cynical! Whatever happened to love being enough, conquering everything, making the world go around? I wanted to believe these things, as we all do. I didn't want to think that these words were simply empty jingles and brave, but essentially futile, hopes. There are so many things that we want to believe in, not because they are true, but because they make us feel better, make life easier to deal with, even if their effect is more akin to opium than anything else. So I kept looking, talking and listening. I heard stories of men who made their wives' lives miserable, treating them terribly and even withholding some of their basic rights – and yet claiming to love them desperately, refusing to let them go, afraid of losing them. I saw women selling themselves short, accepting less than they deserved, harming themselves for the sake of husbands who claimed to love them. They held on, year after year, hoping that those words of love would eventually bring an end to the neglect, insults or beatings – but it rarely happened. When I heard these stories, it became hard to believe in the 'power of love'.

And where I found loving Muslim couples, I saw that, when they encountered problems, it wasn't 'love' they turned to, it was to the *deen*, to their faith. It was to the night prayer, to the supplication, to asking forgiveness, to purifying the soul, to increasing in good deeds. And all this opened the doors of communication and forgiveness, which, slowly but surely, led the way back to the love that they had once shared. Only this time it was deeper, richer and more firmly grounded. Because Allah had brought their hearts back together.

When We Say Goodbye

There is no doubt that, sometimes, marital differences cannot be resolved and the couple have to go their separate ways. It surprises me that, even today, there are people, Muslim and non-Muslim, who believe that a Muslim woman cannot separate from her husband. They think that, once in, there is no get-out clause, no escape – she is trapped for ever. Believe me, before I checked in, I checked that all out!

> And if a woman fears cruelty or desertion on her
> husband's part, there is no sin on them both if
> they make terms of peace between themselves;
> and making peace is better . . .
> Surah an-Nisa: 128

In Islam, marriage is not a sacred bond that can never be 'rent asunder'. The *Shari'ah* recognizes that there are times when all efforts at reaching a peaceful solution fail to yield results – and a couple have to part. Due to its harmful effects on the individuals involved, their children and the wider society, divorce is discouraged and there are Muslim communities where it is still very rare. However, it would appear that, in the current social climate, marriages are becoming more and more fragile, with many more divorces taking place. Is it because we are taught to wish for so much in a partner that we can never find it all in one person? Is it because women who dare to leave a marriage no longer face destitution? Is it that we view marriage as disposable, unlike our grandparents who, for better or for worse, stayed together until their deaths, enduring much hardship and disappointment along with the good times? Islam doesn't say that a terrible marriage is preferable to divorce, but it does emphasize patience, one of the keys to a successful marriage.

In Islamic law, there are three types of marital separation – the revocable divorce, the irrevocable divorce (both are known as *talaq*) and the dissolution of the marriage contract (*khula'*). The *talaq* is performed by the man and the *khula'* by the woman.

> The divorce is twice, after that, either you retain her on reasonable terms or release her with kindness. And it is not lawful for you [men] to take back [from your wives] any of your *Mahr* which you have given them, except when both parties fear that they would be unable to keep the limits ordained by Allah. Then if you fear that they would not be able to keep the limits ordained by Allah, then there is no sin on either of them if she gives back [the *Mahr* or a part of it] for her *Al-Khul'*. These are the limits ordained by Allah, so do not transgress them. And whoever transgresses the limits ordained by Allah, then such are the wrong doers.
> Surah al-Baqarah 2:229

Ideally, after trying all the different methods of resolving marital disputes and making no headway, a man may divorce his wife with the revocable divorce by declaring one *talaq*. The wife then observes her *'iddah* – her waiting period – for three menstrual cycles. During this time, the husband and wife are to stay together in the house – neither of them is to abandon the other. In addition, the woman still has the right to be fed, clothed and housed. This period gives the couple, through daily contact, the chance to resolve their differences.

Also, if normal relations are restored or the couple end up in bed, the *talaq* is nullified. So they have to stay put, albeit separately. If the *'iddah* period elapses, the divorce is final and the couple go their separate ways. If the woman has children, she is entitled to maintenance while they are in her custody. As is stated in the Qur'an, the couple may remarry after drawing up a new contract and the giving of a new *mahr*. They may do this after divorcing two times.

The third *talaq* is an irrevocable divorce. This means that the couple cannot get back together until the woman has had a full and genuine marriage to someone else. After this divorce, the couple must separate and the *'iddah* period is one menstrual cycle.

A *khula'* is when the woman applies to the judicial authority for a cancellation of the marriage contract. Grounds for *khula'* include failure of the husband to maintain his wife, mental or physical abuse, injury, prolonged absence and impotence. The husband is first ordered to divorce her (*talaq*) and, if he refuses, the judge or other authority pronounces them divorced. In this case, the woman gives back her *mahr* as the contract is now annulled. If she does not have the funds to give back her *mahr*, she can claim a debt that her husband owes her as her 'ransom'. She may also apply for *zakah*, the compulsory charity, in order to 'ransom' herself. Her *'iddah* period is one menstrual cycle. The couple are free to remarry with a new contract and *mahr*.

Muslims are encouraged to be patient with all trials, be they spiritual, financial or marital. But sometimes, that patience is not enough to avert the end. I have found Muslim women with marital problems even more reluctant to consider leaving a marriage than other women. They ask themselves whether they can't do more, pray harder, be more and more patient. They think about the effect separation will have on their *deen*, on the children, and the impact it will have on their non-Muslim family's opinions of the *deen*.

But the one thing that most often makes separation inevitable is when the marriage is adversely affecting their *deen*. I have seen many sisters put others' physical, financial and emotional well-being before their own for years on end – but only up until the point where they feel their *deen* is being affected, that they are actually being harmed spiritually.

'I doubted myself and what I believed in. It made me question the *deen* – or what I knew of it. I thought, Is this right? How much have I been brainwashed and how much is from the *deen*? I just thought, If this is the *deen*, maybe I'm just not cut out for it because I'm breaking inside here – I can't go on, I can't live like this.' Layla

If you allow it to, the perceived injustice, unfairness and hopelessness of your situation can make you lose faith in the promise of Allah and, sometimes, even question the *deen* itself. No Muslim ever wants to reach that point.

Layla told me more about her reasons for applying for a *khula'*: 'I just realized that the situation wasn't what I wanted any more – I think we had both changed as people. I had the choice of either losing myself in that, losing my identity, or growing as a person. I had switched off to so much already and I knew I was on my last few switches and I didn't want to switch them off. I knew I was very unhappy and that it was not what I wanted. So I sent the papers off for *khula'*.'

Umm Muhammad and I discussed her own

divorce at length. I had to ask her what made her take the drastic step of seeking a divorce from her husband, the man who had introduced her to Islam.

She replied, 'Due to my husband's psychological problems and the instability that that caused in my home, I decided to leave.'

But didn't she love him?

'When a man is not fulfilling what Allah has told him to fulfil, not progressing in his *deen*, for me, the love starts to diminish. So I made moves to apply for a *khula'* but, because it was quite a drawn-out procedure, I just told him that I needed the divorce sorted out. He tried to convince me not to go through with it but I was quite adamant that it was what I wanted to do. So I got him to do one *talaq*.'

Why was divorce the only way out?

'I felt that I had been hindered with regards to my *deen*, how I wanted to live, how I wanted to practise my *deen*, because his mental illness was really disrupting my life. There were things that I wanted to gain out of Islam and I didn't feel I was gaining them in that marriage. Visiting mental hospitals, prison, being searched – this was not how I wanted to live. I didn't feel secure as a woman and the children were being badly affected too.'

I wanted to find out whether having greater

knowledge of the *deen* or stronger faith would make a woman more or less likely to endure an unhappy marriage. In other words, would a religious woman take more hardship and misery or less? So, when I spoke to sisters who were divorced, I asked them: 'Do you think your divorce was a result of higher *iman* and knowledge or lower *iman* and knowledge?'

Umm Muhammad was quite sure of her answer. 'My going for a divorce was a result of higher *iman* because I knew I didn't need him to live my life any more. That life was not what Islam was about as far as I was concerned.'

But Aliyah was not so sure. Constantly examining her motives, questioning herself and the past, she told me, 'I spend my time trying to seek knowledge, trying to raise my children and in between, every now and again, looking in the mirror, thinking, Why did you do this? or Why did you do that? I still ask myself so many questions, it's unbelievable. Was he ever the person I thought he was when I met him? Were the signs already there?'

Eventually, it was her *deen* that gave her the strength to end their relationship.

'Basically, I thought, I've waited for you to sort yourself out and you haven't done anything. So, you know what? I'm going to divorce you. You're not doing the right thing, you're not fearing Allah the way He deserves to be feared. And you're weakening me and weakening my children. I really wanted to learn about my *deen*, to progress, and he just took me away from that.'

When I left Aliyah's house, I was deeply moved, lost in thought. I could tell from our conversation that her marriage had been fraught with years of difficulty and many trials. And although my heart ached for her suffering, I could not get over the tender mother, the generous host, the loving sister that was before me. Where was the bitterness? Where were the regret, the rage, the anguish? I could see none of this in her, not in her voice, nor in her manner, nor in her words. And I knew why. Because she believed in the promise of Allah – that He would never burden her more than she could bear, that with difficulty comes ease, that no worshipper does a sincere good deed except that she sees its reward, in this life or in the next. It was all these things that made her emerge from her harrowing experience a stronger, better person, filled with optimism and hope.

The end of a marriage comes with a range of emotions. Many of the sisters spoke of feelings of relief and of looking forward to a new phase in their lives. They felt confident and empowered, something that is probably more a reflection on the state of the ended marriage than the divorce itself. Pondering the effects of her divorce on her life, Aliyah told me, 'Since I got divorced, I feel more peaceful. I was always fighting against something, there was always something "going on" in my life. So although I'm now a one-parent family and it's hard, I know that after the hardship comes ease. Now I feel at peace with myself.'

'When I came out of the divorce, I came out with an insight into things. I'm stronger inside now; I know how to control myself better. After hardship comes ease – and if you're patient and you turn to Allah, I think you get more ease and I know I tried really hard to be patient and because of that, Allah just gave me so much ease. When the papers came, I was fine, *masha Allah*.' Layla

But not all sisters are happy when a divorce comes through, particularly if the divorce was initiated by the husband. For some women, Muslim and non-Muslim alike, divorce signals the start of loneliness and insecurity – new friends must be made, new pastimes discovered, new ways of coping found, emotionally and often financially. This is particularly true of divorces that happen later in a woman's life. Having spent years as a dedicated wife and mother, she is now on her own, learning how to live without her 'other half'. For many women, this is accompanied by resentment and bitterness – she feels that she has wasted the best years of her life, that life has passed her by, that she has been used and abandoned.

But I was amazed to find that the practising Muslim woman sees things differently. Although she may be bleeding inside, she is patient with the trial. She doesn't rage against the *qadr*, the decree of Allah, she accepts it. She knows that those years in which she was worshipping her Lord through looking after her family are not lost years – they are safe with Allah, written down amongst her good deeds. She knows that after the hardship comes the ease. She knows that she will not be burdened more than she can bear. And this gives her hope. So, after the tears are spent and the pain has subsided a little, she can begin to look forward, knowing that her identity as a Muslim is not tied to her husband and children. Her sisters will normally rally round, with advice and support or simply a shoulder to cry on. And she begins to look forward to the rebuilding, the re-discovery, the renewal, that will take place in the years to come. And she is grateful to Allah to still have her *deen*, her mind and body. And though that might not seem like much, it is enough to make her want to greet another day and make the most of it. For her, it is not the end of the world. And, fortunately, it is not uncommon in our community for divorcees to marry again and have a second go at creating a successful Islamic marriage.

Ingredients for a Successful Islamic Marriage

Though not exhaustive, this list is based on the guidance of the *Shari'ah* as well as personal experience and my conversations with the sisters.

- *Deen*

> 'The Prophet (s) said, "The best of you are those that are the best to their wives and I am the best amongst you to my wives" and that sums it up. If your husband is a good man and is a good Muslim, if he fears Allah, then he will treat you right and fulfil that saying of the Prophet (s).' Begum

The *deen* is the most important ingredient in a successful Islamic marriage. This means that the couple should respect the *deen* and its principles. They should conduct themselves within their marriage as it is laid out in the Qur'an and the *Sunnah*. The husband should act wisely and put the needs of his family first in a compassionate manner. The wife should support her husband in good deeds and obey him as much as she can. Their manners should be Islamic. There should be no lies, no deceit, no insults, no backbiting, no rudeness, no infidelity, no one-upmanship, no arrogance, no selfishness, no ungratefulness – as Islam has forbidden all these things. Their activities should be Islamic; no alcohol abuse, no drugs, no *zina*, no free-mixing, no nightclubbing – as Islam has replaced these with things that are beneficial and beautiful. A couple should strive in their *deen* together – study the *deen*, memorize the Qur'an, learn *du'as*, remind each other about Allah, correct each other, encourage each other in good – as Allah will bless all of this and bring them closer as a result.

'You try to enjoin the good and forbid the evil, try to do things that are pleasing to Allah together.' Layla

They must give each other their rights and fulfil their responsibilities and always be aware that Allah will ask them about how they treated each other.

'Everything stems from the *deen*. How the Prophet (s) was with his family, your husband should be like that or be striving to be like that.' Safwa

Also, the *deen* is a safeguard against

ill-treatment, as the spouses are not responsible to each other but are ultimately answerable to Allah. All of these things bring a couple together and bring Allah's blessings to the marriage, for it is He who has the ability to make a marriage successful or not.

- *Appreciating each other*

'A Muslim husband should respect his wife for the duties she fulfils – appreciate the food she cooks, acknowledge the way she raises your children, say "*alhamdulillah*" for the way your wife dresses Islamically when she is out, praise her when she looks after the house. For the woman, appreciate the fact that your husband has gone out to work and provided for the family, tell him when you feel content and secure in your home, appreciate what he has done for you.' Umm Muhammad

Indeed, the Prophet (s) said that he who is not grateful to the people is not grateful to Allah. Just saying 'thank you' to each other may sound basic, but it is something that is often forgotten in the ebb and flow of daily life.

• *Communication*

> 'A marriage will only last if both of you know how to solve problems together because there will be problems, all the time. But if you don't know how to solve problems together, that is when you differ so much that you have to part. Also respecting the other person's suggestions. If you can do that constantly, the problem doesn't become a further problem – you reach peace pretty soon after.' Hajar

Couples must talk to each other, share their feelings and resolve their differences openly and honestly. A lack of communication often leads to misunderstandings, feelings of neglect, resentment and alienation. Problems should not be left to fester or be swept under the carpet. Often, the best way of dealing with a problem is to talk about it a while after the initial upset. That way, the couple can discuss it when they have calmed down and are not on the defensive.

• *Patience*

And seek help in patience and prayer . . .
Surah al-Baqarah 2:45

Like all things that bring great rewards, marriage has its tests. A couple will not always agree, will not always please each other and will encounter obstacles along the way. Patience is essential in such times to keep the marriage going and eventually work the problems out. Being patient means not transgressing the bounds that Allah has set – it is not all right to withhold each other's rights just because you have had a falling-out. Being patient also means overlooking and making excuses for each other's weaknesses, faults and mistakes. Marriage is hard work and will not succeed if either partner is hasty, impatient or intolerant.

• *Humility*

Being married to a proud and arrogant man or woman is a nightmare: they will not accept suggestions, criticisms or complaints. This leads to the other partner feeling frustrated and resentful. Both partners should recognize that they are not infallible and that humility is not a sign of weakness – it is a praiseworthy quality. Accepting criticism graciously leads to self-improvement and a mutually rewarding relationship.

• *Gentleness*

Indeed Allah is Gentle and loves gentleness, and He gives due to gentleness that which He does not give due to harshness.

Hadith of the Prophet (s), reported by Ibn Majah

As a rule, couples should treat each other with gentleness. There is no place for harsh words, foul language, raised voices or violence in a successful marriage. If the husband and wife treat each other with tenderness and sensitivity, they will both feel secure and safe within the relationship. This will only increase the love between them and make it easier to deal with any problems they may encounter. Obviously, there are times when gentleness is not possible, but it should be the general principle.

• Fulfilling your responsibilities

Allah has given the husband and wife responsibilities in a marriage and it is vital that these are fulfilled.

'Sometimes, you need to really be inspired and motivated to think, Let me make myself look nice and make a nice dinner for my husband, because if you let that laziness overtake you, then that's it. Because if every day, your husband is coming home to a slob of a wife and not very nice food, what do you expect but unhappiness in your marriage? It's reciprocal — you have to do nice things for him and he has to do nice things for you, it can't be one way or the other.'
Sara

The man should take care of his family's needs

and not become lazy and rely on others to support his family when it is *his* responsibility. They should both make sure that they are fulfilling each other's needs sexually. The wife should not allow her housework to pile up, neglected, for weeks on end. Not only is it sinful to neglect one's responsibilities but it leads to many marital problems. Among these are resentment, loss of respect for each other, quarrels and, very often, separation.

• *Keeping the home fires burning*
The Muslim husband and wife are encouraged to beautify themselves for each other and this has a wonderful effect on the marriage. Contrary to what is commonly done, the Muslim wife should make an effort with her appearance when she is at home, for her husband and herself, knowing that this adds sparkle and passion to the marital relationship. Keep the passion alive by exchanging gifts, little notes, planning romantic meals *à deux*, even if they take place by candlelight on the living-room floor after the children are in bed. The key is finding time for each other, to flirt with each other and make each other feel wanted.

• *Mutual respect*
One of the keys to a good marriage is respecting one another's personalities, character traits and opinions. In fact, the Muslim man is specifically

warned against trying to change his wife's character, in the *hadith* that states: 'The woman was created from a rib. If you tried to straighten the rib, you would break it. So be kind to her, you will then live in joy with her.' It is essential to respect each other's personalities, views and areas of expertise. Neither partner should belittle or insult the other as this leads to either loss of confidence or seething resentment. In a mutually respectful relationship, each partner feels valued and confident in their role within the marriage. There is no need for sarcasm or condescension in an Islamic marriage.

• *Having fun together*
Never overlook the importance of having fun together, of doing little things to break the monotony of the daily grind. The Prophet (s)'s relationship with Aisha was an example of such little things – they teased each other, played games, raced each other, told each other stories and spent quality time together.

'You can't just look out for your own needs. You want him to go out of his way to do nice things for you, so you go out of your way to do nice things for him. Be nice to each other, surprise each other, do things spontaneously, not the same old humdrum things, day in, day out.' Umm Muhammad

Striving to make our marriages an act of worship, obeying Allah, fulfilling our responsibilities and respecting each other are all 'love deposits'. Sharing thoughts and feelings, communicating and doing interesting things together help keep love alive, refreshing it, and adding to the balance of the 'love account' and keeping our marriages firmly 'in the black'.

8

THE MOTHER, THE
MOTHER, THE
MOTHER . . .

Just over a year after my *nikah*, my marriage, I
gave birth to my first baby. For nine months, I had
watched my body changing, blossoming, nurturing this miracle of life inside me. I approached
pregnancy and motherhood with great en-
thusiasm: I ate healthily, did gentle exercises and
devoured every single book on pregnancy and
childbirth that I could lay my hands on. I confidently prepared to have a home birth, having
been blessed with midwives who believed in it and
supported me all the way. I gave birth in the basement bathroom of our little flat, my husband and
midwife in attendance, assisted by nothing more
than water, homeopathic remedies and a healthy
dose of *du'a* (supplication). My son was born
healthy, with my mother-in-law next door and my
little sister cooking chicken upstairs. It was a

wonderful birth. And, just like that, I became a mother.

Bringing Forth Life

I always thought of carrying a new life inside me as an act of worship, of drawing closer to Allah. Why? Because having children is something loved by Allah, encouraged by Islam and a source of good in this life and, hopefully, the next. Because being patient with difficulties and hardships – morning sickness, heartburn, backache, aches and pains – is an act of worship. Also, the various inconveniences of carrying a child and bearing it are part of what qualifies a mother for the high status she enjoys.

Watching your body change, feeling the movements of the active life inside, seeing pictures of the tiny fingers, toes, the perfect little limbs forming, and reading about all the different things the baby is learning and doing – without any work on your part – is a humbling and inspiring experience. Humbling because you know that you yourself were like that once, because you are reminded that you have hardly any control whatsoever over what is going on inside your body – that Allah, the Creator, is in charge, and instinct and natural process have taken over. It is inspiring too, inspiring because Allah has chosen to bless your womb with this new life, because you are participating in a noble and ancient rite of passage, because you feel your body – your womb, placenta, the heart that is pumping all that extra blood around you – striving to fulfil its potential. It is a heady experience.

The same is true of childbirth. The potent mix of anticipation, pain, adrenalin and endorphins can be exhilarating – if you choose to see it that way! Indeed, we can all take inspiration from the story of Maryam, Jesus (peace be upon him)'s mother. According to the Qur'an, her mother had dedicated the child she carried in her womb to the service of Allah. However, when she gave birth to a baby girl, she despaired of her ever being able to fulfil that promise. But Allah had chosen Mary (Maryam) over all the women of Creation, to be the one who would be visited by the Angel Gabriel. He informed her that she would bear a child, a righteous child who would be honoured in this life and the Hereafter: the Prophet Jesus (Eesa). Never having known a man intimately, Mary was shocked, asking how she could bear a child when no man had touched her. The Angel replied, 'So [it will be], for Allah creates what He wills. When He has decreed something, He only says to it: "Be!" and it is.'

And so it was that Mary (Maryam) went into

labour in a lonely valley, far from her people. When the pain seemed almost too much to bear, she cried out in anguish and Allah blessed her with water beneath her feet and fresh dates to ease her suffering and rebuild her strength. He also blessed her with a son, Jesus (Eesa), who grew up to be a great prophet and who called his people to worship Allah and who, in turn, eased the suffering of many by the will of Allah.

There is something special about Maryam's experience – on her own in a lonely valley, a virgin giving birth to a child – something that inspires us to be strong and confident, trusting in Allah, knowing that He created and equipped our bodies for this task.

Our community is quite unique as far as Muslim communities go, in that men are often present at the birth of their children. This could be due to the fact that most of us are from Western backgrounds, where fathers routinely attend their babies' births. However, historically and even today, in most traditional societies, men are kept far away from the birthing process, which is seen as the female domain.

Our husbands act as birthing partners in hospitals, birthing centres and during home births. In hospital, they are indispensable for support, encouragement, and reminding the birthing mother to remember Allah and to supplicate to Him, not to lose hope or become despairing. They also ensure that Islamic guidelines are adhered to, particularly with regards to our privacy and making sure our wishes are respected. These are some of the biggest drawbacks of hospital births, as far as sisters are concerned: as women who habitually cover ourselves in front of strangers, we feel the lack of privacy and control over our labour environment even more keenly. In the privacy of your own home, during a home birth, you are comfortable in your own space: you don't have to worry about male medical students observing you in all your glory, about strangers coming in to give you 'an internal', strapping your legs up or telling you to lie on your back and PUSH! With a midwife normally in attendance, you can labour at your leisure (within reason), free to take whatever position makes you comfortable. You can play recitations of the Qur'an, eat your own food and not worry about the state of your hair after a couple of hours in labour. And afterwards, there is your own bed, your husband and, hopefully, the older children still fast asleep in their rooms.

'Baby Planning'

Much to the chagrin of some of our non-Muslim mothers, most sisters do not use a 'reliable' form of birth control. There are several reasons for this. One of them is that the Muslim believes that it is by the will of Allah if a woman becomes pregnant or not. As human beings, we know that we can 'tie our camels' – take the necessary steps to ensure the outcome we prefer – but, ultimately, we know that the end result is in the Hands of Allah: if one is destined to fall pregnant, it will happen.

As the Prophet (s) said, when he was asked about performing *coitus interruptus*, 'If you pour that fluid that produces children on a rock, Allah would bring forth a child from it. Surely, Allah will create any soul that He wills to create.'

Another reason why birth control is not widely practised is that Muslims are encouraged to have many children – it is part of the *deen*. The Prophet (s) said, 'Marry a woman who is loving and can bear many children, because I will boast of your numbers [on the Day of Resurrection].' As a result, Muslims around the world have some of the highest birth rates – and our community is no different. Unlike the majority of families in this society, it is not uncommon for a Muslim couple to have four children or more.

Now, to many people today, large families are a symbol of backwardness, of days gone by when human beings didn't know how to control their reproductive systems. The Muslim sees things differently: in the eyes of Allah, children are a blessing, not a curse or a 'lifestyle inhibitor'. We don't see our lives as being geared towards a certain standard of living – the two cars, a front and back garden, a holiday abroad every year – and thus see children as coming in the way of that. Children are more precious than all those material things and they are treated as such. So practising Muslims of all financial backgrounds celebrate large families and rejoice at the news of a new addition to the *ummah*, making *du'a* that the child fulfils its potential as a good Muslim, a true servant of Allah.

In addition, many Islamic scholars consider it impermissible to limit the number of children one has due to financial concerns. This is because of the saying of Allah:

> Do not kill your children for fear of poverty. We provide for them and for you. Indeed, their killing is ever a great sin.
> Surah 17:31

Thus we believe that each child is born with its own provision already decreed by Allah, independent of its parents. However, there are times when contraception becomes necessary. According to Islamic law, in a situation in which a pregnancy or birth may lead to the injury or death of the mother, the mother's needs take precedence. In such cases, contraception would normally be used, as well as when there is a need to manage the demands of pregnancy and child-rearing.

'Still No Baby?'

In the past, in most societies around the world, a woman's worth was measured solely by her role as a mother – if she did not conceive she was considered worthless, a waste of space, and her husband was usually urged to replace her with a woman who could provide offspring. In some cultures, this is still the case.

However, this is not the case according to Islam. Allah says in the Qur'an:

> To Allah belongs the dominion of the heavens and earth. He creates what He wills. He gives to whom He wills females, and He gives to whom He wills males. Or he couples them as males and females, and he renders whom He wills childless. Indeed, He is knowing and capable.
> Surah ash-Shoorah 42:49–50

The practising Muslim woman does not consider having babies her sole purpose in life – she was created to worship her Lord. If she is able to do that through having children, that is a blessing, but if she isn't, there are many other ways for her to grow close to Allah and lead a fulfilling Islamic life.

Umm Muhammad told me, 'Very often, cultural Muslim societies do not really understand Islam. We know that we have to believe in the *qadr*, the divine decree, that nothing happens unless Allah wills it. The man and the woman may do the act but it is up to Allah if the woman conceives. Everything is by the will of Allah – whether you have a boy or a girl, whether you're rich or poor, it is the decree of Allah.'

This point led me to consider another 'thorny' issue – that of how girl children are perceived in Islam.

Before Islam, Arab communities practised female infanticide, burying their baby daughters alive and, indeed, in many communities where cultural Islam is the norm, there is still a stigma attached to giving birth to a girl. Allah condemns this in the Qur'an in the strongest terms:

And when one of them is informed of a female [born to him], his face darkens with suppressed anger. He hides himself from the people because of the ill of which he has been informed. Should he keep it in humiliation or bury it in the ground? Unquestionably, evil is what they decide.

Surah an-Nahl 16:58–59

There are also several *hadiths* that speak of the specific reward of raising and taking care of female children. The Prophet (s) said, 'Whoever nurtures two girls until they reach puberty, he will be with me on the Day of Resurrection like this.' And he brought together his index and middle finger.

> 'In our community, if it's a boy or a girl, it's the same. If a sister's had loads of boys, and then she has a girl, everybody's ecstatic and if she's had loads of girls then has a boy, it's the same thing.' Yasmin

The Mother, the Mother, the Mother . . . Then the Father

In so many cultures throughout the world, the mother holds a high and dignified position: she is the bearer of life, the carrier of future generations, the nurturer of tomorrow's people, she heals, she soothes, she comforts, she loves – she is the strong yet tender backbone of society. Islam is no different. Allah says in the Qur'an:

> And We have enjoined on man [to be dutiful and good] to his parents. His mother bore him in weakness and hardship upon weakness and hardship, and his weaning is in two years. Give thanks to Me and to your parents, unto Me is the final destination.
>
> Surah Luqman 31:14

The Prophet (s) was approached by a man who asked him, 'To whom do I owe my good company?'

The Prophet (s) replied, 'Your mother.'

The man asked, 'And then who?'

He (s) repeated, 'Your mother.'

'And then who?' came the question.

'Your mother,' was the reply.

'And then who?' the man asked again.

'And then your father,' answered the Prophet(s).

Based on this and several other *hadith*, the mother is given a very high position in the life of the Muslim. Needless to say, that position is hard-won, and involves making the home a comfortable, safe haven as well as being patient with all the trials and tribulations of rearing children and preparing them for life.

A Woman's Work

As I mentioned earlier, part of the Muslim wife's role is to keep the house in good shape. Initially, I found that very hard, mainly because I had never done that, having grown up in Zimbabwe with housekeepers all my life. Also, I found it tedious and boring, a waste of time, as far as I was concerned. There is no glory attached to being house proud in our society, particularly as a young woman. It is much more hip to be too busy to waste your time cleaning the skirting boards unless, of course, you can claim 'domestic goddess' status – then, it's almost forgivable. But then, when my older sister came to see me from overseas, she said something that made me have a rethink. I was ironing some clothes, complaining about how much I disliked it, when she said to me, 'And what's wrong with nurturing your home?'

And I thought to myself, It's true – what is wrong with nurturing your home, keeping it clean and looking nice? And then I thought of the reward that I knew I would get from Allah, in this life and the next, if I treated my housework as an act of worship – it would mean that all that effort spent keeping the house in working order, no matter how tedious, would be worthwhile. I had become embarrassed by my family's thinly veiled, though good-natured, attempts to make me take better care of the house – I didn't want to be known as slovenly so I literally decided to clean up my act. I stopped seeing it as a waste of time and started looking at it as an act of worship, fulfilling my side of the bargain, getting it out of the way so that I could focus on other things that were more enjoyable. And when I did that, it became so much less of a burden.

> 'I can't say to you that I enjoy housework all the time but because I see it as worship, I can do it – that gives me the ability to do it.' Sara

In the eyes of Allah, the 'housewife' has honour and dignity for the role she plays in the family unit and thus the society as a whole – she is the glue that holds it all together. The prevalent attitude that many men (and women) have, that looking after the home and raising children is somehow inferior and deserving of a lower status, could not be further from the Islamic viewpoint. The *deen* recognizes that the home is the first training ground for all members of society and its care and atmosphere deserve to be prioritized, not left to the end of the list. If the home life is secure and loving, there is a better chance of its products – the children – growing up to be well-adjusted adults. Therefore, the worth of the woman who looks after the home and family should never be underestimated.

Tests and Blessings

In the Qur'an, Allah says,

> Allah has given you spouses from yourselves, has granted you from your spouses, children and grandchildren and has provided you with good things for your sustenance.
> Surah an-Nahl 16:72

Thus, Muslims see children as a favour from Allah, a favour that we are grateful for. They are also viewed as a trust: they are on loan to us from Allah and it is a religious duty and act of worship to nurture them.

'When you have children, it makes you look at the world in a different way – you just want to make it a better place for your children because they are not ours, they're Allah's and they are given to us on trust.'
Layla

As Hajar's son Faris was born to her before she started practising Islam, I asked her about the difference between being a mum as a non-Muslim and as a Muslim.

'My role as a Muslim mother is completely different from that of a non-Muslim. Before I used to act as if I owned my son. Now I don't – I totally appreciate that he is "on loan" to me and I will be questioned about what I did with that loan. Now, I'm a lot more focused on the Hereafter in his upbringing, and then whatever he does with his life is up to him. *Insha Allah*, it will be the right thing.'

Because our children are only on loan to us, we should treat them as we would anything precious belonging to someone else: with care. Thus it is important for us to treat them well, look after their needs, be patient with them, teach them right from wrong and give them all the love, care and attention they need to grow up into confident, well-adjusted Muslims. Sara, who has a little one-year-old, put it this way: 'It's like an *amanah* – a trust – placed in your care by Allah. That's how I try to look at it sometimes when I've been lazy about changing his nappy or any other aspect of caring for him. You've got to remember that he is a blessing from Allah and you have to do your best with him. You'll be answerable for his formation, education, *tarbiyah* – his nurturing upon Islam.'

But parenthood, as everyone knows, is not a

bed of roses. Like everything in life that brings immense rewards, it requires hard work, dedication and, sometimes, sacrifice: children can also test you and push you to the limit. Indeed, Allah describes them thus when He says:

> And know that your possessions and your children are but a trial and that surely with Allah is a mighty reward.
> Surah al-Anfal 8:28

And indeed, children test their parents on many levels – your *deen*, your time, your body and your mental state: anyone who has had to endure a tantrum in the middle of a crowded supermarket knows that. But, because the raising of children is one of our main religious responsibilities, one that we will be questioned about by our Lord, it acquires increased importance in our lives – it is our top priority as Muslim mothers.

Full-time Mums

Between the breastfeeding, the nappy changing and the broken sleep, I unashamedly and unreservedly fell head over heels in love with my baby. I had been amazed by the miracle of birth and now I marvelled at his perfect little fingers and beautiful big eyes.

The style of childcare favoured by most Muslims is based on several aspects of traditional childrearing, among them breastfeeding and sharing a bed or a bedroom for the first months of life. But, most important of all, our version of parenting involves being a full-time mum.

It never occurred to me that I should be out working instead of caring for my baby; that my time would be better spent in an office than reading with him; that I belonged in board meetings instead of the mother and toddler group. I didn't feel demeaned by staying at home to look after my baby – I felt privileged, and grateful that I could afford to make that choice.

For centuries past, in almost every culture and civilization, a mother's place was in the home – taking care of her children. Islam teaches these same values. Although today, the majority of mothers work part or full time and use a variety of childcare options to make sure their children are taken care of, many are choosing to stay at home in order to look after their children full time. Be they traditional women with 'conservative' values or 'earth mothers' keen to raise their children as close to them as possible, a significant number of women (and men) believe that the mother is a child's best caregiver. Amongst Muslim women, this view seems to be held regardless of whether the sister in question is educated or not, whether she previously held a top career or always wanted to be a housewife – once she becomes a mother, her priority is her child. That is not to say that a Muslim mother cannot work outside the home. Indeed, in many Muslim societies and communities, sisters, aunts and grandmothers see to the care of the children while the mother goes out to work as a doctor, dentist, teacher, student or any of the other jobs that Muslim women do.

Part of the Muslim mother's job is bringing her children up with good, strong role models. These are role models that embody the essence of good character: faith in Allah, righteousness, as well as the universal values of humility, honesty, courage, generosity, kindness, compassion, mercy and strength. The greatest of these role models is our Prophet Muhammad (s) and teaching our children about him, encouraging them to love him and follow his guidance, is one of our main priorities. Other Muslim role models include the prophets, the companions and the righteous people of the past, as well as some of the upstanding Muslims of today.

This nurturing also includes cultivating the child's awareness of Allah, his love for Him and his purpose on this earth. It involves teaching him the traditions and rituals of Islam – the ritual cleansing (*wudhu'*), the five daily prayers, the fast in Ramadhan, the various prayers and supplications that are recommended throughout the day – when getting dressed, eating or leaving the house, for example. In essence, the upbringing of the Muslim child is an act that concerns one's religion and working on a career concerns one's worldly life. For the Muslim, it is clear which should take precedence.

However, not every stay-at-home mum is comfortable in that role. As I always have something on the go, some project or other that I am involved with, I have avoided, even if only in my own mind, the title of 'full-time housewife'. Mei admitted quite candidly that being a housewife was not really her thing either, telling me, 'I never wanted to be a housewife, I don't like that word, I don't like that occupation. Even though housewives are highly respected in Islam, that role doesn't suit me. I was brought up to be a career woman. Sometimes, the situation gets to me and I have to remind myself that my family is the most important thing in my life, that they are a gift from Allah and then I get happy, and when I get happy, I find a little more time for myself.'

Teacher

The ideal Islamic family has a strong foundation: the belief in and worship of Allah. This is its basis and its reason for being. Everything in that family – the relationships between its members, their manners, their aspirations, their activities – revolves around it. As converts, this was an entirely new concept. We knew that, as mothers, one of our most important roles was that of teacher. But, in order to fulfil that role, we had to re-examine our own families, our childhoods, the influences that we grew up with – judging between the things we wanted to emulate and the things we needed to cast aside. In our efforts to establish an Islamic family worthy of the name, without examples within our own families, without elders, knowledge or experience to guide us, we found ourselves on a steep learning curve – one that continues to this day.

As reverts, we all made a clear choice – we *chose* Islam over our previous belief systems. Our children have not been through that decision process. Although a child born of Muslim parents or a Muslim father is considered a Muslim, this does not in any way guarantee the soundness of their faith, their *iman*. *Iman* is not hereditary, as many cultural Muslims of today seem to think. Because the teaching of Islam is our main function as parents, we need to explain the *deen* so that it can be understood and appreciated by our children, so that they can develop true faith based on knowledge, not superstitions, cultural norms or fear. As a school-teacher herself, Rabia feels that sisters need to remember what it was like to be new to the *deen*.

'We have to remember the way we learnt the *deen*,' she said. 'Everything was explained to us, we read, we learnt, and that's how we have to teach the children as well. We have to go back to that time when we didn't know anything about the *deen* and teach the children in the same way.'

One of the advantages of living in the West is that Muslims have taken Western forms of media and reinvented them in the service of Islam. One of these is children's media – books, tapes, games, CDs – all these are now available to help children to learn about Islam in a fun way. Through stories and songs, the children learn about all the prophets and their stories, as well as the Prophet Muhammad (s) and his family and companions, giving them an understanding of their heritage and history as Muslims, as well as a certain pride in their way of life.

Islamic Education at School

Almost all the sisters in this book either send their children to Islamic schools or teach them at home. Some people do not understand the attraction of an Islamic school but many practising Muslims feel that it is a 'gentler' alternative to the non-Muslim state school system, in which children are exposed to all sorts of influences, many of them at odds with our beliefs.

An Islamic school environment fosters an awareness of the centrality of Allah in our lives, how the child should relate to his Lord, knowing Him, loving Him and understanding his duties towards Him. At its best, the environment nurtures a love of the *deen*, of Islamic manners and morals, of the Islamic way of life. It affects his relationship with others, how he treats other people, his manners, his language, his actions; and also his own sense of confidence and identity and, eventually, the kind of person he will develop into. It helps to make the Muslim child secure and confident in his or her Islamic identity; they don't feel embarrassed that they can't eat ham sandwiches, they don't feel self-conscious when it is time to pray or when they are fasting, they don't have issues about wearing the *hijab*. In short, they have the opportunity to see the Islamic way of life – their way of life – as 'normal'.

Eid and Christmas

A concrete example of another benefit of the Islamic school environment is that Muslim children don't feel self-conscious about not celebrating Easter or taking part in the Christmas play. According to the *Sunnah*, the Muslims have two festivals (*Eids*) in the year, *'Eid ul-Adha* and *'Eid ul-Fitr*. The month of Ramadhan is a sacred month and each Friday, *Yawm ul-Jumu'ah*, is a special day. These are the celebrations legislated by Allah. So how does the Muslim child feel when he sees all the books, films and advertisements showing the colourful presents under the tree at Christmas, the bright lights of Diwali, the shimmering candles on the birthday cake? It is only natural for a child to want all those things but, as Muslims, we are not permitted to join in these celebrations. So how does the Muslim parent, living in the West, make up for all of that?

Instead of giving in to prevailing norms that are against our religious beliefs, as many feel compelled to do nowadays, we substitute and we improvise. My son has never had a birthday party in his life but, for *'Eid ul-Adha* a few years ago, he had a special party for all his friends, with balloons, Pass the Parcel, races and sweets and presents galore. Some sisters make a point of making each Friday a special occasion and really make an effort for *Eid* and Ramadhan – buying new clothes, doing projects, visiting relatives, organizing children's parties, outings or trips abroad.

'Even if it tires me out, I will go out of my way, I will take them out and do things with them because they have to have that memory of *Eids*, no matter what. It makes them proud of their religion and who they are.' Mei

Curriculum and Islam

Another benefit of an Islamic school is that there is a better chance of achieving a balance between Islamic knowledge and the curriculum subjects like Maths and English. Because the Islamic faith is so focused on learning – and there is so much to learn – it cannot be sidelined in the education of a Muslim child. It is not just about sending your child to learn by rote at the *madrasa* in the evenings after school – there is a lot more to it than that. The child must be helped to truly *understand* his religion and develop a love for it and a pride in it.

'I think that the most important thing for children to have is the *deen* because the *deen* will rectify anything else. The *deen* provides the perspective.' Sara

That is not to say that sisters believe in neglecting the curriculum education. However, it is all too easy to over-emphasize the worldly aspects of a child's education, as Sara explained to me: 'Some parents are very ambitious in terms of academic achievement, they want you to be a professional but that is not the end goal for us, it is a means to an end. I think it's about striking a balance.'

Personally, I want a well-rounded education for my children, an education that includes learning about their *deen*; becoming fluent with written and spoken languages; learning Arabic; understanding Maths, Science, the way things work; understanding and learning how to recite and memorize the Qur'an; knowing world history and culture as well as their Islamic heritage; developing their creative talents through art; learning about discipline and their physical abilities through sport; developing good manners, an honourable character, a love of learning and of reading, and encouraging a curiosity about life and people and a desire to live a life that is full and meaningful. It is that balance of spiritual, mental and physical development – of *deen* and *dunyah* – that, as Muslim parents, we strive to attain.

Balancing the *Deen* and the *Dunyah*

On a day-to-day basis, it is easy to get distracted by the concerns of the *dunyah*, the worldly life.

We may be working so hard on a particular project, or getting so stressed out at work, that our *deen* takes a back seat: we find that we are not studying as we used to, no longer praying with focus and concentration, not reciting the Qur'an. Our society presents us with so many distractions in the form of work and leisure pursuits that it is not hard to find one's mind completely taken up with all these activities – and neglecting the worship of Allah. That is not to say that we are expected to be praying or reading the Qur'an every minute – the Muslim is commanded to be balanced and that is the example of our Prophet (s). However, just as the student who is studying for an important exam cannot afford to regularly abandon her books to go and hang out on the high street, so the Muslim cannot afford to leave the worship of Allah for worldly pursuits for too long. We therefore have to strike a balance between our religious life – our *deen* – and our worldly affairs – the *dunyah* – with ourselves and also with our children.

Like Sara's father, there are some Muslim parents who so desire the *dunyah* for their children – a good education, material comfort, status, entertainment, leisure pursuits – that they completely neglect the *deen*. This is often the result of prioritizing the *dunyah* over the *deen*. It is a narrow, materialist view of what is important in life.

There are also Muslim parents who deny their children each and every aspect of the *dunyah*, claiming that 'all they need is *deen*'. These children may not be schooled adequately, have no time or space for leisure and grow up to be ill-equipped for life in the big bad world. Theirs is a narrow, restrictive view of what Islam is about.

The way of Islam is balanced, halfway between these two extremes. None of us wants children who have no knowledge of their *deen* and, similarly, we do not want to handicap them by denying them the knowledge of the *dunyah* and the pleasurable aspects that are *halal* (lawful), within reasonable limits.

So many of the things in this world that are detrimental to our mental and physical health are bright and attractive, sweet and tasty – and this is even more so with our children. Today, all these things are beautifully packaged and aimed right at our children – on their TV channels, during their cartoons, at their eye level in the shops – it's all calling to them.

'I think children are given far too many rights to decide in our society,' Hajar told me, 'which means they make far too many mistakes in their choices. I think they have to accept the fact that we are their parents and, at this stage, we are the ones who know better.'

When she said that, I thought of tantrums, good food left on plates, endless pestering for sugary snacks and junk food, eyes goggling at the TV screen all afternoon, little girls dressed up to look like Christina Aguilera – and I found that I agreed with her. Indeed, when many of us were new to the *deen*, with young children, we tried to shut the door to all of it.

Taking us back a few years in the life of our community, Rabia told me, 'When the sisters first started having their children, there was this kind of "shut them off from the rest of the world" trend. Very strict: no this, no that.'

However, as the children grew older and we grew more experienced, things began to change.

'Then the children got to six or seven and started to have voices and they started to ask questions. Then they got to ten, eleven, and they started to get attitudes. So the sisters started to change their approach as well: you can't shut them off and hide them in a box. They realized that it wasn't an ideal world where the children were going to grow up to be perfect Muslims.'

Indeed, we came to realize that it was not going to be possible to shut out the outside world, the *dunyah*. It was everywhere and we couldn't ignore it – neither could our children. So we had to begin negotiating space, knowing when to allow and when to restrict, knowing what to expose them to and what to keep from them, at least for the time being.

'You can't cushion them, put cotton wool around them – you can't do that. My husband and I are more realistic. His approach is: let them be exposed to it – not too much – but always be there to explain. When you're too strict and then you let them go, they just go right across to the other side.' Mei

Hajar put it this way: 'I feel that I can't cocoon my son. If I lived in Yemen and knew that we were going to live and die in Yemen, I would give him a "solely Islamic" upbringing, but all the communities that I have lived in have had a strong *dunyah* element that has been hard to ignore. But if I tried to deny him all of that, I would become the oppressor, and I don't want to be the oppressor in his life.'

Old School, New School

In the Qur'an, Allah puts great emphasis on children obeying, respecting and being kind to their parents. In many different verses, being dutiful to one's parents is mentioned immediately after worshipping Allah alone, the foundation of the Islamic faith.

> And your Lord has decreed that you worship none but Him. And that you be dutiful to your parents. If one of them or both of them attain old age in your life, say not to them a word of disrespect, nor shout at them but address them in terms of honour.
> Surah Al-Isra 17:23

'It's a mixture of love and respect. When I think of my upbringing, I think, Why did I obey my father? Not because I was scared of him, I obeyed him because I loved him and I had this huge respect for him.' Sara

When I asked Umm Muhammad about her parenting style, she told me, 'I would say, yes, my parenting style is that my children must obey me but at the end of the day, I've got to deal with things in a way that they understand – I cannot dictate Islam to my children. I've got to *teach* Islam in a way that makes them want to follow it.'

This emphasis on obedience must be tempered by the gentle, loving nature of the relationship between the parent and the child, as described in the Qur'an and the *hadith*. The Prophet (s) himself was very loving and gentle with children.

Once, a man saw him kissing his child and said, 'I have ten children and I have never kissed any of them.' The Prophet (s) said, 'He who does not show mercy will not be shown mercy.' The Prophet (s) also said that Allah grants to gentleness that which He does not grant to harshness.

> 'You can be as strict as you want as long as you have communication, respect and fairness. And show them lots of love so that they know you love them.' Hajar

So, although Muslim parents expect high standards of obedience and respect from their children, there is also a great emphasis on having a loving relationship with them. And, when it works, I have been impressed by children who are respectful to their parents, who do as they are told but who are also not afraid to express themselves and laugh and joke with their parents. The difference is, they know when to do one and when to do the other.

My own parenting style is in a constant state of flux. As a practising Muslim, it's not possible for me to adopt a *laissez-faire* approach to childrearing – allowing my children to do whatever takes their fancy, without any regard for the limits set by Allah. As parents, both mother and father are responsible for teaching their children right from wrong, as well as the morals and manners of Islam, and they will be questioned by Allah about that.

But, like many parents of our generation, we are faced with a bewildering array of opinions on the best way to achieve this. We waver between the traditional approach – obey your parents, respect your elders, do as you're told, no talking back – and the modern liberal approach – respect your child's opinion, give him choices, communicate with him. I find that neither of them works all the time and I have to mix and match them to suit different situations. There are times when I only have to remind my son about Allah and what He loves for him to do the right thing. At other times, like mothers the world over, I find myself talking constantly, bargaining, negotiating, banging my head against a brick wall – the frustration is terrible. Like many other parents, Muslim and non-Muslim, we are still negotiating a space halfway between these two very different parenting styles – the battle is not yet won.

Teenage Years

The teenage years are a turbulent time for every young person, but particularly for the Muslim. There are so many conflicts, so many difficult choices, so many temptations. In Western society, the teenage years are like a grace period, a time when you have independence but few responsibilities, when you are developing your own persona but are still under your parents' roof. Thus, a certain amount of rebellion and general rowdiness is expected, if not by every parent, then by every parent on an American sitcom!

In Islam, the human being is accountable for his actions as soon as he reaches puberty. There is no grace period during which bad behaviour is tolerated or indulged – in the eyes of Allah, there is no difference between the teenager on drugs and the adult on drugs – their sins and misdemeanours are equal, except that one might have the excuse of lack of knowledge.

There are few Muslim teenagers in the West today that appreciate this fact and, as a result, even Muslim homes are witness to rows about hair, clothes and body piercings. More often than not, these are more a result of culture clashes than religion. There are some parents who, having grown up with certain cultural norms, try to force these on their thoroughly Westernized children who, of course, are having none of it. These parents think that it is OK for their child to learn the ways of their host country from nursery to senior school, at which point they try to re-assert a sense of culture and national identity that the child does not possess. When I read about cases such as these, my heart bleeds for the frustrated parents and the even more frustrated and confused teenager. However, I have witnessed instances of teenagers growing up in the *deen* and sticking to it, content to submit to the laws of Allah, not because their parents are Muslim but because they themselves believe in Islam. This is usually the result of a high level of knowledge, worship and study within the home and efforts to provide *halal* outlets for the usual teenage frustrations.

While most teenagers are into the latest pop group or soul diva and look up to them, emulating their behaviour and their style, this is not the case with the practising Muslim teenager.

Sixteen-year-old Rumaysah told me: 'I look at some of the qualities of the women *sahabah* – the companions of the Prophet (s) – and I look at my mum's friends. I think that they are strong human beings: they've been through different hardships and they're still strong.'

However, although anyone seeing her on the street, clad in black from head to toe, would have trouble believing it, there are many things that she and her peers have in common with every other teenager: 'I think I am the same as other teenagers, apart from the fact that we're Muslims and there are certain things we don't do that they do. We like the same clothes, fashions, like everyone else.'

So, I asked her what she wanted to do with her life, to which she replied, 'I want to do a lot of things. I do want to improve my knowledge of the *deen*, plus I want to do certain things for my future so that I can get a better job so I can have nice things like a nice house, nice car – being OK financially as well as in my *deen*. I'd like to travel to many different countries and I'd like to be a beautician or a dental nurse too.'

Phew! And is she in a rush to get married?

'I'd like to get married and have children but it's not that high on my list of priorities – I want to finish doing what I'm doing first.'

I asked her mum if she worried about her children becoming weak and leaving the *deen*, turning away from their Islam. With her usual level-headedness, she said, 'It's not a fear for me. It's something that I wouldn't want to happen but it's not something that I fear because, at the end of the day, Allah is the One who guides.'

Something that has always bothered me, when it comes to Muslim teenagers, is the moral double standards that are rampant in so many Muslim communities, resulting in girls being locked up in the house in an effort to safeguard their chastity and the family honour, while their brothers are allowed to go out and stay out, drinking, doing drugs and sleeping around. It is as if, as in so many societies around the world, it is all right for the boys to break all the rules, but woe betide the girl who puts just one foot out of line. However, this attitude has no basis in Islam: both boys and girls are expected to obey the laws of Allah.

Umm Muhammad and I discussed the issue of raising girls and boys and I found her approach refreshingly different to the prevailing tradition.

'It's no harder raising a girl than a boy, as far as I'm concerned,' she said. 'Islamically, whatever they gain in this life, their reward is the same with Allah. So, in my mind, my son should be brought up the same as my daughter. It's not that my daughter should be pious and my son should run round the streets, sleeping around with girls – that happens in many cultural Muslim households. I feel my son should follow the same principles as my daughter, because this is Islam – Islam is not about letting your sons do one thing and your daughters do another.'

I asked Yasmin what her hopes were for her zany teenage daughter Sumayyah and she said, 'Firstly, I would like her to be a good Muslim, knowing her Lord, knowing her *deen*, knowing her rights – it's important to me for my daughter to know all that.'

Work/Life Balance

As Muslim mothers, our lives are shared out between our *deen* (study, acts of worship, time to contemplate), our families (household chores, childrearing, looking after hubby) and ourselves (improving ourselves, pampering ourselves, relaxing), and, as with most mothers, this last aspect is often the most neglected! It is obligatory for us to study our *deen* and to continually strive to improve ourselves as worshippers of Allah. Not only do our families have rights, but, as is mentioned in a *hadith*, our bodies have rights too, to be looked after and kept in good health.

'I have to make that special effort to make sure I spend time on myself, my body and to study the *deen* – if I don't do that, then I feel worthless.' Mei

Although most of my sisters are full-time mothers, not all of them are at home, doing housework all day, with loads of children running around. There are sisters from our community who manage impressive balancing acts, often juggling family commitments and work or study. It is not easy, though, to find a job that is Islamically appropriate, that allows us to cover the way we want to and that fits in with our families.

However, this obstacle has been overcome by many sisters who either own their own businesses or work freelance or from home. One of the sisters from our community, Karima, runs a very successful catering business outside London where *she* calls the shots: she works in her *niqab* and her food speaks for itself. She has always told me that, if your work is good enough, people will hire you no matter what you look like. But, like so many other 'working mothers', that role comes with its own challenges and its fair share of angst.

I started working when my son was just over three months old – I guess I couldn't help myself. With the encouragement of some of the mums who lived near me, I began a little Islamic home school for the children in the area. A year later, we had nine children and covered all the curriculum subjects – it had become a major part of my life.

However, as my little son grew, I began to feel more and more guilty. He was no longer going to play at a sister's house in the mornings and he wanted to be involved in all the children's work – with quite disruptive consequences. And then, when I went to visit my friend in Wales, I found that her niece, who was the same age as my son, was already saying words and naming pictures. I was horrified – I hadn't had the time or the imagination to read those little books with my son, and I felt terrible. What was I doing? Allah was not going to question me about those other children – He was going to ask me about my own child. How could I justify neglecting my primary responsibility for the sake of work that I was not even compelled to do for financial reasons?

I decided that my son had to be my first priority and I told the parents that we would not be re-opening in the new term. And I was able to devote my time to exploring, discovering and developing my son's talents. But still, I felt restless. I knew that what I had done was right in the eyes of Allah – after all, my child was my responsibility and I couldn't neglect that. But my creative juices were flowing and I began writing children's stories and rhymes and picking up my paintbrush again, knowing that these were things that I could comfortably fit around my baby's needs. And that was the main criterion for me – I knew that I wanted to work, to use my time creatively and have outside interests, but I didn't want to neglect my primary role in doing that.

However, I loved the outlet that the creative activity of being a writer and illustrator afforded me and I enjoyed working with my publishers. It was also a privilege to produce imaginative children's books about the *deen* and, hopefully, contribute to a better understanding of Islam.

Other sisters who work express similar feelings about their jobs – they are a release, a change of scene and a social activity, as well as a source of income.

> 'It's hard, but I enjoy it. I enjoy my job, I enjoy socializing and meeting people. I love being around the sisters: it lifts my *iman*, we'll talk about things, we'll laugh, we'll discuss. So even when I have a holiday, I'm happy for the break but I do miss being around the sisters every day.' Umm Muhammad

But there was never any doubt in my mind that my primary role was that of a wife and mother and, now and again, I had to remind myself of that, putting the work aside to attend to the needs of my family. I have always felt very strongly that, if I take care of my obligations, Allah will bless whatever else I do with success. And, *alhamdulillah*, He has proven me right so far.

And so, combined with having a close relationship with our young ones, teaching them about Allah, explaining our way of life and the world around them, spending quality time with them, having fun together and creating a rich and varied family life, we as Muslims in the West hope to give our children the best that an Islamic childhood has to offer. And if it works, our children will not feel hard done by – they will find happiness, fun and fulfilment within the fold of Islam.

'I was proud to be a Muslim and I want my son to have that. I think if he feels privileged to be a Muslim, it will combat all the stuff out there that appeals to his desires. I don't want him to feel like he is lacking in anything.' Layla

Establishing a true Islamic family is not an easy task – but it is a noble one. It is essential to the well-being of our community and of future generations, for it produces upright children who, hopefully, grow into upright adults and go on to produce more upright Muslims. In this way, through sticking to our principles and living according to the will of our Lord, Allah, the true Islamic family serves as a fine example of what the Islamic way of life can offer society.

9

ROOTS AND
FOUNDATIONS

If becoming Muslim, getting married and having a baby were adventures that I embarked upon within Islam, learning about and appreciating Islamic values – submission to Allah, patience, seeking knowledge – was one of the greatest and most enduring. Learning submission to my Lord was the hardest after years of glorified rebellion. Patience was an easier lesson to learn, bringing with it serenity and self-control. Seeking the knowledge of the *deen* started with those first uttered verses of the Qur'an – how halting they were at first and then, year upon year, they soared with confidence, with the knowledge of Arabic. And knowledge brought precious gifts of inspiration, understanding and introspection. For the life of the Muslim is not just governed by the daily workings of the *halal* and the *haram*, the lawful and unlawful. Muslim women are not merely defined by their *hijab*, their marriages and their children. At their best they are, like their Muslim brothers, human beings trying to master their desires, trying not to succumb to impatience and despair and, in what is one of the greatest journeys, seekers of knowledge. They are students of the *deen*, always searching, enquiring, memorizing and acting on what they have learnt. It is these values, and not the mundane acts of everyday life, that give us our strength, our courage, our resilience and our hope. These values underpin who we are and give coherence to our way of life.

I have addressed many of the most controversial issues surrounding the topics of Muslim women, as well as issues that are at the core of our daily lives – the way we dress, our marriages, our children. All these are like blossoms and fruits in the branches of a tree. But it is important to remember that the tree is made up of more than its foliage – it has a trunk and deep roots. These roots underpin our values and must be explored in order truly to understand what it is to *live* Islam.

Striving to Submit

There are few words that are as unpopular in today's society as 'submission' and 'obedience'.

These concepts are the antithesis of the 'freedom' of our modern-day liberal democracies. In fact, using English words to describe certain Islamic concepts is a very dicey business. There are so many words that we use regularly in Islamic parlance that have negative or pejorative connotations in the modern Western context, among them, 'submission', 'obedience', 'righteousness' and 'piety'. In fact, nowadays, it seems that anything that smacks of religious devotion is ridiculed.

This is not the case amongst Muslims. We do not share society's scorn of these and other values that are encouraged by Islam. This is possibly one of the factors that makes the Muslim world so incomprehensible to the West: in our communities, God still matters and, amongst practising Muslims, He is at the centre of our affairs.

> 'One of the questions I ask myself is: Have you really submitted? I suppose even to this day, I wonder if I really have. I would say I have, but Allah knows best what is truly in my heart.' Aliyah

Indeed, submission is at the core of our faith and the way we live our lives. This submission is, firstly, to Allah and His Laws. This means loving what He loves, staying away from what is displeasing to Him, believing in His Word and living according to His rules. All of this entails submission because, as Sara told me, 'when you find the truth, the truth isn't always going to be what you like'. There are times when what we know we *should* do is in conflict with what we *want* to do – pay the bills instead of flying off for the weekend, reading some of the Qur'an instead of watching television – life is a constant battle between duty and desire. Indeed, it is stated in a *hadith* that, while the Hell Fire is surrounded by pleasures and temptations, *Jannah* (Paradise) is surrounded by hardships, things that take sacrifice and struggle. Of course, once you have done your duty, you experience the satisfaction that comes with knowing that you have done the right thing. In Islamic parlance, striving to do your duty instead of giving in to your desires is called fighting your *nafs*.

> 'For me [submission] means giving up what I want to do for what Allah has told me to do.' Layla

I asked sisters what 'submission' means to them and, for all of them, fighting their desires is a central part of it.

In Sara's words: 'Submission is about finding peace with Allah, finding peace within yourself and being able to be honest with Allah. It's about putting aside your desires because everything that He asks us to do is good for us in one way or another. We may not appreciate it, we may not understand why, but everything He asks of us is good for us. That is why you find peace in obeying Allah. When you're not obeying Allah and you know that His Word is true, that His Command is true, you're in turmoil. Personally, when I'm not obeying Allah, I am not at peace with myself.'

Our society is infatuated with rebellion. We consider it admirable to go against the status quo, to challenge authority, to push the boundaries. So how does that fit in with a culture in which the authority in question is the Lord of the heavens and the earth? When the boundaries are set by Him, for all time and for the whole of mankind? Clearly, in this context, rebellion cannot maintain its glamorous image.

Contrary to the Western view, obedience, and not rebellion, is considered a good character trait in Islam. Obedience has been prized by societies the world over for thousands of years and, in those societies, citizens were expected to obey those in authority, their elders and the various traditions and taboos. Much has changed in recent decades. However, in Islam, although obedience is praised, it is not unconditional: it is only permissible to obey when being commanded to do good. There is no obedience in tyranny, oppression, sin, transgression, deceit or wrongdoing. And obedience in Islam is based upon proof. Submission and obedience do not mean that we blindly follow any mullah that happens to say two words about the *deen*. They must prove their statements and, if what they have brought is the truth, then, and only then, do we hear and obey.

Patience

In numerous places in the Qur'an, Allah commends the quality of patience. He praises the prophets – Nuh (Noah), Ayyub (Job), Ya'qub (Jacob), Muhammad (s) and the righteous people – Maryam (Mary) and Assiyah (Pharaoh's wife). They are all praised for their fortitude and forbearance, particularly with the hardships involved in obeying Allah and calling people to worship and obey Him.

> Verily, Messengers were denied before you [O Muhammad (s)], but with patience they bore the denial, and they were hurt, till Our Help reached them, and none can alter the Words of Allah. Surely there has reached you the information about the Messengers (before you).
> Surah al-An'am 6:34

The quality of patience goes hand in hand with submission because, of course, submission isn't always easy. The *jihad-un-nafs*, the spiritual battle with one's desires, is neverending and needs constant vigilance and a lot of patience. Patience with obeying Allah, patience with the trials that this may bring, patience with other people, patience with the promise of Allah. Patience will enable you to keep that *niqab* on in the height of summer; patience will stop you giving up on a troubled marriage; patience will make you strong enough to complete the fast when your stomach is literally crying out for food; patience stops you cursing fate when things don't go your way.

Patience is indispensable in the life of the Muslim. It is our refuge in times of hardship – we are patient with our situation, knowing that Allah will replace the hardship with ease, that He answers our supplications and that He is the Most Merciful to His slaves. Patience is our safeguard against doubt and despair and is the key to our serenity.

> *Salamun 'Alaikum* (peace be upon you) because for that you persevered in patience! Excellent indeed is the final home!
> Surah Ra'd 13:24

Liberation

All this talk of submission, obedience and patience makes us sound like long-suffering martyrs. Is this really the life of the Muslim? Hopefully, what has preceded in this book will allay any such fears. But, lest it be thought that the life of the Muslim is a type of incarceration, a type of oppression in itself, I asked the sisters whether they were liberated. And I refused to allow easy, sound-bite responses!

Firstly, and most importantly, Islam liberated us from not knowing the purpose of our existence. It answered so many of our questions: 'Why am I here?', 'What is the purpose of my life?', 'What is the meaning of life?' A man once said to me that he never asked himself any such questions, that he was quite happy living life from one day to the next, taking each day as it came. Perhaps he was telling the truth. But every civilization that man has produced has, in its own way, sought to answer these questions, through religion, philosophy, mysticism. Humans are undoubtedly spiritual beings, we have higher aspirations, greater expectations and we have always tried to reach the ultimate understanding of what we are here for. We are not like animals who are born, eat, mate, have offspring and die purely by instinct. We have free will and we make our own choices. And our Islam showed us the choice that is beloved to Allah, that will lead to our happiness in this life and the next.

Umm Muhammad, the former party girl, said this: 'I'm liberated from the unknown. I used to come home from parties and sit at the window and think, This is not life. This cannot be what I was created for. I believed there was a God and I believed that He was out there. I used to say, Please show me what I'm here for. I cannot be here just to jump up and down at this party, come home and sleep, go shopping the next morning and go to work on Monday. This cannot be my purpose. I'm not going to just die and discover that that was my purpose. But now I feel totally liberated and I feel happy with my *deen*. Allah has opened my heart. I've understood why I was created and I'm pleased with that. I'm happy with my Lord wanting me to worship Him. Why shouldn't I want to worship Him? I feel quite liberated because I'm not a slave to society and I'm not a slave to anybody's ideas of Islam. I'm a slave to what my Lord has asked of me.'

Islam also freed us from seeking fulfilment and happiness with the fleeting, transient things in this world. As Claire told me, 'Islam liberates you from certain things, like your image, presenting yourself to society as you think you should, achieving academic or career goals you think people want you to achieve. You still want them when you become a Muslim but you have a strong framework and principles to work by.'

> Whoever's worries were the Afterlife, Allah puts richness in his heart. He corrects his affairs and the world will be compelled to come to him. But whoever's greatest worries were the world, Allah puts poverty in front of his eyes. His affairs are put in disarray and no worldly gain will come to him except what has already been written for him.
>
> *Hadith* reported by At-Tirmidhi, weak but made hasan by supporting chains, Al-Albani

Unlike many, we do not believe that money buys happiness. Even if we are blessed with material comfort, we do not look to that alone to bring us happiness. For happiness does not come from having great wealth or fame – it comes from being content with what Allah has given you. We are not victims of the materialist brainwashing that has consumed so many in the world. For us, wealth is a means to an end, not an end in and of itself. We know that it is from Allah and that it is a test as well as a blessing – we will be questioned about how we spent it. Did we squander our money with wanton extravagance, with never a thought for how we could use it better to help others and to help ourselves in the next life? All this makes us free from the consumerist values that the media seek to impart.

> 'Before Islam, I never had enough, I was always running, running, running. In Islam, there is liberation: I've found I have enough now, and I'm happy, *alhamdulillah*.' Claire

It is all too easy, when one has reached a certain level of material comfort, to keep looking ahead, aspiring to the next level. If one does not achieve that level, one becomes frustrated and discontented. Relationships come and go, children leave home, jobs change, houses are sold, health deteriorates – all the things we rely on to make us happy, that give meaning to our lives, are transient. For Muslims, it is only Allah, The Ever-Living, that is constant, through good times and bad, and it is only submission to Him and love of Him that will carry us through all those times.

As Muslims, we do not champion the latest beliefs, the fashionable religions, the trendy ideologies. We know what we believe, we know right from wrong, and we don't feel the need to fit in to whatever ideas are popular at any given time. What we have and hold onto is constant and solid. It is a rock in the middle of a turbulent sea, where 'truths' are as many as those who peddle them.

> 'I thought I was happy – until I came to the *deen*. Then I realized how unhappy I was because I was always conscious about looking a certain way, trying to socialize and keep up to date with people, keeping people happy – so many things to live up to. But when you come to the *deen*, you realize that you don't have to do that to be liked.' Sadiqa

Pondering more on the subject, Claire mused, 'Coming to grips with the demons in my own character – impatience, lack of self-control, pessimism – compared with the lessons of patience, self-control and optimism that Islam has taught me. I think you let go and when you let go, you feel free.'

Because Islam sets such high standards – in terms of belief, worship, character, manners and relations with other people – it has given us something noble and lofty to aim for. We are no longer content to live vapid, shallow lives, never working to improve ourselves or purify our souls. We are constantly striving, never standing still and, because of this, we have been saved from mediocrity. Our every act has meaning, a meaning beyond the everyday, the worldly.

'Islam has liberated me from self-pity and self-obsession. Islam gives you so much optimism, I think, even [in] simple things like looking at those worse off than you, appreciating the things that you have, realizing Allah's favours upon you.' Claire

Because we believe in Allah's word and trust in Him, we are free from despair and hopelessness. There is never a time when we feel that there is no more hope, that things will never change, that life is not worth living. To be a Muslim is to be confident, never despairing of Allah's aid.

The Islamic lifestyle is one that protects those who live it from many of the most harmful aspects of today's society. We are safe from addictions, alcohol and drug abuse, sexually transmitted diseases, unwanted pregnancies, abortions, sexual harassment, among so many other things.

On issue after issue, sisters echoed each other's sentiments and, in essence, they all said the same thing: we feel liberated by our submission, by our Islam.

'Iqra!'

Iqra! [Read!] In the name of your Lord who created, created man from a single clot of blood. Read, and your Lord is most Merciful . . .
Surah Alaq 96:1–3

Ever since these first verses were revealed to the 'unlettered prophet' (s), Islam has been a religion of study and scholarship. The companions – *sahabah* – learnt their beliefs and the rulings of Islam from the Prophet (s) himself. They, in turn, taught it to the next generation – the *taabi'een* – who passed that knowledge to the generation after them. And after them, throughout Islamic history, scholars have kept the knowledge of Islam alive. They established cities and centres of learning, from Madinah to Baghdad, Andalusia to Timbuktu. Scholars, men and women, pondered over ancient texts and considered responses to the challenges and issues of the day.

But such study is not the sole preserve of the scholars. The Prophet (s) said, 'Seeking knowledge is obligatory for every Muslim', and, indeed, from the beginning of our Islam, we wanted to learn for ourselves. So we read, asked questions and discussed what we had learnt. We weren't prepared to accept anyone's statement unless they could back it with proof – Qur'an, *sunnah* or the statement of one of the scholars of the past – something that would prove that it was truly Islamic and not someone's uninformed or jaded opinion.

'Ilm and Iman

Having come to the *deen* with little serious study behind me, I was still learning about Islam as I went along. Often, I would express very strident views that were in complete contradiction to Islam, arguing my point with ferocity, until I would read something, a verse, a *hadith*, that would show me that Allah said something different. That was one of the biggest tests of my submission: letting go of long-held ideas once I realized that they were in conflict with what Allah and His Messenger said. Unless it was something I already agreed with, it was often only after reading and poring over the proofs and pondering the arguments that I would actually abandon something that was not allowed.

And that is what gaining knowledge of something does to you: it makes you see things differently, and your priorities change. It happens all the time. For example, at some time in your life, you may have considered Mills and Boon sophisticated literature, but once you've read Shakespeare, you know differently, and your views on Mills and Boon soon change – I hope!

It is the same in the *deen*. When you learn about the importance of the prayer and how it wipes away sins like a clear stream cleans away dirt, you feel differently towards it: you take more time with it – and you expect more from it.

When you learn about the wisdom of fasting and how it erases all the sins of the previous year, you feel differently towards it: you are more determined to do it, determined to control your desires.

When you learn about the immense rewards you get for reading the Qur'an, you will make greater efforts: you won't give up when the Arabic twists your tongue or when you stumble and stutter, you will only try harder.

'There is such a vast amount of knowledge out there and obviously whatever you get, you have to try and act upon it. That's the scariest thing about knowledge: once it comes to you, you have to act upon it. It is a big responsibility. If you read something or you learn something or you're told something, the pressure is on you to actually act upon it.' Aliyah

Knowledge also increases your faith. You become firmer in your beliefs and the path that you have chosen. When you read about the reve-lation of the Qur'an, the reasons for its revelation, the way it was gathered, its miracles, it strengthens your faith and your resolve.

When you learn about Allah's names and attributes – He is The Most Merciful, The Oft-Forgiving, The Kind, The Appreciative, The

Loving – you never despair of His forgiveness and you are keen to offer your good deeds.

This is the effect of knowledge on a person's *iman* – their faith.

And all this makes you a better Muslim, a better person, an example to those around you. Indeed, the effects of knowledge on the individual and the society should never be underestimated.

Seeking Knowledge

My own experiences of seeking knowledge began when Sandra, Hanah and I would travel across London to attend Islamic talks. Through these journeys, we began to become familiar with the most common terms used in the field of Islamic knowledge – *fiqh* (Islamic jurisprudence), *'aqeedah* (belief), *'akhlaq* (morals and manners) and *tajweed* (the art of Qur'anic recitation). Attending talks was not only our spiritual nourishment, it was our social scene as well. I remember going with my usual crew to a talk being given by a prominent American speaker in Central London – there was so much excitement, seeing other people we knew, some in *hijab* for the first time, meeting new sisters, other reverts, all of us participating in this great event that was not only enjoyable but rewarding as well – it just felt like the best, most beneficial type of weekend activity.

After I got married and moved near a mosque with a large revert community, I found myself in a community where seeking knowledge consistently was prioritized. Here, the emphasis was more on regular Islamic classes rather than occasional Islamic talks and, thus, my learning became more focused. For the first time, I attended regular lessons, keeping my notes diligently and memorizing whatever the teacher had set for us. My husband and I both attended these classes and we would often look over each other's notes, conferring and testing each other.

One of my best experiences was when the mosque, along with some other centres, organized a weekend conference in a town in the north of England. I have never had a weekend like it.

They had hired the grounds of a university and the student halls of residence were to be our rooms for the weekend. Coach loads of people had arrived, from all over the UK, and the whole place was full of Muslims, all gathered for a noble purpose: to gain knowledge. Amongst the women, there was an atmosphere of warm sisterhood; everyone smiled when exchanging *salaams*, shared what they had, spoke to strangers. The teenage girls all hung out together, looking grown-up in their *abayahs* and half-*jilbabs* and scarves, catching up on a year's worth of news. The children flitted about and played on the wonderful green lawns, secure in the knowledge that their mothers were never far away.

On the Sunday morning, I left my husband and baby sleeping in our tiny room and walked across the grounds in the early-morning calm after the dawn prayer, secure and unafraid, to the food hall where a number of sisters had gathered. There, an older Pakistani lady gave an Islamic talk, a rousing talk that touched our hearts, brought tears to our eyes and smiles to our lips. Afterwards, we spoke for a little while, exchanging our thoughts and feelings, and then we got up to pray the extra prayer that can be offered at mid-morning. And when we had breakfast together, a serenity settled around us.

It is hard to describe the feeling in the air between people when one is involved in seeking knowledge as part of a group. The one time I felt this more than any other was when we had a week of seminars on Islamic disciplines, taught by foremost students of Islamic knowledge. That week was one of such intense concentration and study that it welded us together. To me, all those early mornings, walking through the still-quiet estates to the school where the seminar was held; the days spent next to each other, close, learning, listening, taking notes; the evenings spent revising, discussing and memorizing, in the *masjid* and in individual houses dotted around the city, put a special light in the sisters' faces, a sparkle in their eyes. In one *hadith*, it says that when Allah is mentioned in a gathering, the angels gather round and make *du'a* for the people in that gathering. During that special week, it was as if we could hear the rustle of the angels' wings, hear their murmuring voices and see the light that settled on everything. We were elated, quietly, still absorbing the magnitude of the experience. We had sought refuge from all our *dunyah* concerns – no one was rushing off to work, to school, to quiet a crying child: if only for this week, we were not mothers, wives or daughters: we were students of knowledge. The world outside seemed to fade away as we listened to the cadences of the teachers' Arabic, followed the rhythm of the translators' speech, felt the grip of the pen and the scratch of the paper beneath it. And all the while thinking, What an amazing *deen* . . . what a wonderful *deen*! We were learning so many things that we hadn't known before, clarifying things that were previously unclear, and we felt privileged to be taught by such eminent scholars.

I won't forget sitting in the *masjid* on one of the afternoons after class, revising what we had learnt that day with a group of sisters. We asked each other the proofs for different religious rulings, the conditions for the various *hadith* gradings, the rules of *tajweed*, the core beliefs of Islam. And, while all this was happening, I happened to catch sight of some of the younger girls, newer to the *deen*, who had come by the *masjid* to pray. The look on their faces – the admiration, the awe and the envy – was a reflection of the beauty of what we had. Very few Muslims ever get to study the *deen* in any kind of depth, let alone in such a heady atmosphere. Our *iman* was so high, our faith so strong, that we felt like we could easily have given up the *dunyah* (worldly life) and everything in it just to keep sitting there in that classroom, learning about the *deen* for ever.

A few lines of poetry that I wrote at the end of the seminar were read out during the closing gathering and I think they truly summed up how we felt about the scholars, the '*ilm* and the *deen* at that time:

Your sisters in this *deen*
Are overwhelmed by *yaqeen* [certainty]
That seeking knowledge is the nourishment
For Muslimaat and Muslimeen [Muslim
    women and men]

How grateful we are
For the favours of Allah,
That we shared in this honour
And took hold of our *deen*
With firm hands,
Firm hearts,
Your sisters hate to part
From our beloved scholars
We have grown to love so much.

The tears haven't dried,
The hearts are still sad,
That our leaders are leaving us
To the mercy of this land.

We hate to return to old ways,
That dull, lifeless *dunyah*
After this exquisite nourishment
That has brightened up our hearts.

Our appetites have been whetted,
Our thirst far from quenched,
May Allah make it a thirst that drives us,
Seeking knowledge to the end.

So now, we give our *salaams*,
Insha Allah, these aren't the last,
May Allah unite our hearts once more
After this time has passed.

Jazakum Allahu khairan
From your sisters in Islam,
May we strive together, establish the *deen*,
Taste the sweetness of *iman*.

Seeking knowledge sincerely leaves you changed as a person. Your manner is different, your outlook changed and your actions altered. It is a similar feeling to the fast in Ramadhan – you are involved in worship non-stop and it feels so *good*. For someone who has never experienced the high that comes from spiritual or religious study, it must sound strange to hear it described in terms more befitting a psychedelic trip. But, at its best, that is what it is: it is food for the mind and the soul and its effects are long-lasting, seeping into every area of your life. I remember how, as newlyweds, my husband and I used to battle with public transport, travelling out of London, for a couple of hours at least, to attend an Islamic talk that took place in a family home. Then we would make our way back across the city, tired, late at night, the last few passengers on the train. We did all this for the reward, the buzz, the boost of learning about the *deen* and being with other people who, with their gentle manners and kind smiles, were there to learn about Allah too.

The 'Ilm Will Set You Free

There are many theories about the reasons for the general malaise that is to be found in certain Muslim communities around the world. Some blame it on the failure of those societies to modernize, to democratize, to catch up with the West. Others say that it is a result of poverty and ignorance. And still others blame it on Islam.

Throughout the world, Muslim communities are beset by different trials – low employment rates, disaffection of the youth, discriminatory attitudes towards women, as well as political and religious turmoil. It would take a different book to address the causes of all these problems from the Islamic perspective, something I am not qualified to do, but the one factor that is common to nearly every one of these societies is the general lack of Islamic knowledge. Gone are the days when Muslims studied their religion seriously and put what they learnt into practice. And if one were to wonder why one makes a fuss about Muslims having knowledge of their *deen*, one only has to look at the results of a lack of knowledge and understanding: political upheaval, terrorism, materialism, greed, corruption, domestic violence, amongst other social woes.

Returning to the authentic Islamic knowledge

and putting it into practice has many benefits, on both the personal and the social level. At its best, when a person begins to learn about Islam and practise it, his character changes – he becomes God-fearing, knowing that Allah can see and hear everything he does and that it is being written down and that he will be questioned about it all; he becomes more careful about what he says and how he says it, controlling his temper and staying away from lies and backbiting; he is careful with how he treats other people, knowing that they have rights over him; he is cautious in his business dealings, staying away from dishonesty, trickery and *haram* transactions, such as usury (interest); he is more socially responsible, seeking to alleviate the suffering of others, giving charity and helping others where he can. And even when problems arise and mistakes are made, he returns to Allah, seeking His forgiveness, and to the Qur'an and the *Sunnah* to resolve them according to the laws of Allah. In essence, he begins to embody the noble characteristics of Islam: the *taqwa* of Allah – humility, generosity, honesty, kindness, mercy, amongst so many others. A society made up of such people would be a great society indeed.

And a society that is established upon the sincere worship of Allah would be showered with His blessings as all things are possible for

Him, be it good rains, good governance, peaceful families or the happiness of the individual.

I suppose what I am saying is that Muslims possess the tools for their own regeneration within their *deen*, but they will only be able to access those tools with *'ilm* – the sincere study of the *deen* and the application of all that they learn.

Some may find this an over-simplification of the problems that face us – but, as Muslims, we must believe in the promise of Allah:

> Allah has promised those among you who believe, and do righteous good deeds, that He will certainly grant them succession [to the present rulers] in the earth, as He granted it to those before them, and that He will grant them the authority to practise their religion, that which He has chosen for them. And He will surely give them in exchange a safe security after their fear [provided] they worship Me and do not associate anything [in worship] with Me. But whoever disbelieved after this, they are the *Fasiqoon*.
>
> Surah An-Nur 24:55

Not everyone cherishes the ideal of a society run according to secular principles, a society established on capitalist, materialist values, a society without moral boundaries, a society where neighbours are strangers, a society where women are sexual objects on every billboard and magazine cover, a society where there is no mention of Allah, no remembrance of Him. However much some would like to believe it, to many this is not the climax of human culture and society. Indeed, Muslims see a different way forward, because their foundations and roots are completely different. I believe, as Islam teaches, that gaining knowledge of the *deen* is one of the first steps towards building societies that are shining examples to the whole of mankind, Muslim and non-Muslim alike. There are those who will scoff at all this, claiming that Islam's time, like the times of the Greeks and the Romans before it, is over; that the supremacy of the liberal democratic '*deen*' has been established once and for all. To these people, especially the Muslims amongst them, I ask them to question themselves: did Allah create them? Did He truly reveal the Qur'an as guidance to the whole of mankind, for all ages? Was His Prophet (s) true to his call? If the answer is no, then they are free to say whatever they like – Islam has no hold on them. But if they answer yes, then they must be prepared to look at the world in a new light, in the way that Allah sees it, as He has made clear in His Book and through His Messenger. For us

Muslims, the revelation is not some passing
fancy – it is the truth, and it is binding.

> But whosoever turns away from My Reminder
> [this Qur'an] verily, for him is a life of hardship,
> and We shall raise him up blind on the Day of
> Resurrection. He will say: 'O my Lord! Why
> have you raised me up blind, while I had sight
> [before]?' [Allah] will say: 'Likewise, Our verses
> came unto you, but you ignored them and, like-
> wise, on this Day, you shall be ignored.'
> Surah Ta-Ha: 124–126

I believe that the lack of authentic Islamic knowledge in our societies is felt most keenly by us, its
Muslim women. It is we who suffer most when
general levels of *deen* are low, when we do not
know our rights and when the men either don't
know them or don't fear Allah enough to give
them. It is in societies such as these that we do
not inherit, cannot divorce, and are barred from
the mosque. It is we who are oppressed by
patriarchal cultures and chauvinist attitudes. It is
we who are cut, carved and killed, depending on
the prevailing customs. It is not Islam that
oppresses Muslim women, it is the lack of
knowledge or the application of that knowledge
that oppresses.

In the beginning, Islam was a liberating force

for society as a whole and women in particular. Before Islam, women in Arabia, like most parts of the world, had hardly any rights – they could be married off at will, had no rights to property or inheritance, were treated like chattels, and, worst of all, the shame of having a daughter was so great that it was customary to bury baby girls alive. Islam gave women protection – the right to life instead of death, to their own legal and social identity, to be educated, to trade, to consent to their marriages, to sexual satisfaction, to stipulate conditions for their marriages, to receive the dowry themselves, to end those same marriages if needs be, to attend the mosque, to study the *deen*. At that time, women questioned the Prophet (s), were taught by him, migrated with him, fought wars alongside him and died for the cause of Islam. There was Khadijah bint Khuwaylid, business woman, first believer in the Prophet (s)'s message and his loyal supporter; there was Sumayyah, the first martyr of Islam, who refused to renounce her faith while the men around her did so; Asma bint Abi Bakr who, alone and under cover of darkness, took food and news to the Prophet (s) and her father while they were in hiding; Basibah bint Ka'ab who fought so bravely during the Battle of Uhud, and many others. It was during this time that the first female scholars of Islam came into being –

women like Aisha bint Abu Bakr who not only taught the women as is to be expected, but taught the men also. She was the first of a long line of female scholars who excelled in their study of the *deen*, narrated *hadith*, memorized whole volumes, taught thousands of students, dictated books and produced some of the most famous scholars in Islamic history, including Imam Malik and Bukhari, the great compiler of *hadith*. These great women, and others like them, all had different personalities – some were wise, some impetuous, some knowledgeable, some courageous, some defiant, some compliant. But they were honoured by Allah and hold high positions in the history of Islam and amongst the Muslims – all this at a time when women in the West and elsewhere were still fighting to be recognized as beings with souls and as legally separate from their husbands.

And then, somewhere along the way, this noble tradition began to die out until, today, one can count the number of female scholars on one's fingers. And, as the general level of knowledge declined, so did the knowledge of the women and so did their status and position in society. And where women do not understand their *deen*, they do not know their rights, and when they do not know their rights, they cannot fight for them. And so generations of daughters grew up seeing their mothers living this way and they accepted it, and generations of sons saw their fathers acting this way and they accepted it – until all their society could lay claim to was the name 'Muslim' and their society looked nothing like that which the Prophet of Allah (s) came with. This is the great tragedy of ignorance – that it breeds a culture of ignorance, a culture that, in the end, stifles the beauty of what the people might have had.

It is thus my belief that only when Muslim societies return to the knowledge of their *deen* will they begin to fulfil the great promise of Islam and truly reap its rewards, in this life and the next.

> This precious knowledge
> Has been placed
> In the care of our hearts,
> Glowing like the midnight star,
> A candle in the dark.
>
> May it flow through our hearts
> And limbs
> The speech upon our tongues
> May it reflect on those around,
> Our husbands
> And young ones.

May Allah make that bright light shine,
Light up our families,
Brighten up our hearts and homes
And our communities.

If our communities are strong
And strive to know Allah,
The great goodness will manifest
And grow, *insha Allah*.

And as it grows, it will bring forth
Children who will strive
For *'ilm*, for closeness to *Sunnah*,
For good in both their lives.

O Allah, make that sweet light shine
And change the things we do,
Change our souls,
Our families

And change this ummah too.

10

THE ULTIMATE SISTERHOOD

My sisters
are descended
from Caribbean slaves
and Spanish slave-owners,
from African queens
and colonial masters,
from Berber nomads
and Prussian farmers,
from village peasants
and landed gentry,
from rich
and poor,
from Black,
White
and Brown,
from Muslim,
Jew,

Christian
and Hindu.
They have been brought together
by Islam,
in this time and in this place.
Their lives have brushed mine,
changing it,
enriching it.
Blessing it.

In between the *hijab* and *jilbabs*, the courtship and the marriages, the children and the new value system, I discovered another jewel in my Islamic life: sisterhood. I felt it in the mosque, when the greeting of peace – *salaams* – and the low hum of recitation would fill the room. I felt it during the congregational prayer – the *salah* – when female bodies stood close together, shoulder to shoulder, uttering silent prayers, bowing and prostrating. I felt it at the newborn celebrations and the *waleemahs* – celebrations of women, children and food. I felt it during Ramadhan, when we broke the fast together and when we stood together for the long *Tahajjud* prayer. The closeness, the solidarity, the security, the love: the warm glow of a sisterhood based on so much more than a shared gender. For this is the sisterhood of Islam, a sisterhood to surpass all others, a precious and sparkling jewel that lights up the women's faces as they speak about their feelings for their sisters in Islam.

'She Thinks She's So *Nice*'

I grew up without a sense of true sisterhood. In the cut and thrust of adolescent social politics, there was no room for sentimentality and feminist romanticism.

To be fair, as a teenager, I had a few close female friends but we were never part of a big group of girls who all got along – there was too much rivalry for that. So we clung to each other, happy to be just two, maybe three together. It was regularly said about us, 'They think they're so *nice*!' by other girls who considered us a threat. There was certainly no sisterly love – just jealousy, one-upmanship, and an incredible bitchiness. Confidences were betrayed, promises broken, and boyfriends stolen.

But of course, having said all that, a lot of the time, we were just the same as most other girls around the world: we gossiped and talked about other women behind their backs, or in front of them, depending on the occasion: 'Some people should be looking in the mirror *before* stepping outside!' or 'Eeh, she ain't doing herself any favours in those trousers!' So, we were not innocent victims: we too could be heartlessly cruel as we belittled other women and showed them up in company. There was no loyalty, no sense of solidarity, no looking out for each other: it was every girl for herself.

A glance at most of the magazines that are aimed at teenagers and young women will show the kind of mindset that we were encouraged to have. Invariably, the main topics are men, sex and fashion. Or sex, men and fashion. Or fashion, sex and men. Maybe with a little make-up and male centrefolds thrown in for good measure. And these magazines trumpet the whole 'liberated woman' image, selling themselves as magazines that cater for the 'woman of today'. Had they not, in fact, exchanged the banality of cleaning implements and apple pie recipes for the equally banal obsessions with appearance, status and sex, sex, sex? No wonder most of us never had anything important to talk about if this was what we were aspiring to!

And although the girls I hung out with were like our peers with regards to our teenage cattiness, we considered ourselves to be just a little bit more intellectual than the majority of the girls we knew, girls who rarely read a book or the paper, watched the news, asked questions, formed opinions or explored beyond their own little worlds. Although there were a host of societal reasons why many girls didn't apply themselves, we didn't care: all we knew was that we wanted a challenge – and 'chilling' with the girls was not the way to get it.

As those teenage years drew to a close, we came to spend more time in adult male company. Friendships with these grown men were different from the ones we had had with schoolboys. While it was rare to find a girl who could hold a decent discussion on anything beyond guys, relationships and clothes, men were versatile: they could discuss current affairs, politics, philosophy and the more important things in life. They had opinions and weren't afraid to express them or argue their points. Also, they didn't spend the evening bitching about their friends and gossiping about other people's private lives. They didn't moan about how there were no good women left, complain about their girlfriend or about the size of their beer bellies. Sure, they had a tendency to ramble a bit when it came to sport or cars but, by and large, their company was fun and stimulating.

But, as I mentioned earlier, friendships with men were rarely ever free from the frisson of sexual attraction. If the girl didn't harbour secret feelings for the guy, he undoubtedly harboured secret feelings for her, feelings that were just waiting for an opportunity to express themselves. So, although spending time with men was more fulfilling in many ways, it was a double-edged sword: one was always self-conscious and had to be careful not to show *too* much flesh, be too vivacious, too 'free', lest a girlfriend or, worse still, the guy himself, get the wrong idea. As a result, there could never be total trust and confidence in the platonic nature of the relationship – an out-of-town girlfriend, a late-night ride home, a particularly fun night out, all of these were opportunities for the guy to finally make a move and tell his 'best friend' his true feelings. Often, this would be followed by a complete breakdown in that relationship – how could things ever be the same now that she knew that he saw her 'like that'?

Women Friends

However, when I went to university, I found myself amongst young women who were intellectually and emotionally stimulating and who didn't spend all day talking behind each other's backs. These were young ladies like myself who questioned things, who analysed situations, who argued their points coherently. We had political and intellectual conversations *all* the time, and we shared our thoughts and feelings on personal issues too. Many women experience this change in their adult friendships with other women.

However, one of the things that most sisters mentioned when talking about their friendships before coming to Islam was the level and frequency of backbiting, gossiping and bitching. It is not possible to tell how many 'women-hours' are used up talking about each other or other people, telling secrets, spreading rumours, lies, fabrications, most of it masquerading as friendly advice or the latest news. As Sara put it, 'You would say, "I'm not bitching or anything *but* . . ."' And while it is fun to be the one 'dishing the dirt', making everyone laugh with your barbed insults and sarcasm, it is not quite the same being on the receiving end, when others are bitching about you, pulling apart your dress sense, your taste in men, tearing your whole life to shreds over cups of cappuccino. But, often, this is not something that we stop each other from doing – we just fall into it naturally and everyone conspires to keep this great feminine tradition alive.

Although there *are* instances of men and women relating to each other in a mature, sexually neutral way, in my experience, these relationships are few and far between. It is as if men come with their own energy – their testosterone, their machismo, their self-confidence – that reacts with the female energy and makes women start batting their eyelids, flicking their hair, changing their tone of voice and suddenly that camaraderie, that solidarity and dominance of the female energy is gone. There is a new tension in the air and men are at the centre of it.

Claire told me about an incident that reminded her of all this. A friend of the family had come to visit her mother and she could hear them talking. All of a sudden, the woman's tone of voice completely changed – it became girly and playful – and she couldn't figure out why. Then she found out: a man had just walked into the room. 'Some women just can't help themselves in front of men,' she mused, 'and you see the change in them. It's like it's not the same person – it's *quite* profound.'

It is the male presence that makes women see each other as rivals for their attention and makes them compete for the spoils of the mating game. And while men occupy this central role in female relations, true solidarity and sisterhood will remain an elusive dream, a slogan on a T-shirt.

Love for Your Sister . . .

In Islam, relations between women are governed by the norms and forms of Islamic sisterhood. Muslims are taught to view each other as brothers and sisters in the faith and to love each other for the sake of Allah.

As Allah says in the Qur'an:

The Believers are but a single brotherhood . . .
Surah 49:10

In a *hadith* reported in Sahih Muslim, the Prophet (s) said, 'It is sufficient honour for those who love one another for the sake of Allah, men and women alike, to know that their almighty Lord will take care of them on the Day of Judgement and will say, "Where are those who loved one another for My glory? Today, I will shade them in My shade on the day when there is no shade but Mine." '

Sisters have rights upon each other – to exchange the greetings of *salaams*, to visit each other when sick, to advise each other, among others. And the same manners that apply to our other relationships are applied to our friendships amongst women – we respect each other, only speak well of each other, are honest, kind, generous. Indeed, the *hadith* literature is replete with exhortations and advice on how to conduct ourselves as brothers and sisters in Islam. One example of this is the statement of the Messenger (s), 'Beware of suspicion, for speaking on the basis of suspicion is the worst kind of lie. Do not seek out one another's faults, do not spy on one another, do not compete with one another, do not envy one another, do not hate one another, and do not turn away from one another. O servants of Allah, be brothers/sisters!'

However, there are other factors that make Islamic sisterhood a force to be reckoned with. The Islamic way of life – the social structure, the division of male/female space, the *hijab* and the role of the family – is uniquely suited to fostering close, trusting and supportive friendships between women.

In the Islamic social structure, the home is considered the female domain. It is her responsibility and she is queen of it. It is there that she removes her covering, that she lets down her guard, that she spends time with those closest to her – she is herself there. Great emphasis is also placed on generosity and hospitality – there is reward in feeding your guests and Muslims are encouraged to visit one another. It is therefore not uncommon to go to a sister's house and find it full of women reading, relaxing, cooking, talking: being free. We find a women-only space, a sanctuary where men are excluded. Men cannot enter a room where there are other women – they have to stay out and call their wives or children if they need them. Most men have no problems with their wives spending time with the sisters without them, as they too spend time with the brothers.

Another factor that greatly influences our

relationships is the fact that men and women do not mix socially. This was explored earlier and there is no doubt that not free-mixing is one of the reasons why we, as women, are so close.

As there are no men in our social gatherings, we do not feel self-conscious: there is no one sizing us up, comparing us, judging us. We therefore do not see each other as rivals or compete with each other – there is nothing to compete for.

We never worry about our husbands being attracted to our friends for they do not spend time with them and will probably never have seen them uncovered.

Incidentally, many mistake the Muslim woman's reserve in front of men as timidity. Although this isn't necessarily the case, as a rule, we do not behave in a familiar, informal way with men. We don't crack jokes with them, we don't make casual conversation with them and we certainly don't flirt with them. We save the fullness of our personalities – our humour, our brashness, our teasing, our sensitivity, our tenderness, our singing and dancing – for those closest to us: our families and other women. That is where you will see a sister's true character, somewhere where no harm is done and no mis-understandings can occur. As women, we learn together, party together, work out together and have fun together – in an environment completely free of unease and potential problems – *fitnah*. We are free to be ourselves and to trust each other, now that the male energy is no longer part of our social sphere.

Among Sisters, Among Friends

So many things changed when we came to the *deen* – our beliefs, our dress, our lifestyle and our relationships with other women. When we started practising, we knew that hanging out with guys was not really the done thing. So we had to re-orientate ourselves towards the Muslim women that we knew. We had to work at having female friends, talking exclusively to women, learning how to relate as sisters in Islam.

For some, it was easy: they fitted right in with 'the sisters'. Others found it harder: the absence of a male presence was strange, the way the sisters related to each other was so different from in *jahiliyyah*. For a start, sisters were always smiling at each other. They were always pleasant. They were always polite. Whether you met them in the corridors on campus or in the prayer room itself, they always gave *salaams*, smiling, often shaking hands or hugging as well. They were just *different*.

And then, after a while, we started to change too. We found ourselves smiling at all the sisters we met, greeting them with *salaams* too. There was something so benign, so positive about the way the sisters treated each other. Although Sandra, Hanah and I would still tease each other quite mercilessly, we never did that to the sisters – they just seemed too nice. This was possibly due to the fact that, while we were reverts, they were mostly Asian girls, born Muslims. I was to see sisters of other races behave a bit differently with each other. However, some factors didn't change: no matter what the racial background of the sister, they were unfailingly friendly, non-confrontational, warm and welcoming. And this was definitely a new feeling. We couldn't help but return it.

As young sisters who were still in full-time education, we would mainly see each other after class and at the weekend. That time was spent visiting each other, talking, listening to Islamic tapes or going shopping in the various markets of Green Street. We would visit each other, sleep over at each other's houses and stay up talking and having midnight feasts till the time for the dawn prayer. I can honestly say that we didn't miss having men around. We were happy together, content with each other's company – at ease.

I have seen the Muslim teenagers in our community have the same experiences as we did as young Muslim converts – and, happily, they are not affected by the factors that marred *our* teenage friendships. They too spend time together, studying their *deen* and other subjects and talking about their plans for the future. They also visit each other's houses, go to the mosque, go shopping together, rabbiting on about not very much! And yes, they too talk about fashion and all that 'bling-bling'! But, unlike other communities, the teenagers and single sisters do not segregate themselves from the older, married ones. Typically, they attend the same classes as us and the same gatherings. And although they often disappear to the nether regions of the house for a giggle and a catch-up, emerging all made-up and sparkling, they often like to sit with us and listen, exchanging views, asking questions and gleaning the wisdom of their mothers and their mothers' friends. And they are never far away on *Eid* days because they know that it is their mothers that really know how to have a good time!

The wedding party I described earlier is a beautiful example of the wonderful female energy that pervades our social gatherings. With the men in another room or, better still, in another house, the sisters will celebrate the wedding of their friend with songs, tears and laughter. For marriage is an experience that binds us together and adds a new dimension to our relationships with each other. Typically, once a couple get married, they disappear from the social scene for a while, too wrapped up in each other to want to hobnob with the brothers or sisters. Some couples stay like that, most comfortable with each other, not wanting to socialize too much. However, the vast majority soon get back into the swing of things – the mosque, the dinners, the get-togethers, the swimming sessions, the gym, the park. After all, a loving marital relationship is wonderful, but there is still nothing like a good gathering of sisters to strengthen the *iman*, refresh the mind and have a bit of a laugh.

Having children adds another dimension to the bonds between sisters. Unlike some first-time mums, we seldom find ourselves in a situation where we are the only ones in our peer group to have a child and have to experience the isolation that that entails. Much to my midwives' surprise, I never needed to attend antenatal classes or join a mothers' group because I had experienced mothers all around me who answered my questions on pregnancy, childbirth and childcare. For many of us, our children have grown up together, in each other's houses, calling us 'Auntie'. We often organize parties, treats and outings for the children together, either a few close friends or the whole community. I remember one Sports Day that was organized by the teachers at my son's nursery at a beautiful park in the area. Although it was a public park, it was divided into sections by rows of trees and flower beds. It was a wonderful day: all the sisters came loaded down with food – sandwiches, fried chicken, naan bread, watermelons and strawberries – and drinks, eager to cheer their children on in their very first Sports Day. The weather was glorious and everyone got into the spirit of things, so much so that, as soon as the children's races were over, the sisters' races began – and they didn't stop! They ran races solo, they had relay races, they had skipping races and hopping races – the children went mad with excitement. I don't know what the few passers-by who caught a glimpse of us made of the sight of all these 'veiled women' having so much fun.

Another area of co-operation is our work arena. By and large, when sisters in our community work, they work in female environments, be it the community school or their own business. The sisters who work in our school enjoy the effects of their sisterhood every day. Other sisters who are freelancers work together in that same spirit of co-operation when we organize events together – pamper days, bazaars and family days out. I have fond memories of the many pamper days we have organized in the past, with the beauty therapists upstairs, the masseuse in the back room, the hairdresser in one of the bedrooms, the braider and henna artist in the lounge and the catering sisters in the kitchen. And the house itself bulging with sisters who had come to be pampered, to support the sisters in their efforts or simply to get a break from the children and relax. Although those days were quite hectic, one always had a good feeling afterwards, particularly if some benefit had been gained or a juicy discussion had. And sisters always wanted to know when the next one would be.

Whether in our homes or in the mosque, at a function or at work, in our domain, we are free to be confident and uninhibited, unafraid of giving anyone the wrong ideas, of being judged, of sending mixed signals. In those gatherings, be they formal or informal, sisters are able to be down to earth, share their experiences and discuss pertinent issues. We laugh together, cry together and share like sisters.

'I went to the *masjid* and there was a gathering of sisters there. All I remember from it was how smiley all the people were – all sisters, all women, all beautiful *masha Allah* in their own way, once they are out of their *niqab*. They were all so genuine. It was such a revelation. I had never been in a circle of all women like this before . . .' Sara

My own mother experienced our lively social life when she visited from abroad – she was invited out on most evenings while she stayed with me – and loved 'the sisters', as she called them. As a woman, she appreciated the warmth, the laughter and camaraderie that we share, recognizing it as something beautiful and special. When people commiserate with my father about how his bright, vivacious daughter could have become a Muslim, hiding herself away behind a veil, he always tells them not to feel sorry for me; that I am having a whale of a time and not leading the joyless life they seem to expect.

Nothing but Love . . .

And He has united their [i.e. believers'] hearts. If you had spent all that is in the earth, you could not have united their hearts, but Allah has united them. Certainly He is All-Mighty, All-Wise.

Surah al-Anfal 8:63

The bonds between Muslim women stretch beyond the ties of womanhood. They encompass a shared outlook, common goals and a belief that unites them in a way that worldly considerations cannot. As sisters in Islam, we strive to love one another for the sake of Allah. This means that our reasons for loving a person are not superficial or materialistic: we love our sister because she has submitted to Allah. This love for religious and spiritual reasons is one that transcends the boundaries of race, age, wealth and class.

Sara told me: 'In *jahiliyyah*, we hang on to certain company because we see certain benefits in it for ourselves. In Islam, it's not the same. There could be a sister who is the least fashionable of people, be the dowdiest of people, she could have all these traits that you would have looked down on in *jahiliyyah* but she may be extremely pious, she may be a good listener, someone you can speak to about all your problems, who gives you good advice all the time. And you don't care what anyone else thinks about your friend now because you know what the best reason is to love a person and that is for the sake of Allah.'

Loving someone for the sake of Allah entails loving all that is Islamic about their character – their love and worship of Allah, their manners, their positive influence, their sincerity, their trustworthiness and understanding. However, as with any other individuals, there are other factors that will draw particular sisters closer together, such as shared experiences, shared history, culture, sense of humour or intellectual interests and hobbies.

But surely one can't be expected to get along with every sister. What about when there are personality clashes or just the wrong chemistry?

'Even if you wouldn't normally get on with such and such a person,' Sara explained, 'you love them because they've submitted to Allah and because she's your sister in Islam – and I love that sincerity. For me, that is the only thing that can make somebody sincere: doing things for the sake of Allah. That is pure sincerity and a pure intention. You can *feel* it amongst sisters when that sincerity is there.'

Indeed, there is a lot of love, a lot of open love, amongst the sisters. You see it in their smiles, you hear it in their laughter and you feel it, almost tangibly, in the air, in the atmosphere. Aliyah expressed her feelings about her sisters this way: 'I love my sisters more than *anything*, even more than my family.

'I am so happy on days like this,' she continued. 'When I join ankle to ankle with my sisters, when I pray to my Lord, I pray that whoever's either side of me, or in front of me or behind me, that Allah joins us again and that we will be together in Paradise, *insha Allah*.'

And it is strange, but the times when I have been most aware of that love are those times when we are together seeking knowledge, or reciting the Qur'an, or praying the night prayer or discussing an aspect of the *deen*. At times like these, when the eyes are bright and the hearts soft with the remembrance of Allah, you can almost feel your heart swelling with love for those around you, your sisters, your companions on this journey.

Trust

I asked Umm Muhammad about her feelings on sisterhood and she mentioned 'trust' as one of the main features of her friendships in the *deen*.

'I had some good friends that I was close to in *jahiliyyah*,' she told me, 'but, in Islam, I feel that I can trust sisters more than I could trust women before. I feel that, first of all, they fear Allah, and they're not going to harm me in any way. I had had friends [in *jahiliyyah*] that I had been very close to for years but I felt like I could tell the sisters things that I couldn't tell them. I felt very open with them, a lot of trust, openness. And I felt happy with all the sisters that I met – these were my sisters. It wasn't as if I was a loner in *jahiliyyah*, but I felt loved and wanted by the sisters.'

> '*Alhamdulillah*, when I came to Islam, I found true friendship. I can turn to any sister [within reason] and ask for anything or ask about anything and they will feel fine about answering my questions. It could be a personal issue, it could be a money issue. In *jahiliyyah*, I could never turn to any of my friends and ask them for money, I'd rather do without.' Aziza

Because our behaviour is moulded by Islamic guidelines, we all have the same standards and we all know what kind of treatment to expect from each other. In *jahiliyyah*, quite often a secret shared was a secret spread, but there is no fear of this happening with sisters. We trust each other, we will not lie to each other, we will not try to cheat each other, or backbite, and we will not try to harm each other in any way. And because we share these values, we are able to relax in each other's company, safe from mistrust, suspicion and doubts.

Equality

> 'In *jahiliyyah*, you'd look at people's houses, you'd look at their status, you'd look at how they look. And if someone didn't "look the part" then they couldn't go to a party with you. In Islam, it doesn't matter whether you're tall or short, pretty or ugly.' Umm Muhammad

In our community, the sisters do not discriminate against or compete with each other over material possessions. Amongst sisters (and brothers), the young speak with the old, the rich sit with the poor, the revert learns with the born Muslims. Because we love each other for the sake of Allah, we do not choose our companions based on their looks, their status or how rich they are.

> 'My friends now are not all out for themselves, it's not "all about me". Before, I did have a vast array of different friends from different backgrounds. But I would say that there are people who I would not have had any time for in *jahiliyyah* and they would not have had any time for me. They may have looked down on me in *jahiliyyah* or I may have looked down upon them. But we are friends, we are sisters now, we talk on the same level: we are equals.' Sara

Islam is a great equalizer and, among sisters, it is mainly knowledge of the *deen* that will earn a sister the greatest respect. We also respect the older sisters, the 'aunties', and they respect us in turn. However, respect such as this doesn't equate to elitism, arrogance or snobbery – either in the *deen* or in our sisterhood.

Manners

Another reason why our sisterhood is so strong is that we treat each other well, with good manners, according to the guidance of the Prophet Muhammad (s). It is rare to find sisters speaking to each other in a nasty way, being sarcastic or rude. And it is *extremely* rare to see sisters shouting at each other, swearing or fighting. Disagreements just don't get to that point. And if they ever do, the two sisters end up asking each other's forgiveness and seeking Allah's forgiveness. The Prophet (s) said in a *hadith*, 'It is not permissible for a Muslim to be estranged from his brother for more than three days, both of them turning away from one another when they meet. The better of them is the one who is first to greet the other.' As it is forbidden to stop speaking to a Muslim for three days, there is a strong incentive to make up. More often than not, sisters will speak about any issues that may come up, not wanting to hold evil thoughts in their hearts.

Our manners also stop us from backbiting or slandering each other, or from standing by and listening to someone else do it. We also express our love for each other in words, which is encouraged by Allah and His Messenger (s). Sisters will exchange gifts, help each other out, give each other advice, feed each other, visit each other when they are sick, pray and supplicate for each other and try to be there for each other – all in a spirit of Islamic sisterhood.

> 'I had a lot of good experiences with sisterhood when I came to the *deen*. Sisters who would give me their last pennies without telling me and do things like leaving it under my pillow. I had a lot of really good examples, really good role models when I came to the *deen*. Sisters who were very, very strong then and, *masha Allah*, who are very strong now . . . they were like my oxygen.' Ghaniyah

As with any friendship, there are a host of reasons why certain sisters will get along with some better than others but, the beauty of it is, the manners we are meant to have apply to those who are our close friends as well as those who are on the periphery. Every sister has been given rights in Islam and that ensures that, even if you don't necessarily gel with a person, you will still treat her with respect and courtesy.

> 'Obviously, you'll meet people in life that you don't gel with and they're not your best friends. Islam teaches us that everyone has rights and you have to give them their rights.' Umm Muhammad

The Ultimate Sisterhood

'We are all striving for the same thing, we all want the same thing, *insha Allah*.' Aliyah

This book is a celebration of my wonderful sisters. They were its inspiration and they were part of its creation. Through their strength and spirit, I have experienced a life that even I never thought possible: a life with sisters that I love and trust around me. It is a good life. It is a noble life. It is the life that I love. Islamic sisterhood is special. It transcends colour, it transcends class, it transcends all manner of worldly things. It is close, it is warm, it is tender and strong. It is unlike any other because it is based on the most solid of foundations: the love of Allah.

GLOSSARY

Adhan	The call to the congregational prayer
Ayah	A phrase or verse from the Qur'an
Deen	The Islamic religion or way of life
Dhikr	Remembering Allah and mentioning Him
Du'a	Supplication
Eid	A day of celebration in Islam
Hadith	Reports of the Prophet (s)'s sayings, actions and approvals
Hajj	The pilgrimage to Mecca
Halal	Lawful
Haram	Prohibited
Hijab	The covering of the Muslim woman. Also refers to the headscarf
Iman	Belief or conviction
Isnad	Chain of narrators of a *hadith*
Jahiliyyah	The time of ignorance and disbelief

413

that preceded the revelation of the Qur'an. Also refers to the time before one accepts Islam

Jannah	The gardens of Paradise
Jihad	Striving or fighting for Allah's cause
Masjid	Mosque
Qadr	The Divine decree or predestination
Salah	The prayer
Shahadah	The testimony of faith
Sunnah	Guidance or teachings
Surah	A chapter from the Qur'an
Taqwa	Fearing Allah and revering Him
Ummah	Nation or followers
Wudhu'	Ritual cleansing in preparation for the prayer
Zakah	Obligatory charity on one's wealth
Zina	Adultery or fornication

FURTHER READING

Here is a list of further reading for those interested in finding out more about Islam. All books are available in quality Islamic bookstores and online.

Authentic Etiquette of Eating and Hosting from the Qur'an and Sunnah with 150 Recipes from Around the World, M. Ariff, I. Azad, A. Benkhelifa, N. Driscoll, Path to Knowledge Publishing, onlineislamicstore.

Beneficial Speech in Establishing the Evidences of Tawheed, Shaykh Muhammad Bin Abdil-Wahhaab Al-Wasaabee; Salafi Publications, P.O. Box 6294, Birmingham, B8 3JE.

A Brief Illustrated Guide to Understanding Islam, I. A. Ibrahim; Darussalam, Publishers and Distributors, Houston, Texas, USA. (Free samples of this book are available online.)

Explanation of the Creed, Imam al-Barbaharee; Al-Hidaayah Publishing and Distribution, Birmingham B10 9AW

Explanation of Faith, Shaykh Muhammad ibn Salih al-Uthaimeen, translated by Dr Saleh as-Saleh; Message of Islam, Hounslow, Middlesex TW5 9YX

Explanation of the Three Fundamentals, explained by Shaykh Muhammad ibn Salih al-Uthaimeen, Al-Hidaayah Publishing and Distribution, Birmingham B10 9AW

Fundamentals of Tawheed, Dr Abu Ameenah Bilal Philips; International Islamic Publishing House (I.I.P.H), 486-Atlantic Avenue, Brooklyn, NY, 11217, USA.

Ibn Taymiyyah's Essay on Servitude, Shaykhul-Islaam Ibn Taymiyyah; Al-Hiddayah Publishing and Distribution, P. O. Box 3332, Birmingham B10 9AW.

The Ideal Muslimah, Dr Muhammad Ali al-Hashimi; International Islamic Publishing House (I.I.P.H), 486-Atlantic Avenue, Brooklyn, NY, 11217, USA.

Increase Your Knowledge on Islam (A Pack of Six Books); Darussalam, Leyton Business Centre, Unit 17, Etloe Road, Leyton, London E10 6LU.

Islam the Natural Way, Abdul Wahid Hamid, Muslim Education & Literary Services

(MELS), 37 Rollo Road, Hextable, Kent, BR8 7RD.

The Magnificent Journey (a translation of *The Message from Tabuk*), Ibn ul-Qayyim al-Jawziyyah; Al-Qur'an was-Sunnah Society of North USA. (Quransunna@aol.com.)

The Noble Qur'an in the English Language, Translated by Dr Muhammad Taqi-ud-Din al-Hilali and Dr Muhammad Muhsin Khan.

The Prayer: Its Effects in Increasing Iman and Purifying the Soul, Husayn al-'Awaayishah; Al-Hiddayah Publishing and Distribution, P. O. Box 3332, Birmingham B10 9AW.

The Prophet's Prayer, described by Shayth Nasiruddin al-Albani; Jami'atul-Ihyaa Mimhaj as-Sunnah

The Purpose of Creation, Dr Abu Ameenah Bilal Philips; Dar Al Fatah, P. O. Box 23424, Sharjah, UAE.

A Simple Call to One God, Dr Asra Rasheed, Edited by Dr Abu Ameenah Bilal Philips; Dar Al Fatah, P. O. Box 23424, Sharjah, UAE.

INDEX

INDEX

INDEX